ISBN: 978129027329

Published by:
HardPress Publishing
8345 NW 66TH ST #2561
MIAMI FL 33166-2626

Email: info@hardpress.net
Web: http://www.hardpress.net

WILLIAM HONE
HIS LIFE AND TIMES

WILLIAM HONE.

WILLIAM HONE

HIS LIFE AND TIMES

BY

FREDERICK WM. HACKWOOD

AUTHOR OF
"THE GOOD OLD TIMES," "INNS, ALES, AND DRINKING
CUSTOMS OF OLD ENGLAND," "GOOD CHEER,"
ETC.

WITH 27 ILLUSTRATIONS

T. FISHER UNWIN
LONDON: ADELPHI TERRACE
LEIPSIC: INSELSTRASSE 20
1912

PREFACE

THE Author acknowledges his indebtedness to Miss Soul (granddaughter of William Hone) for the careful collation of the family papers entrusted to him, among which were many transcripts of notes taken down by Mrs. Burn from the dictation of her father in the later years of his life, and which constitute the main sources of the information relating to the personal side of his subject. The material placed at his disposal was voluminous, of subjects varied, and arranged in fairly good chronological order. William Hone erected his own literary monument, and the biographer therefore confined his efforts to presenting this material more as a revelation of the man's intimate personal life.

Transcripts are not always safe material to work upon, but the accuracy of these family documents being found fairly reliable, they have been departed from only when found in direct conflict with independent testimony. Strange to say, very few references were found to the most interesting of all Hone's friendships—that with Charles and Mary Lamb. However, an admirable chapter dealing with this period has been supplied by Major Butterworth, to whom the Author takes this opportunity to tender his most sincere thanks ; for without this contribution the work would have been decidedly incomplete. For the ready permission to print the two letters from Lamb to Hone (dated respectively 25 July, 1825, and 7 February, 1834) grateful acknowledgement is made to Messrs. J. M. Dent & Co. To his old friend Mr. George T. Lawley he also expresses his deep sense of obligation for assistance rendered during the progress of the work, and particularly in the arrangement of the Bibliography. The biographer also puts on record his gratitude for expert assistance relating to the Queen Caroline period received from Mr. Charles E. Pearce.

CONTENTS

CHAPTER		PAGE
I.	INTRODUCTORY	11
II.	AUTOBIOGRAPHICAL	22
III.	EARLY STRUGGLES	64
IV.	A BOOKMAN'S ACQUAINTANCES	80
V.	POLITICAL ACTIVITIES	91
VI.	AN ALERT PUBLISHER	103
VII.	IMPENDING PROSECUTION	118
VIII.	THE ARREST	132
IX.	THE FIRST TRIAL	149
X.	CLOSE OF THE TRIALS	159
XI.	AFTER THE TRIALS	174
XII.	THE CRUIKSHANK CONNECTION	189
XIII.	A BANK RESTRICTION NOTE	198
XIV.	INDUSTRY WITHOUT BUSINESS METHODS	206
XV.	POLITICAL PAMPHLETEERING	218
XVI.	THE QUEEN CAROLINE AFFAIR	231
XVII.	ANTIQUARY AND CONTROVERSIALIST	243
XVIII.	THE "EVERY-DAY BOOK"	246

8   **CONTENTS**

CHAPTER		PAGE
XIX.	THE "TABLE BOOK"	259
XX.	WILLIAM HONE AND CHARLES LAMB	266
XXI.	GETTING OUT OF KING'S BENCH PRISON	282
XXII.	THE "YEAR BOOK"	294
XXIII.	HONE'S POLITICAL AND RELIGIOUS VIEWS	299
XXIV.	CONVERSION	304
XXV.	LIFE AT PECKHAM	319
XXVI.	SUB-EDITOR OF THE *PATRIOT*	327
XXVII.	RETIREMENT AND DEATH	339
XXVIII.	HONE'S FUNERAL—A DICKENSIAN EPISODE	347
	APPENDIX : BIBLIOGRAPHY	357
	INDEX	369

ILLUSTRATIONS

WILLIAM HONE . . . . . *Frontispiece*

FACING PAGE

WILLIAM NORRIS, AS HE WAS CONFINED IN BETHLEM . **95**

ELIZABETH FENNING **99**

SKETCH, SUPPOSED TO BE BY GEORGE CRUIKSHANK, OF HIM-

SELF AT THE AGE OF 20 . . . . **110**

FRANCIS PLACE **120**

CARTOON OF HONE AS A TOM-TIT TWITTING HIS PROSECUTORS **172**

LAW *VERSUS* HUMANITY ; OR, A PARODY ON BRITISH LIBERTY **174**

A MEMENTO PUBLISHED BY J. HEAD, OF 141, FETTER LANE

(FEB. 6, 1818) **185**

AN ACCOMMODATION BILL BETWEEN AUTHOR AND ARTIST . **192**

BANK RESTRICTION NOTE **200**

A ROUGH SKETCH, DATED 12 JANUARY, 1819, SUPPOSED TO

SHOW HONE'S PENCILLINGS **203**

"THE WEALTH THAT LAY IN THE HOUSE THAT JACK

BUILT" **221**

FACING PAGE

THE FIRST ILLUSTRATION IN "THE QUEEN'S MATRIMONIAL LADDER" 223

SPECIMEN OF PIRATED ILLUSTRATIONS TO UNAUTHORISED ISSUES OF HONE'S WORKS 224

THE MAN IN THE MOON 226

"THE HOUSE THAT JACK BUILT" 230

HONE AND CRUIKSHANK 230

TRANSPARENCY WITH WHICH HONE ILLUMINATED HIS SHOP 235

THE PICTURES ON THE TWO LEGS OF THE CARDBOARD TOY LADDER 236

MARY LAMB 280

CHARLES LAMB 280

REV. DR. RAFFLES 292

REV. SAMUEL PARR, LL.D. 292

THE ILLUSTRATION TO HONE'S PARODY, "A VISION OF WANT OF JUDGMENT—BY SLOBBER'D MOUTHEY" . . 297

THE WEIGH-HOUSE CHAPEL 321

FACSIMILE OF VERSES WRITTEN BY HONE, JUNE 3, 1834 . 343

"THE QUEEN'S MATRIMONIAL LADDER" . . . 361

WILLIAM HONE

I

INTRODUCTORY

WILLIAM HONE may be taken as a type of Englishman into whose brains had distilled the doctrines of the French Revolution, which inspired him, not to action but to thought ; a type of the phlegmatic, slow-moving Englishman to whose opinions, and the proper constitutional advocacy of them, may be traced the roots of so many of our modern reforms.

How much the progressive thought of this country owes to William Hone and the men of his stamp is too often lost to view. Though these men had the roots of the matter in them, the country in their day and generation was not in the least prepared for the political reforms they would have planted. Yet they lived in hope and died not in despair. Hone, be it remembered, was born in the eighteenth century, the era of oppressive and cynical politics, when class prejudice was rampant and political honesty but lightly esteemed.

The times in which he lived were out of joint ; and it is when, in tracing the events of his life, we leave the main stream of history for its eddying and whirling side currents, that we are enabled to see how the garbage of decayed feudalism was largely swept away by the first flood of modernity.

Hone long contemplated the publication of an Autobiography, and to that end made innumerable memoranda, particularly of the events and memories of his childhood days.

" Then," he says, " I considered and paused, for upon close self-examination I discovered deep within me the hidden old roots of feelings and tendencies planted in my earliest years, which from defective training had grown wild and vigorous in my youth and manhood."

His notes had become too voluminous to be brought within the narrow compass of a pamphlet, and a project for the writing of a more extended " memoir " then took possession of him. From this more formidable undertaking he was also long deterred, not only because he could ill spare the time such a task would entail, but chiefly because his inmost reflections failed to inspire him to the mood for making the attack. He found no spur to the effort when he recalled what he describes as the events of his " wayward life."

" At length," he continues, " having selected a few hints and notes, throwing aside the bulk of my accumulations, and being now at leisure, I resume my first purpose, and begin with recollections of my earliest life and the way in which I was brought up, until I left my parental home. And now, ' with the blossoms of the grave upon my head,' the scenes of my young days recur familiarly and vividly as those of yesterday. ' I feel as a child.'

" Pascal writes that the last thing we can settle in the composition of a work is how to begin it. This thought has been verified in me. In the course of my brief life the most astounding events of modern times have happened ; to these I have not been an indifferent observer, nor always an observer only. Of the numerous changes in our own country, crowds of incidents have affected me personally."

The Autobiography, as far as he got with it, reflects the ingenuousness of the simple terms in which he thus introduces it.   An appended note reminds the reader that the date of his birth was memorable as a period of passionate conflict, when the insurgent storm of popular tumult in England culminated in the excesses known as the Gordon Riots.   London was in possession of an excited mob, which fired the prisons, liberated the prisoners, broke into, sacked, and burned private dwellings and destroyed valuable property.   In after-years his mother vividly recalled the intense fever of public excitement which prevailed at the moment her firstborn was ushered into the world ; and, mother-like, she cherished an impression that her child's energy and earnestness of temperament were the tincture of the stirring times in which he was born ; for though shrewd and sensible in other respects, she failed to perceive in that which she attributed to national influences an inherited phase of her own character.   In William Hone were unmistakably blended the mild, benevolent, and cheerful disposition of the father, with the inquiring mind, the perseverance, and untiring energies of the mother.

Hone himself was fond of dwelling upon this portent, and used to relate that he was told by a young woman who had been the landlady's assistant at Copenhagen House that in 1780 a body of the Lord George Gordon rioters passed this house of resort, with blue banners flying, on their way to attack Caen Wood, the seat of Lord Mansfield, and that the proprietress was so alarmed at this incident that at her request Justice Hyde sent a party of soldiers to protect the establishment.   Hone seemed to derive some sort of satisfaction from the contemplation of the civil commotion with which his advent into a stormy world was heralded.

The " waywardness " of spirit to which Hone alludes had reference to the freedom of religious thought in which he had indulged himself in his early manhood rather than to his advanced political ideas. His inquiring mind had fostered a habit of omnivorous—and, during his callow youth, an ill-regulated—reading ; a habit which, combined with a tendency to self-introspection and self-communing, could but engender some slight morbidity of mind.

If his political trials had brought him fame, they had also—politics being inseparable from partisanship—excited considerable party spirit against him. His political enemies had not hesitated to make as much capital as possible out of his well-known flounderings in the quagmire of religious doubt, the most effective way of doing which was to dub him " atheist." And as an unbeliever he was consequently reviled by those who differed from him.

Now, while Hone possessed much independence of political thought, and maintained these convictions with a fine courage, in matters of religion he manifests in the " Confessions " of the Autobiography, a trembling sensibility which at times is almost distressing. No man, indeed, can climb beyond the limitations of his own character.

To the real atheist that appellation is never a term of opprobrium ; in the sincerity of his religious convictions he rather regards it as a mark of distinction. How much Hone in his later life resented the application of the term to him, spurning it as a wilfully false estimate of his character, is evidenced by his private papers. Thus the Foreword to his projected life history is couched in these terms :—

" From certain occurrences which are matters of history, and some of my productions which are not yet forgotten, the public continues to deal with me as a public man ; and, according to the differences of individual views, to entertain different notions concerning my opinion on religion. Hence it seems incumbent on me to make a plain declaration of my religious sentiments. This I now do without reserve in the following narrative. I sincerely wish it could be read by all who ever heard my name."

The title-page, drafted in his own bold and well-formed handwriting, appears as :—

VIEWS OF RELIGION

AND

RELIGIOUS VIEWS.

A NARRATIVE

BY

WILLIAM HONE.

This is a memoir explanatory of my mind from its perversion in boyhood by the principles of a wretch-making philosophy, until I found happiness in the submission of my will, and by divine grace was enabled to surrender my heart to God in Christ.

This is dated 1835. The same perturbation of mind is disclosed on his draft title-page of the " Memoirs from Childhood ".; again we have precisely similar phrasing allusive to " Perversion in Youth by a Wretch-making Philosophy : Struggles under its Influence through Life, and the Final Submission of the Heart to God in Christ . . . by William Hone, Editor of the EVERY-DAY BOOK," &c.

In an attempt to justify the celebrated Parodies for which he was put on trial, but more particularly in his burning desire to rehabilitate himself in the public mind, Hone prints at the end of the pamphlet containing his father's " early life and conversion " (which he edited and published the year before his death) the following extracts from " Mr. Simpson's New Edition of his father's ' Plea for Religion ' "—it is a note, he says, " written by a very dear friend, who knows me intimately " :—

" There is a delicacy to be observed in referring to living individuals ; and, without infringing on it, a slight allusion may be made to Mr. William Hone, whose name, a few years ago, stood associated in the public mind with profaneness and infidelity.

" It is but justice to Mr. Hone to state that the object of his Parodies was political, and that they were not composed for the purpose of bringing religion into contempt, although that was their unquestionable tendency. While, however, this is admitted, it must also be admitted that if the promotion of infidelity did not enter into the plan of the Parodies, yet, that no person could have aimed at a political object by such means, whose mind was not, at the time, under the complete influence either of infidelity or indifference— of opposition to religion or carelessness about it."

This puts the case very fairly. The Parodies were neither pleasant nor witty, and possessed of no literary distinction whatever. It was common knowledge that Hone's mind at that period was (to put it mildly) assailed by religious doubts ; and it was therefore a perfectly legitimate inference that his flippant treatment of serious subjects should be accepted as internal evidence of his well-known attitude of mind.

" Mr. Hone, in early life, was led to reject Christianity, and to adopt sceptical, if not atheistical, opinions. At the time of his celebrated trials his opinions may have been less extravagant, but neither his intellect nor his heart had submitted to the authority of revealed religion. After that period he became convinced of the truth of the Bible, as a communication from God, but satisfied himself with something like Unitarianism. This, however, he found would not satisfy the heart. About six years since his conscience was awakened to a just sense of man's condition as a sinner, and the need in which he stands,

both of an atoning sacrifice and a sanctifying Spirit.
After many painful exercises of mind, serious examination of the Scriptures, prayer, and attendance on
the preaching of the Gospel, he came fully to accept
the faith which once he destroyed and to acknowledge that Saviour whom he had formerly dishonoured.
The change in the minds of his family was equally
remarkable. One after another was brought to 'the
knowledge and belief of the truth,' though at first
contemned and resisted, till at length, in the close of
the year 1834, Mr. Hone, his wife, four of their
daughters, and a son-in-law were received to Christian
communion by one of the Congregational Churches in
London, and three of his children and three of his
grandchildren were baptized. The interest excited by
the circumstance was intense ; the scene was felt to
be one over which angels might be supposed to rejoice,
and which demanded the thanksgiving of Christians
on earth.

" The substance of this statement is communicated on
the best authority, and is purposely brief and general,
as there is reason to hope that Mr. Hone will give
to the public, from his own pen, some account of the
change which he has experienced."

To this there is a Postcript added by Hone, dated
3rd June, 1841, in which he, curiously enough, applies
to himself those terms to which, from others, he
strongly objected :—

" The history of my three days' Trials in Guildhall
may be dug out from the Journals of the period—the
History of my Mind and Heart, my Scepticism, my
Atheism, and God's final dealings with me, remains
to be written. If my life be prolonged a few months,
the work may appear in my lifetime."

After the public excitement occasioned by the historic
trials of 1817, the culminating period of his life, there
was not unnaturally a call for some biographical account
of the man around whom all the excitement had centred.

2

The popular expectation was not gratified. But the accumulation of the necessary material, by the subject himself, went steadily forward ; and during his last illness Hone gave a number of instructions relating to the use and disposition of his papers and books, with which it was long the study of his family to comply. But, chiefly through the lack of the necessary leisure, the years passed unheeded, and it was not till 1873 that a serious attempt was made to collate the family papers with a view to publication, a task undertaken by his eldest daughter, Mrs. Burn, then long resident in Australia, which never attained fruition.

One cause of the original delay was, strangely enough, the formidable bulk of the material which Hone had collected for the purposes of his defence ; for the contemplation of these vast stores of literary wealth resolved itself into a design for a more elaborate work which was to embody " A History of Parody."

According to Mrs. Burn, her father had

" mentally sketched out his plans, and wanted but the necessary retirement, and freedom from daily inroads upon his time, to enable him to effect his purpose. That season of retirement never arrived. Circumstances compelled him to a reluctant abandonment of his more ambitious project, and reduced his design to that of a simple Autobiography."

Even that demanded more time than he ever had at disposal, with the result that he had only accomplished the history of his youth when accumulated physical and mental infirmities gradually revealed the sad truth that for him the pen was ever at rest.

" The brightness of his intellect had sensibly waned," writes Mrs. Burn, " and the vigour of a strong frame had progressively yielded to repeated shocks of paralysis, when in August, 1842, he became alarmingly ill. Dropsy supervened, and the family prepared themselves for the most solemn of earthly partings."

The end was uncertain ; some weeks might elapse ere the closing scene, but they were assured by medical friends that the fiat had gone forth.   The daughter's narrative continues :—

" His active connection with the *Patriot* had terminated in 1840, when, aided by friends, after a prolonged illness, he retired for a short time to Richmond, and thence to Tottenham, a locality which had for him choice associations, for there and at Edmonton he had strolled the green lanes with his ever dear friends Charles and Mary Lamb.

" He chose for his last earthly home a cheerful house suitably situated, and enlivened by passing vehicles and pedestrians.   To the last he retained his innate love of genial society and of rural beauty, and was pleased to have his air-bed moved toward the window in view of a row of fine elms which bordered the opposite pathway.   He would sometimes remark : ' How beautifully the sun shines on the leaves,' when it was his impaired vision which failed to detect that it was the autumn sear that was gilding the fading foliage.

" On the 6th November, 1842, he entered upon his eternal rest.   During the long months of watching his sorrowing wife and family were surrounded with the kindly sympathy of their many friends, and especially supported by the generous kindness of their excellent neighbour Mr. Woolaston, whose medical skill in the alleviation of the patient's sufferings was hardly less welcome than his friendly visits at all hours, when his cheerful voice and the occasional introduction of another visitor raised the invalid's spirits, and relieved some of the pain and weariness.

" Soon after the final rites there were many inquiries and a widespread expression of urgent wishes for the production of a Biography.   Much diversity of opinion existed as to the period it should embrace, as well as to whom the task should be entrusted.   Several friends kindly proffered their services, and certain others were suggested.

" Some   well-intentioned   persons   proposed   the political years of his life only as worthy of record ; others, again, considered that those of later times would convey the most instructive lesson to posterity ; while his family judged a memoir should comprise a history, however brief, from the dawn to the close of life.

" Time in its flight has effaced from memory many incidents, but sufficient material remains to illustrate truthfully the political, literary, and social aspects of a life of varied usefulness and real patriotism."

Through the years that have intervened public opinion has not withheld that approval which his public conduct merited, nor denied him those high commendations which, by his literary talents and private worth, were justly his. At the same time, certain ill-informed and unscrupulous persons " of the baser sort " have not hesitated to put forth misrepresentations of his character, which to those who ever had the faintest conception of the man and his work could not fail to be recognised as scurrilous and contemptible calumnies.

From various causes, as we have seen, the projected Autobiography was never written, except the " Memoirs from Childhood " reviewing the first twenty years of his life. The few anecdotes embodied seem somewhat apocryphal. To preserve the chronological order of our narrative as closely as possible we propose to begin with this uncompleted Autobiography as compiled either from his own notes or dictated by him to one or other of his children, and dated in his own hand the 20th December, 1838. An appended short note is dated Tottenham, 1841.

In the long years that have intervened the purpose of one member of the family after another to produce an authentic Biography of the father they revered has been thwarted time after time by untoward circumstances. William Hone in his lifetime suffered much obloquy for his opinions, and even at his death remained a maligned and much vilified man. Not unnaturally, his family developed an over-sensitiveness in their solicitude for the honour and probity of his memory.

His letters show him to be a man very much in earnest, but not always particularly lively. In considering the personality of William Hone, his private papers and correspondence will be drawn upon as frequently as possible in order that the man's *ipsissima verba* may reveal his attitude of mind, and, so far as he indulged in them, his ideals, enthusiasms, and prejudices. In the vigour of his manhood he was an ardent politician, and before the days of *Punch* his cartoons and caricatures made the features of leading politicians familiar to the public.

If occasionally he strikes the reader as a *poseur*, a nearer approach will quickly dispel the impression and show it to be merely the attitude of a naïve simple-mindedness, exhibited with somewhat of the natural vanity of an artless child.

II

AUTOBIOGRAPHICAL

My Father was the eldest son of a farmer who lived upon a grazing farm near Ripley, in Surrey, which he held under Lord Onslow, until he lost it through bad management, owing to convivial habits. He died of a broken heart, leaving my Grandmother with a large family, which dispersed, and my Father became apprenticed to a law stationer in London.

At the expiration of his apprenticeship he was deluded into intimacy with persons attached to the theatres, and was under an engagement to go upon the stage. A severe illness, however, seized him the day before he was to have appeared ; it resulted in religious impressions, which were deepened by the remembrance of his mother's pious teachings in his childhood. Upon his ultimate recovery he remained decidedly religious ; to avoid his companions he engaged himself as clerk to a corn merchant [1] at Bath.

There, in 1779, he married Miss Frances Maria Stawell, and there their first child, myself, was born on the 3rd of June, 1780.

I have heard my Mother relate that when I could just run about, while she was engaged in household affairs, she suddenly missed me, and ran about for a considerable time seeking in vain, until, looking into a stable, she found me stooping down close behind a large spirited carthorse, playing with his fetlocks, an

---

[1] He was first employed as clerk to a solicitor.

incident which she regarded as ominous of a fearless character. After I could walk alone, my Father sometimes took me with him to the counting-house, to show me the moving craft, and the swans on the river, and the horses in their stabling.

When I was about three years of age my Father returned alone to London, for the sake of hearing a particular minister, and having obtained settled employment in the office of Mr. Ludlow, Solicitor, of Monument Yard, he sent for my Mother and me, as had been previously arranged. We settled for the summer in the eastern corner house of Grafton Street.

Paddington was then an inconsiderable village, having a single stage-coach, which daily made one journey to and from the City.

Our next residence was on the west side of Tottenham Court Road. All beyond Warren Street, which had been lately commenced, was open meadow-land and dairy farms as far as the eye could see, except the " Adam and Eve," then resorted to as a country tea-garden house, at the west corner of the Hampstead Road, and the " Old King's Head," at the opposite corner, with a few humble buildings.

My young eyes were attracted by the numerous moving objects I beheld from our windows. Opposite was a cow-lair, and great gravel-pits adjoining, while beyond meadows extended to Gray's Inn Lane ; one of them, conspicuous at a distance, formed the bowling-green, now a public-house, in Cromer Street.

From far and near on Sunday mornings in the different fields crowds assembled around preachers, boxing-matches, dog-fights, and duck-hunts. To these scenes resorted pickpockets, who, when detected and pursued, were brought by large mobs to ponds in the gravel-pits and mercilessly ducked, with uproarious shouting.

On Sundays London poured towards the country a populous tide of individuals, differing much in appear-

ance from our present Sunday swarms to the suburbs ;
many were personally afflicted, youths walking on
crutches or with one crutch, girls suffering under dis-
orders of the hip-joint, rickety children, with jointed
iron straps on their legs—at least one-tenth of the
passers-by were crippled or diseased.

On Sunday afternoons tradesmen or respectable
journeymen and their wives were profusely powdered.
Men wore scarlet coats and long-flapped, figured waist-
coats ; cocked hats, with their hair behind in long
or large clubbed pigtails, and at the sides in large
stiff curls ; silver or plated buckles, curiously wrought
or bespangled, on their shoes.

Daily there were processions of Freemasons' funerals,
or long trains attending the Irish burials, to Old Pancras
Church ; and frequently school " breaking-up " processions. We soon removed to Warren Street, of which
only five houses were then built.

My recollections of this early period are vivid ; of
my Father reading to me, Bible in hand, while I stood
between his knees ; of his talking to me about Adam
and Eve, Noah's Flood, Cain and Abel ; and of my
questioning him about the Garden of Eden, the Dove
with the olive-branch, the Ark with its animals, and
the Rainbow after the Flood.

My childish imagination drew pictures of Paradise
from the upland horizon of Hampstead and the verdant
intermediate scenery which fascinated my young eyes
and filled me with indescribable emotions.

Nature was my first book ; my father's only one was
the Bible, and he constantly read in it. He was a
good man, and he taught me the alphabet and reading
from the Bible.

I saw but little of him except on Sundays, when,
going to hear the Rev. W. Huntingdon preach, he
took me with him. On other days his employment
in a distant law office drew him out early and detained
him late. He often inveighed so bitterly against the

Arminians and John Wesley that I imagined the Arminians to be much more wicked than common wicked people about the streets, and that John Wesley had some peculiarly terrible aspect. My Father and his friends were in the habit of speaking much and bitterly of John Wesley. They frequently called him " the Old Devil," and I had a most terrific idea of this satanic personage.

Although my Father and Mother had taught me to read tolerably well, I was too young for a boys' school, being under six years of age, and as the family was increasing I was sent to a neighbouring dame, who taught young children from the Horn-Book.

That implement of education was a thin piece of oak of small duo-decimo size and form, covered on one side with a piece of horn, through which appeared, printed on a paper which was pasted on the wood, an alphabet of capital letters, headed by a cross, a lower-case alphabet of small letters, the vowels, a few syllables of two letters, the Lord's Prayer, and the *Gloria Patri*.

I was soon Dame Bettridge's head scholar. She was very fond of me, and I was always good with her, although, perhaps, naughty enough at home. She lived in one room, a large underground kitchen ; we went down a flight of steps to it. Her bed was always neatly turned up in one corner. There was a large kitchen grate, and in cold weather there was always a good fire in it, by which she sat in a carved wooden arm-chair, with a small round table before her, on which lay a large Bible, open, on one side, and on the other a birch rod.

Of the Bible she made great use, of the rod very little, but with fear we always looked upon it. There, on low wooden benches, books in hand, sat her little scholars. We all loved her, I most of all, and I was often allowed to sit on a little stool by her side. I was happier there than anywhere.

I think I see her now, that placid old face, with her white hair turned up over a high cushion, and a clean, neat cap on top of it. One morning I was told I was not to go to school. I was miserable and cried to go to my Dame; it was a dark day for me. The next day I got up hoping to go to school, but no! I might not; then they told me she was ill, and I cried the more from grief. It was my first sorrow. That day, too, I passed in tears, and before evening I became so distressed that my mother, to appease me, obtained leave for me to go to school the next day. I went to bed and cried myself to sleep.

The next morning the servant was told to take me. All was so still as we approached the house that I had an awful feeling that there was something not right. The door was shut; so the servant tapped, and a girl opened it. Instead of the benches and my school-fellows in the room I saw the bed, let down and curtained, and my good Dame lying on it, pale and altered.

"Here is Master William; he would come," said my bearer, and a low, hollow voice from the bed replied, "Let him stay; he will be good." Shocked at her appearance, I stood and cried, until she motioned me to approach, and then scrambling up to her on the bed, she soothed me to quietude.

I saw the little round table covered with a clean white cloth, and something upon it which I did not understand, covered over with another cloth.

I sat still until she inquired of the little girl who attended upon her the exact time of the day, and then she told me a gentleman was coming. I asked her respecting the gentleman, and receiving an unsatisfactory answer, shuffled off the bed to the little girl, who had gone into an adjoining room, and learned from her that the expected gentleman was Mr. Wesley. I eagerly asked, "What Mr. Wesley?" Her answer confirmed my fears. It was the terrible John Wesley!

At that moment the knocker rapped, and while Lucy went to open the door I ran back to my Dame and round the bed, and looking through the window I saw his black stockings. I turned and gazed in stupor at my poor Dame, until the sound of his footsteps startled me to attempt instant escape, but before I could reach the door I saw the black legs, with great silver buckles, coming down the stairs, and there came into the room a venerable man, his long, silvery hair flowing upon his shoulders, his countenance cheerful and smiling and ruddy as a youth's, and his eyes beaming kindness.

Nevertheless, as he went up to the bed I trembled. With an eager, gratified look my poor old Dame drew her withered hands from under the bedclothes and clasped his proffered hand. He touched her cheek with his lips, and, continuing to hold her hands, he breathed out short sentences of consolation.

The room seemed illuminated by his presence, but I recollected having heard something about " Satan coming as an angel of light." He looked at me and said something. She said, " He is a good boy ; he will be quite quiet."

After much talk he uncovered the table, and I saw the bread and wine as I had often seen it at my Father's chapel. Suddenly he said, " Let us pray," and then he kneeled at the bedside. I was full of wonder ; I knew not what to think, but determined not to kneel. He began to pray and my tears flowed, and then I dropped upon my knees weeping, but feeling happy, I knew not why.

After prayer and all else was over he conversed affectionately with the poor afflicted woman, and, taking her hand, he again pressed his cheek to hers, and with a solemn benediction he bade her " Farewell " ; then, laying his hand upon my head, he said, " My child, God bless you, and make you a good man," and then silently withdrew. I wondered was this

" the Old Devil " ? I never saw Rev. John Wesley again.

From what had passed I feared my Dame was going to die, and I burst into convulsive sobbings. She beckoned me to her once more, and again getting on the bed, I cried myself to sleep in her arms. I was removed from her before I awoke, and never saw her again, for in a day or two she died.

Although a child, yet from that time I reluctantly listened to, and always distrusted, Mr. Huntingdon ; for of John Wesley nothing could now make me think ill. I feared to tell my thoughts, nor did I mention this scene until I heard the hawkers crying a new elegy upon the death of Mr. Wesley. Comparing his writings, which I have read within the last few years, I do not hesitate to declare that my childish preference for John Wesley is confirmed.

William Huntingdon was an illiterate man of vigorous mind ; my father was attached to his high, exclusive doctrines, and extended his attachment to the man. He had an occasional intimacy with him, and some years later corrected for the press several of his works, which I copied—particularly the " Bank of Faith " and " The Arminian Skeleton." In " The Last Will and Testament of William Huntingdon " he bequeaths to every heir of promise in the Christian world " that golden phœnix in its cage " called " The Pilgrim's Progress."

About the time of my Dame's death my Father told me he would buy me " The Pilgrim's Progress," that it should be my own. My father himself was a man of exemplary piety. He constantly carried a Bible of small size in his pocket, and had a larger one at home, daily used, and a volume of Crisp's Sermons.

Our family library consisted of a mutilated copy of Milton's " Paradise Lost," " Mrs. Glasse's Cookery," in worse condition, an old book of Farriery, and some Pamphlets of Mr. Huntingdon. With any other books

I was wholly unacquainted, and the addition of such a book as " The Pilgrim's Progress " to such a collection as ours was to me an event.   I eagerly longed for its coming home, and well recollect my emotions of heart when my father, eyeing me with affection, slowly drew from his pocket a good old woodcut copy of the famous " Pilgrim."

The first glance at the frontispiece delighted me. It represented the upper half of the Author, sleeping in a sort of cave, with his head upon his hand, and above him Christian, in a large hat and flowing coat, walking upwards towards the " Gate Beautiful," with a lion standing on each side of the way.   All the cuts were rude, yet they all pleased me ; but the pleasure I derived from the work itself is indescribable.   I read in it continually, and read it through repeatedly.   I read without the least conception of the Allegory, forgetting, too, that the narrative was a dream—I supposed it to be real and literal.   I earnestly desired to become a man that I might travel and find the places described.

One day upon some remarkable occasion my Father took me into the City, where I had never been before. He entered the Royal Exchange at full " 'Change " time, and perched me on his shoulder to enable me to see the quadrangle and the statues.   It was a sight wholly new.   I think there were some old flags hanging about.   I read the inscriptions on the columns, denoting the walks of the different foreign merchants and tradesmen, and hearing the strange din and buzz of the crowd and the ringing of the bell, I suddenly imagined we were in " Vanity Fair," and, clapping my hands, shouted out, " Father !   Vanity Fair !   This is Vanity Fair ! "

Some of the bystanders looked oddly, and one of them, a calm-speaking, elderly man, said, " What does the child mean? "   My Father answered: " Sir, the little fellow is a stranger to the place ; he has been reading a book called ' The Pilgrim's Progress,' and he fancies he is in Vanity Fair."   The old gentleman

smiled and observed, " Perhaps he is not far wrong."
I firmly believed that I beheld the spot where " Faithful " came to his end, and it was difficult to dissuade
me from the notion.

My admiration for " The Pilgrim's Progress " was
excessive, and after a while I entreated my Father
for another book of the same kind ; he astonished
me by saying he did not know another like it.   I
thought there must be many, and went moping about.

He bought me " The Holy War," but though this
was by Bunyan, it failed to interest me as did " The
Pilgrim's Progress."   In " The Holy War " I found
no " Christian " and " Hopeful " ; no " Wicket-Gate,"
no " Valley of the Shadow of Death," no " Giant
Despair," no " Vanity Fair," no " Interpreter's House,"
no " Delectable Mountains " with the shepherds, no
river with " Christian " helping " Hopeful " through
the flood—the " Shining Ones " on the other side.

My Mother had a cousin married to a Mr. Rees, a
Solicitor and Commissioner of Bankrupts, in Feather-
stone Buildings, Holborn.   He occupied, as a country
residence, the Manor House of Belsize, Hampstead,
and when the intimacy of relationship between Mrs.
Rees and my Mother was renewed I was left in the
family, a numerous one, chiefly of grown-up sons.
Leading to the mansion was a noble avenue of elms,
in which I was allowed to walk alone, keeping within
sight of the house ; in the rear were the offices and
gardens, an orchard, and a walled park, where I had
liberty to wander at pleasure.

I recollect that Belsize awakened in me newborn
senses.   There, near the park wall, I first marked
the different odours of flowers growing in the gardens,
the delicious smell of apples lying in the storeroom.
Then my ear educated itself to sounds, and I listened
breathlessly to silence—to its eloquence—my young
heart escaped in sighs, for I felt wonder.   There I
first heard the sound of the wild bee, and can still

point out the spot where I heard his drowsy hum among the flowers in the sultry heat of a summer's day.

I had an almost constant companion in the youngest son, a kind-hearted youth of about fourteen, tall of his age, and verging into a decline of which he afterwards died from too rapid growth. I was a favourite with him, although so much younger than himself. I helped him to build high among the branches of an ancient mulberry-tree a summer-house large enough for us both, in which we sat and read childish books, reasoned, and talked of birds and insects new to our eyes and of all innocent things.

We could occasionally hear from the heart of London the solemn striking of the hour by St. Paul's clock, and in quiet evenings a favourable wind bore to us the clear silver tones of the chapel bell of Lincoln's Inn. Often we were warned into the house by the clanging of the dinner-bell. Sometimes when we were with the family, and the weather indicated a storm, we slipped away from the house, and, clambering to our airy height, awaited the coming of the tempest, and abided watching the lightning, while the thunder rolled and crashed and the rain poured ; and then, when all had passed away and the sun shone out, we scrambled down through the drenched leaves.

Here, too, after sunset we were accustomed to sit, listening to distant sounds, looking for the appearance of the first star and the coming out of other stars until the firmament was gemmed with sparkling and shining lights. In whispers we talked of the freshening odour from the drenched earth and the clearing up. Often our outstretched eyes followed little flecks of cloud while they evaporated and were lost in the transparent rain ; we gazed on the clear sky and strained our sight to look through it into Heaven.

To this summer-house in the mulberry-tree we climbed daily. From such scenes and habits of childhood I derived a love for quiet and the country which has yearned in me throughout life, and has frequently detached me from alluring society and busiest occupations to bury myself awhile in rural solitude and nourish peaceful thoughts " far from the haunts of careworn men." I sought to be *alone*. In my solitary rambles about the place or in the adjacent lanes I used to sit and indulge in childish musings till some living thing caught my eye, and then I watched the motions and habits of insects, or examined little wild flowers and mosses, and closely observed things I had never before noticed.

On my return home from the delights of Belsize I had little liking for play, but continually hankered for books. Odd pence were sometimes given to me, and always expended on something to read, which was trashy stuff, sold at little shops ; in those days there were no " Penny " and " Saturday " Magazines, no works of healthy entertainment or of information for the young mind. Inquisitive [1] and imaginative, and often getting improper answers to my childish questions, I examined my own thoughts, and gathered education from them.

One day my Father brought home a little book which affected me to tears—Janeway's " Token for Children."

---

[1] To his son Alfred he relates that during one of his pleasant sojourns at Belsize, when they were making the grape wine, he was attracted by the odour of the mushed grapes in a large open tub standing in one of the outhouses. The juice was so tempting that, boy-like, he leaned over to get a drink, but, losing his balance, he toppled over, and his head was immersed till he was in imminent danger of suffocation, from which he was only saved by the timely arrival of the gardener. Rescued with head and clothing smothered in grape-skins, the culprit was stripped, bathed, and put to bed—an episode he never forgot, and which admirably served him " to point the moral " to his own boys.

I could read " The Pilgrim's Progress " or " The Holy War " in the presence of my Father and Mother, or of any one, but not " The Token for Children." With this I got away alone, into private places, where I could read and weep unseen. My Father occasionally talked to me about the things in this little book without my being able to talk to him ; had I spoken, I should have betrayed feelings which I strove to conceal.

My desire for reading became distressing to myself and to those around me, and I moped in my Mother's way until my Father sent me to a boys' day school. The scholars were numerous and well taught for beginners, but my situation was amongst advanced scholars, who were arranged on forms and at desks. Mr. Perry was a kind, religious man, loving and preserving order, and the scholars were exercised three times a day. The whole school, standing, sang out of Watts's " Divine Songs for Children." I especially admired " The Summer Evening," and thoughts recurred to me in after-life of other than of Watts's songs.

While I was at this school (1787) in my seventh year I rapidly improved, but within three months from my going I was attacked by the dreaded disease of the age, virulent smallpox, under which not all the medical skill nor watchful care employed could preserve me from sinking, apparently to death, and preparations were being made for the funeral, when I showed signs of recovery—young life was not extinct, Nature had sought repose in simulated sleep or trance, and the converse of my Mother and Aunt in relation to my funeral, which I overheard, in the struggle of agony forced an utterance, which arrested their attention.

My recovery was very slow. Soon afterwards my parents removed to Old North Street, Red Lion Square, and I went no more to that school. I missed the green fields close to the house, where I had been

allowed to roam. As I had not learned to write, my
Father, who wrote a fine distinct hand, taught me by
keeping me close at copying specimens he set before
me, and he took great pains to form mine. For four
years the greatest part of my time was employed in
learning to write and in getting lessons thoroughly by
heart from the Bible.

I was about nine years old when my Father went
to preach at a chapel in Paradise Row, Lambeth. I
was with him, and we were invited to dine by Mrs.
Johnson, a widow lady, who had an only daughter. The
friendship of our parents continued ; an attachment
between the daughter and myself strengthened with our
years, and in the year 1800 we were married.

About this time my inquisitiveness about sects and
opinions induced my Father to buy a " Dictionary of
All Religions," in two volumes, which I deemed scarcely
better than " Josephus," although I often turned to it
for one fact which riveted me upon the first reading.
The compiler relates that at the time of the Crucifixion
of Christ some mariners, being at sea, navigating on
a calm day and near a desert island, were surprised
by dolorous sounds and lamentations which seemed to
come from the desolate place. They steered close to
the coast ; there were no living beings to be seen,
and yet terrifying shrieks and wailings of distress ran
along the shore. The mariners were silent from
astonishment, and then they heard a loud voice mourn-
fully proclaim, " The Great God Pan is dead ! " I
never read this account without feeling a mysterious
awe and solemnly pondering.

Another circumstance roused some new thoughts. In
July, 1789, a boy whom I knew suddenly stopped
me in Hand Court, Holborn, from driving my hoop,
and with mysterious looks and voice he said, " There's
a Revolution in France." Little instructed, the word
" Revolution " was new to me ; I stared at him and
inquired, " What's a Revolution? " " Why, the French

people in Paris have taken the Bastille, and hung the Governor, and let loose all the prisoners, and pulled the Bastille down to the ground." "How do you know?" "My Father says so; he read all about it in the newspaper just now—and he says it's a Revolution." My informant's Father was a Captain in the City Trained Band.

I had a young brother who had long been in a decline, and his condition lay heavily on my Father's mind. The poor little fellow wasted fast in the heat of summer; he was too enfeebled to walk or to stand, and my Father sometimes came home early and carried him into the fields till sunset. On these occasions my brother Joseph and I went, and to him and to me these walks were delightful—what they were to my Father I can now well imagine, as with tears in his eyes, bearing this poor dying child on his bosom, he seldom spoke, except to him, while gently shifting him from one arm to the other. Sometimes my Father drew long sighs, and his features expressed sorrow and anguish, but his looks soon calmed, and his countenance radiated unspeakable peace. And thus he bore about his dying child as long as he could be lifted from the bed on which he lay.

When he ceased to breathe my Father was absent. On his return home, seeing us in black, he knew the sad truth, yet ceased to afflict himself—his looks expressed " Thy will be done." He immediately passed into his own room ; we listened and heard him praying, and presently he rose from his knees, and came in with a calm countenance. While the child lived in suffering the Father's tribulation was great, but when he died it ceased.

After the funeral my Father borrowed for me " Foxe's Book of Martyrs." The plain narrative of their sufferings and fortitude animated me to enthusiasm. I read the controversies they held at an apposite moment.

A family in the same house with ours were of the Catholic religion. Being out one morning, I was overtaken in Lincoln's Inn Fields by a little girl of this family, who told me she was going to her chapel, and asked me to go with her. I hesitated at first, but she was a good-tempered child, about my own age, and her persuasions prevailed with me.

On entering my eyes were attracted to a procession of singing boys in white vestments and shining scarlet, passing towards the stairs of the gallery ; but when in the body of the chapel I looked in amazement at the Altar, covered with white linen and decked with flowers, a shining pix and crucifix, altar-piece above, massive golden candlesticks on each side, vases burning with lambent flames, and priests coming from a side door in rich habits.

The service began with dulcet music, and proceeded with the singing of sweet voices, the chanting of the priests, the swinging of censers, emitting aromatic odours, and now and then the tinkling of a bell. I comprehended nothing of what I saw, but, indescribably lost in wonder, I long outstayed the hour by which I ought to have been home.

The scene, so different from anything I had witnessed in places of dissenting worship, operated to make me imagine I felt more religious, and, to indulge in this feeling, several times afterwards I strayed into their chapel. What I saw and heard was void of meaning to me, but my senses were charmed, and, with what the little girl told me at home of the devotion of the Catholics, and the hardships they endured, I began to think that the Romish religion was the only religion in the world.

It was at this juncture that I fell to reading the " Book of Martyrs." There, independent of their fortitude under torture, and the triumph of their deaths, I found enough to determine me from my notions, and to enable me to read and to understand in some degree, that " God is a Spirit, and must be worshipped in spirit and in truth."

Soon after this one or two persons known to my Mother lent me several books, to which she did not object, but thought my Father would, and I therefore read them unknown to him.

We young ones were sickly children, and I in particular was deemed consumptive. While recovering from one of my illnesses I read Brooke's " Fool of Quality," a book which I then thought delightful, and am almost certain that were I to read it again, after a lapse of forty years, I should think so still. It must have been a work of merit, for it was abridged by John Wesley. Except the " Book of Martyrs," it was the only book that religiously affected my mind at that age. But my serious thoughts, such as they were, quickly disappeared, and soon afterwards an accident befell me, fully adequate, it may be supposed, to their revival.

I kept some little fish in a decanter of water on the sill of a back window, on a second-floor landing. This window was almost beyond my reach, and one forenoon, being desirous of watching the fish at my ease, I clambered up and sat straddling across the sill. Suddenly I thought I heard my Mother coming, and fearing to be caught in that position, I hastened to get my leg in ; but by an awkward movement in trying to avoid the fishes' decanter I lost my balance and rolled out of the window. Catching a leading branch of an old vine that grew against the house, I held fast, my dangling weight freed the vine right and left, and I came down, ripping the immense branches above and around me, until I found myself flat on the gravel walk.

I struggled through the mass and found myself unhurt ; the alarm which had caused my fall had been false, nobody had seen the accident, and how the vine could possibly have fallen was a matter of wonder. I told my Mother, some years after, of my narrow escape from death, which had not produced in me the slightest reflection.

Shortly before this accident a favourite bird escaped from a staircase window ; I leaped after it to find myself in a neighbour's garden, and a prisoner. In my alarm I ran through the house, opened the hall door, and escaped—rejoicing that I had not been detected by the owner, Mr. Ayrton, who was believed to be very austere.

As a youngster I was not exempt from the perils of boyish adventure ; all through my life I have felt the splinters of a glass bottle, which shattered in my hand while firing a train, and inspired me with a wholesome distaste for gunpowder.

When not otherwise employed I amused myself with colouring children's common prints, and cutting out different figures from writing and coloured papers. My greatest indulgence was being permitted to go to the office of a neighbour, a copper-plate printer, where I watched him and his apprentice work ; much of my time was spent with him, observing these processes. I believe in the course of three years I saw every plate sent in to him. During this period I read only two books, a sixpenny dull " Life of Frederick the Great " and the " Life of Philip Quarll," with an account of his monkey " Beau Fidèle." These were purchased from my savings.

I was not eleven years old when I made my first attempt to purchase an old book. With an economy befitting my parents, their allowance of pocket money was suited to my age ; I had a penny a week to spend as I pleased. On a fine summer day of 1791, two weeks of that amount were in my pocket when I first saw the great book-stall outside the front of Nunn's large book-shop in Great Queen Street, at the corner of Wild Street. Of the money value of old books, and of the value of money itself, I was utterly ignorant, but I was suddenly possessed with the determination to buy one of the hundreds of volumes temptingly spread before me. I vainly examined several, for all were marked beyond the sum I held ready to my hand ; and those at the lowest price—sixpence—were in a box at the door.

There were none here that attracted me excepting a fine clean copy of " Garth's Dispensary," with a view of the old College of Physicians, Warwick Lane, for a frontispiece. While poring over it, out stepped the bookseller, J. Nunn—a large, formidable, farmer-looking man, in a sort of brown frock-coat, with amplitude of skirt—and desired me to go away. I offered him my twopence, telling him I wanted to buy that book, and proposed that he should keep it for me until I brought him the remainder of the purchase money. He took the money, looked at me in my pinafore (for in those days, and many years later, boys wore pinafores until twelve years old), and smiled as he turned from me to put it away.

The copper-plate printer permitted me to read all the odd sheets of printed paper that came to him in the course of business, and he gave me an old copy of Gesner's " Death of Abel." This book was a continual feast to me. It brought to my recollection Belsize—I imagined the country round it to be like Paradise. Since then I have not read the " Death of Abel " ; yet, even now, I remember the pleasure I then derived from the description of Eve's emotions on finding a dead bird, when she did not know what death meant. It impressed me deeply.

Within the range I was allowed for walking was the shop of a staymaker. One day, while sauntering up and down with my " Death of Abel," the staymaker beckoned me to him, looked at the title of my book and smiled, which encouraged me to ask him to lend me one. He fetched a volume from the parlour, the only book he had, and said it was too hard for me.

It was an " Essay on the Weakness of the Human Understanding," by Peter Huet, Bishop of Armagh. I took it with me, found it puzzling, yet I comprehended, by attention, something of the meaning. Huet's Essay first led me to *reflect*. I was then eleven years old.

I was in the habit of making my own every scrap of printed and written paper, whether from cheesemongers' or other shops, and one day met with an old printed leaf, which seemed to be part of an energetic defence of some man ; I could not discover who he was, nor could my Father. I took uncommon pains, and at every opportunity strolled into booksellers' shops, showing my leaf and anxiously inquiring. At last I obtained the information from a bookseller who possessed a copy of the book. It was the " Trial of John Lilburne."

By patience, industry, and extraordinary management I accumulated half a crown—I had for some time improved my resources by the disposal of toys and boxes which I made of card, and I bought the book. Since " The Pilgrim's Progress," no other book had so riveted me ; I felt all Lilburne's indignant feelings, admired his undaunted spirit, rejoiced at his acquittal, and detested Cromwell as a tyrant for causing him to be carried back to the Tower, after the Jury had pronounced him to be free from the charge. This book aroused within me new feelings, and a desire of acquainting myself with Constitutional Law, which in a few years afterwards I had an opportunity of acquiring.

In my twelfth year I was again sent to school. It was not so well conducted as the one I had been at five years before, but the boys were well taught. I was put at once into Arithmetic, and got on rapidly. The master liked me, and my fondness for reading, and he lent me an old " Annual Register," and a volume of a magazine. These seemed to afford new views, and I imagined if I could get the other volumes of the sets, I should possess an inexhaustible field of knowledge.

I had commenced the " rule of three " when a boy at the school ill-used me ; he was the son of a parish officer, and as my master favoured him, my Father took me away. This ended my scholastic attainments.

My Father kept me at home, instructing me an hour at midday and another hour in the evening. By myself I could make no progress in arithmetic, and home instruction became irksome to me. It was high summer ; we lived in a street on the suburb side of Red Lion Square, at that time open to the meadowland, but now forming the sites of Queen Square, Great Coram Street, the New Road, Pentonville, &c.

Every breeze that blew brought odours from the new-mown grass, and told of green fields. I remembered, and longed to renew, the rambles I had been accustomed to at Belsize. Had I been at school, desires of this kind would have been diverted by my occupations in company with the other boys, and my advance in learning, in which I really delighted, would have reconciled me to confinement. It was true I had a brother at home with me, but he was three years my junior, and our dispositions were different ; he cared but little for reading, and I cared for little else ; we would neither read nor learn together.

I saddened into listlessness, wrote without care, and had tasks set me in the Bible, which rendered the Book itself distasteful. I felt my faculties were wounded ; they seemed benumbed. Of the real condition of my mind and feelings my Father was ignorant. I spoke but little, and dispiritedly, and one morning on leaving home at breakfast-time, he required that (for some fault I had committed) I should get by heart a heavy task before he returned to dinner—at any time it would have been heavy, but in my condition then it was impossible. He put the Bible into my hands, telling me imperatively that if I did not learn it perfectly he would strictly chastise me. I sat on the stair-head gazing in dull vacancy on the open chapter without seeing a word, and closed the book in despair. On my Father's coming home, he required my task; I could only shed tears, without power to explain, and he punished me. My poor Father was not aware of the mischief fraught in me by this severity; from that time I regarded the Bible as a book of hopeless or heavy tasks.

My Mother, unknown to my Father, relaxed in my favour; she permitted me to go out with my brother, and together we rambled in the fields, always taking care to be within doors before my Father came home. In time she brought him to acquiesce in this indulgence, and I gradually recovered my usual spirits. Still, I was in want of proper instruction, and without books to read.

There is a cobbler's stall in Theobald's Road, London, that I go out of my way to look at whenever I pass its vicinity, because it was the seat of an honest old man who patched my shoes, *and my mind*, when I was a boy. I, involuntarily, reverence the spot, and if I find myself in Red Lion Square, with a like affection I look between the iron railings of its enclosure because, at the same age, from my Mother's window, I watched the taking down of the obelisk, stone by stone, that stood in the centre, and impatiently awaited the discovery of the body of Oliver Cromwell, which, according to local legend, was certainly buried there, in secrecy, by night. It is true that Oliver's bones were not found, but then "everybody" believed that "the workmen did not dig deep enough." Among these believers was my friend the cobbler, who, though no metaphysician, was given to ruminate on "causation." He imputed the non-persistence of the diggers to "private reasons of state," which his awfully mysterious look imported he had fathomed, but dared not reveal.

From ignorance of wisdom, I venerate the wisdom of ignorance ; and although I now know better, I respect the old man's memory. He allowed me (though a child) to sit on the frame of his little pushed-back window, and I obtained so much of his goodwill and confidence that he lent me a folio of fragments from Caxton's "Polychronicon" and Pynson's "Shepherd's Kalendar," which he kept in the drawer of his seat, with "St. Hugh's Bones" and the instruments of his "gentle craft." This black-letter lore, with its woodcuts, created in me a desire to be acquainted with our old authors, and a love for engravings, which I have indulged without satiety. It is impossible that I should be without fond recollections of the spot wherein I received these early impressions.[1]

---

[1] Thus he tells how he occasionally whiled away a half-holiday with one of those good-natured, elderly gossips who encourage and are pleased with the inquiries of young children ; and we learn how early were impressed upon the unsullied page of his memory some of those experiences which were to develop into mature thought, and engender aspirations which soared far beyond the range of the humble cobbler's simple wisdom or archæological knowledge. We have, too, an early intimation of the maternal influence. His mother was an ardent admirer of the character of Cromwell ; she would frequently talk to him of the great Protector—or of "Oliver," as she styled him, with the familiarity one uses towards an intimate. Circumstances favoured her predilections, for while living at Hammersmith she became intimate with one who claimed to be a descendant of her hero—Mr. Thomas Cromwell, a brewer. Again, on removing to Clerkenwell, she had the satisfaction of sending one of her grandsons to school to one of the stately old mansions in the rear of St. James's Church, which was said to have been one of the residences once occupied by Cromwell. The house was destroyed by fire about 1845.

Entick's "Dictionary" had been bought for me before I went to school, and then Bailey's "Dictionary," upon which, for want of other reading, I incessantly pored. By this practice I became such an adept in spelling, that I tried to compile a Spelling-book. I found I should not be able to get it printed without money, and on that account my first attempt at authorship was abandoned.

The French National Assembly had declared war against Germany. My Mother began to have, daily, a newspaper, which I read to her and her sister, who lived with us. They commented, and I took great interest in what they said. A large folio "Geography of the Whole World" by James Theodore Middleton, Esq., borrowed from a neighbour, contributed largely to our information, and with the aid of papers issued by the "Associations for preserving Liberty and Property against Republicans and Levellers," we became politicians.

In the Geography were some lines addressed by Addison to "Liberty," and others in imitation of them to "Slavery" by the Geographer. These lines seemed to me a subject for panegyric. I arranged them side by side, and below Addison's, stated in prose the blessings of Liberty in England, and beneath the Geographer's, denounced the National Assembly and the horrors of Slavery, the cruel death of the King, &c., in France ; and wrote above "The Contrast." Then I composed what I called a "poem" and put it beneath the prose.

These doings obtained praise from my Mother and from my Aunt, who was very fond of me, and a smile from my Father. We raised the money for putting it to the press, and finally "The Contrast" appeared in print upon a quarter of a sheet of paper, without any name but with these words dictated by my Father at the foot—"The Author of the above is only twelve years of age." A copy sent to the Association, at "The

Crown and Anchor " in the Strand, procured for me
a flattering letter of thanks from the Secretary. I
received presents from those who promoted the publication equal to its expenses, with a few shillings surplus.[1]

Bishop Watson's " Apology for the Bible," in answer
to Paine's " Age of Reason," was given to my Father,
and he gave it to me. I only knew the " Age of
Reason " existed by his conversing with a friend upon
it as a mischievous work ; its nature I soon understood
from the Bishop's book. Until the " Apology " informed me, I never conceived the Bible had been, or
could be, doubted or disbelieved, and, strange to say,
although I thought Bishop Watson proved the untruth
of much that Paine had written, yet the Bishop's work
alone created doubt in me who had never before
doubted. I mention this much as a fact, without
remark. My wish is to relate truly, every circumstance I can remember, that tended to produce extraordinary states of mind, with the thoughts and

---

[1] The boy's " poem " commenced :—

" Come Britons unite, and in one Common Cause
Stand up in defence of King, Liberty, Laws ;
And rejoice that we've got such a good Constitution,
And down with the barbarous French Revolution !

" There's *Égalité* Marat, and famous Tom Paine
Had best stay where they are, and not come here
    to reign.
Be staunch for your King, and your good Constitution,
And down with the barbarous French Revolution ! "

The same burden runs through the whole of the six
verses, of which these two are a fair sample. The
letter of acknowledgment, dated from the " Crown
and Anchor," April 27, 1793, evinces the pleasure of
the Association in perceiving " a spirit of loyalty in a
person so young," and trusts that a continuance in the
same sentiments will make him a valuable and useful
member of the community.

reflections and views of religion which in these pages will be fully disclosed.

For two or three months a gentleman whom my Father had long known—and a man of religion—allowed my Father to send me to his office, in Canterbury Square, Southwark, that I might see something of business. The two hours allotted for dinner, I chiefly spent in wandering alone over the neighbouring wharves, and walking about the Borough. After leaving the office at eight o'clock in the evening, I sometimes went to a little bookseller's auction, in Tooley Street, where I contrived to buy a few books, with savings from my dinner money and my pocket allowance. This was almost all the pleasure I had, for the clerks delighted to tease me, except the eldest, who took me two or three times to public tea-gardens and places of what he termed innocent amusement, to see, as he said, a little of life—nor seemed to think a boy of my age could be harmed by observing scenes of licence and depravity.

My Father must have observed a change in me for the worse, for he took me away, just as I began to make myself agreeable to the persons who had sneered away my simplicity.

I was now in my thirteenth year, and became very importunate with my Father to find for me a situation in which I could earn something by my handwriting. His intimacies were few, and his inquiries ended without success. By a bold step for a boy of my age, which my Father laughed at as impossible to be availing when I proposed it to him, I got such a situation in a few hours, at City Chambers, Bishopsgate Street, with a gentleman just entering into business as a solicitor. I was his factotum. While his office was there, I was punctual and attentive and gave him entire satisfaction ; but he removed to Nicholas Lane, and there unhappily, in the room in which I sat alone, he placed a book-case, filled with the works of the Poets and

Dramatic authors, with the door unlocked. The books irresistibly attracted me—reading them occupied time I should have devoted to my business ; my employer remonstrated with me upon my neglect, without knowing it had been occasioned by his own omission to lock the book-case door.

I promised and strove to amend ; but the book-case, seductively open, infatuated me ; while daily resolving to read less and less, I heedlessly read more and more. Conscience did its office, and I determined to leave off reading entirely, after I got through the contents of the fatal book-case. That period never came, for I was suddenly, and deservedly dismissed, with an imagination inflamed to intensity by the infatuating reading in which I had recklessly indulged.

Although this was a disgrace under which I shrank, it had one advantage—absence from the books by which I had been infatuated, discovered to me that I had become disqualified for sober reading. I knew there were Poets, and when " Cook's Poets " commenced, I bought the poems of Thompson and Goldsmith, as they came out, in weekly numbers.

They were the first poems I read, and I derived from them lasting benefit. The simplicity and tenderness of " The Deserted Village " and " The Traveller," and the just descriptions and noble sentiments in the " Seasons," refined and elevated my mind. I saw nature with a new-born sight ; in its quiet scenery I felt emotions of peaceful delight unknown to me before—my affections went forth to every living thing ; my heart expanded with rapturous joy.

I had no other schooling than what has been mentioned, but from the time I could hold a pen, I had been taught, by my Father, to write. His handwriting, like every trait in his character, was pure and distinct, each letter well formed and clear, and all so plain and compact that each word he wrote, like every word he spoke, could not be mistaken or doubted.

I had been actively employed in the office, and now to copy the examples which he wrote for me before he left home in the morning was but mechanical, and I was confined within doors. It was summer, an irresistible longing to ramble in the fields and meadows came over me ; I was allowed this indulgence, as I always had been, before, but not after, breakfast. Yearning with a desire to indulge my young imaginings, I was compelled to earn means for my support among the realities of life.

I presume it was with a view to have me under his own eye that my Father got me into the office with himself, at Clerkenwell, where he assisted in managing the concerns of the Parochial Board, and my business was to help him. His firm religious character and gentle disposition commanded general esteem, and while with him I was safe. Here I had access to a good English Library, and in my leisure hours read many books, particularly Rollin's " Ancient History," " Plutarch's Lives," Pope's " Homer," and most of Swift's works.

I now began to think what station I should be likely to fill in life, and conceived myself doomed to be an attorney's copying clerk. This occupation I looked upon with horror. All persons whom I knew in that situation were thoughtless beings, weak, mindless, and scarcely paid for their labour. Under the apprehension of being devoted to this drudgery, I became melancholy, and in the summer evenings stalked about the fields, anticipating and brooding over the hardships of my imagined destiny.

I found myself fixed to a desk under my Father's eye. The establishment was large, and there were wild young men under articles of clerkship, and a number of other clerks. In his presence all was well ; for he was strict with me, and not sparing of mild but effective remonstrance with them when their language deserved censure. They were mirthful upon his being a Methodist, as they called him, yet they respected his rectitude and open conduct, and uniform good temper. Their playful and vain endeavours to entrap him into some neglect of his business duties were exceedingly amusing ; his position gave him no authority over them, but his character shamed and restrained their licentiousness. In his absence they were unbridled, and more successful with me than with him, and when they got me into fault, betrayed and exposed me to his censure.

I was becoming unhappy, and wished myself away, when a popular performer at Sadler's Wells was about to have his benefit, and he being a client of the office, the partners of the firm took a quantity of tickets for themselves and the clerks. This being announced, there was much speculation as to the manner in which my Father would receive his. On one being presented to him by a gentleman of the firm, he respectfully declined it.

The partner who had given me the ticket undertaking to ward off my Father's displeasure, two of the clerks carried me with them into the theatre.

At breakfast the next morning, my Father seemed hurt, but both he and my Mother were silent ; I was silent too. There was noisy discourse at the office on the performance, and ludicrous attempts were made to draw my Father out, but he would not be brought to speak.

The effect was produced which I conclude my Father had foreboded. At busy times, the clerks and I were occasionally sent long distances in the evening, after business. These walks I had found irksome, but now I coveted them ; at my solicitation, many were frequently transferred to me, and by extreme running I effected my business errands in time to get to some theatre at the half price, and I became play-house mad.

Gratification increased my desires ; my limited weekly allowance of pocket-money, which had sufficed for book-buying, went a very little way towards the expense of my headlong indulgence, and I teased my Mother till she added another sixpence to it, and then I sold all of my books that I could get together. I was soon exhausted, and became restless and uneasy. Happily I had formed no intimacies, and therefore had not been seduced by associates into the vices inseparable from theatrical acquaintances.

A dissolution of partnership making a change in the business arrangements of the office, induced my Father to provide me with another situation, in every respect better. My new employer (Mr. Pelletti) had recently begun business as a solicitor, and just married when I became his clerk. I had heard my Father say he was a Unitarian, but though I had completed my fifteenth year, I did not know what " Unitarian " meant. Soon after I went to him, he dispatched me to a distant bookseller's with " Ben Mordeccas's Apology," and a number of other books which I afterwards knew to be Unitarian. I brought back in exchange, as had been previously settled, a set of William Law's works. I read as I came along and was very much interested.

This gentleman was mild, quiet, and strict ; he sat in the same room with me, and for many weeks occasionally read to himself in one or other of these volumes, which now and then he happened to leave on his table—then I read, too. This he discovered, and took an opportunity of talking to me upon the importance of religion—lent me one of Law's pieces, which he said might be suitable for me, and which I kept in my desk and read with great interest. He afterwards started short conversations, and caused me to consider my passion for the theatre. In a day or two my kind employer quitted town, taking with him Law's works. I bought the " Serious Call to a Devout and Holy Life " and read it through with thought and reflection, but being left alone with much leisure on my hands, I renewed an intimacy with an old schoolfellow, and through him gradually became acquainted with a young man who, as our familiarity increased, drew forth all my notions, and then amused himself with laughing at them.

He calmly insinuated that I was in " leading strings," and should be good for nothing while I read silly authors, and took things upon trust. I knew not what to answer, and in a few conversations I thought him unanswerable.

He was my elder by three years, well educated, and seducingly eloquent. He had settled to his own satisfaction that religion was a dream, from which those who dared to think for themselves would awake in astonishment at their delusion ; that the human mind had been kept in darkness, and men held in slavery, but that the reign of superstition was over ; that when intellect should be cultivated to the extent of its powers, the majority of virtue would proclaim its omnipotence ; the rights of one would be the rights of all ; governments would disappear, and every individual would be self-governed.

My new friend told me this was the " New Philosophy." Had these opinions been stated abruptly, I should have shrunk from them with horror ; but each was plausibly introduced—unfolded by degrees—and maintained with much eloquence, by a succession of arguments, plain, and, I thought, undeniable.

I was in my sixteenth year when I became a convert to this wretch-making " New Philosophy," as it was then called, which Mr. Robert Owen has since revised and systematically attempted to diffuse, under the name of " Socialism."

I acknowledged a great Creator—who, satisfied with what He had made, left the creatures of His creation to do the best they could for themselves, and, if there was a future state, it would certainly, be better than this. I looked upon the obsolete religions of antiquity as worn-out erections, which Christianity had somehow or other suppressed, and to which it had succeeded. I imagined that with the cultivation of the intellect, Christianity also would disappear, and Reason become omnipotent. With the growth of these notions, I contrasted Scripture authority — treated its historical accounts as absurdities—ridiculed its sacred characters —and regarded Christianity and its doctrines as impositions and childish dreams.

In the writings of Plato and his followers I sought in vain for satisfaction. To me, their philosophy seemed mere imaginings, and I resolved to inquire no more. At a moment when my mind was disengaged from these speculations, my eye happened to fall upon a New Testament which lay open at the fifth chapter of Matthew, and I read the Saviour's discourse upon the Beatitudes with an interest I never felt before.

At that moment I determined upon a thorough perusal of the New Testament. I read it ; and having read about the same time in one of my then favourite books a parallel between Socrates and Christ, I concurred in the conclusion of my author—that the character of Christ stood out as an example of inimitable virtue. The devotedness of the Disciples to their Master and the successful preaching of the Apostles after His death, were facts not more unaccountable than the wide diffusion of Christianity in after times, and the certainty that among the multitude in my own time there were, at least, some who were real believers.

The standard and rule of Christian conduct seemed to me to be the example and teaching of Christ Himself, and this conception was strengthened by my reading an " Essay on the Internal Evidence of Christianity," which so powerfully insisted upon *lowliness, meekness, love of righteousness, absence of resentful feeling,* and *purity of heart,* that I was charmed into admiration, and thrown into despondency of ever being able to attain such virtues.

The effect produced upon me by this tract rather increased than diminished during thirty years of after life. I frequently recurred to it at seasons when I was little supposed to be occupied by solemn thinkings, and I was accustomed to imagine my own father to be the only real Christian whom I knew.

When about sixteen, I became a member of the "London Corresponding Society," [1] very much to the

---

[1] The London Corresponding Society met in the Strand, sometimes at the Globe tavern, sometimes at the "Crown and Anchor"; the objects and method of working appear with tolerable clearness in the pages of a pamphlet published by the Society in 1794. An address to the "citizens" of England ridicules the notion that "the Constitution of England is the perfection of human wisdom" (a tenet to which, by the way, Hone had subscribed in the first published poem); appeals to Magna Charta and the Bill of Rights against "the usurped power of the judges," particularly against "the unconstitutional and illegal Informations Ex Officio," whereby the arbitrary will of the King's Attorney-General was made to usurp "the office of the accusing jury"; and ends with a passionate plea for the redress of grievances to be obtained only by "a fair, free, and full representation of the people." (Here, in fact, we have the first glimmerings of the era of reform.) Then is printed the King's Speech which was delivered at the opening of Parliament on the 21st of January of that year, with its detailed allusions to the French War then in progress, " for the maintenance of our Constitution, Laws, and Religion, and the security of all Civil Society " (the Address, in its opening sentences, had alluded to the "immense numbers of our countrymen slaughtered in one campaign"; to "our trade, commerce, and manu-factories almost destroyed"; to "many of our manufacturers and artisans ruined, and their families starving"; had deplored the taxes which add to the

distress of my Father. My connection with that and
other debating societies completed the mischief. I
disregarded his admonitions, eluded his restraint, joined
a society which kept me out late at night, and
opposed my Father's remonstrances by questioning his
right to control me. I became self-willed, and determined not to be swayed.

An extensive circulating Library supplied me with
romances and novels, which I read rapidly and
incessantly. My desire for works of this class was
insatiable, and I believe there were none then existing
in the English language which I had not sought out
and perused. This class failing me, I was compelled
to recur to miscellaneous and depraved reading.

My mind had thus become enfeebled when, unhappily, a book was warmly recommended to me by
a youth named Jackson, who distinguished himself as
a speaker in the " School of Eloquence." This work
was then publishing in sixpenny numbers, by Kearsley,
a respectable bookseller in Fleet Street. It caught
my imagination and it wrought upon me to believe,
what its object was to prove, that in Nature there was
nothing but Nature. (I forbear to mention the title.) [1]

I had reveries upon the notions eloquently set forth

---

nation's affliction and the intolerable load of imports
with which it was already overwhelmed—and all in
a   fruitless   crusade   " to   re-establish   an   odious
despotism in France "). On the last leaf of the
pamphlet is appended a letter of appeal, signed by
John Horne Tooke, asking for contributions in aid
of the defence of a Scottish delegate to a similar
society, in Edinburgh, who for his strenuous advocacy
of the cause of constitutional reform had been indicted, and stood in imminent danger of fourteen years'
transportation, to which two of his countrymen, for
a precisely similar " offence," had just been sentenced.

[1] The reference is believed to be to the philosophy
of Holcroft and Godwin.

in the works I had studied. For two years I speculated on them as facts. At length it occurred to me to collect a few *evidences* of the truth of their assertions. Vain were all my researches for a single specimen of *proof*, and I began to doubt the verity of the New Philosophy.

Researches, however, of this nature were the means of my gleaning some particulars of the habits and manners of the living authors who had seduced me to believe in their teaching, and led me to doubt whether my instructors were better or happier, or would live longer than other men.

There occurred an opportunity of seeing one of these distinguished characters. I had been told where, on a certain evening, he might probably be met. I went, and at the moment of my entering the room the " perfectibility " philosopher, to my utter astonishment, was violently energising under a momentary disappointment, in itself so trivial, that, if it had caused similar passion in a child, such violence would have been inexcusable.

Before I left the house, I learned that similar paroxysms of ungoverned temper were habitual to him. Until then, his works had been great favourites with me ; I never looked at them again, nor ever afterwards saw, or desired to see their author.[1]

---

[1] Apparently the " author " and " perfectibility philosopher " to whom allusion is here made was William Godwin, who, in his " Enquiry Concerning Political Justice," states that education, literature, and political justice " are the three principal causes by which the human mind is advanced towards a state of perfection." Godwin's temper was at times tempestuous and violent—there is a story that once he took a knife and threatened to stab himself unless Shelley advanced him money. He was a republican and an atheist ; it was his powerful defence of Holcroft and Horne Tooke in the *Morning Chronicle* that did so much to break down the charge of high treason against them.

I was in my seventeenth year, and my home was at my Father's. He certainly had not discovered the lengths to which I had gone, but I am inclined to think Mr. P. suspected something of the matter, and warned my Father, for he obtained a situation for me with Mr. Jeffreys, a Solicitor, in the busy town of Chatham, which was surrounded by a beautiful country.

I was compelled by my employer to attend every Sunday at the Parish Church. My connections in this place were with a few respectable young men of about my own age, all thoughtful Churchmen. During our intimacy, I gradually disclosed my opinions, yet without desire to force them. My disbelief was to the uttermost, but I was not easy. I forebore to disguise my thoughts, but I concealed the discomfort of my feelings. When we were not together, which was seldom, I took solitary walks, and climbed the hills, or strolled in the woods.

I frequently walked far into the country,[1] beholding the quiet scenery of Nature with a new-born sight ; contemplating in solitude the wonder of silence, until the darkness warned me home. Although impenitent and unbelieving, yet sometimes in the presence of my Father, I reverenced in him the inexplicable *something* which, opposed to my wickedness, seemed to heave my heart.

Religion had no charm for me, save as in " Watts's

---

[1] His musings at such times he occasionally expressed in verse. Here is an extract from a composition he wrote in 1797 :—

" Oft when pale Ev'ning throws her mantle o'er
   The clear bright prospects of declining day,
I frequent roam till past the midnight hour,
   And, to its secret influence, homage pay..

    *   *   *   *   *

These scenes assuage the pain of inward grief,
Draw forth the silent tear, and give the heart relief."

Songs," which brought to remembrance the Dame School of my infancy, and then the home of my Father. About the end of my eighteenth year I returned to London, and entered the office of Mr. Egerton, of Gray's Inn Square, and while there continued to indulge my habit of reading.

My home was now at Lambeth, with a pious widow lady. Every Sunday I attended with her at Surrey Chapel. The personal peculiarities and the fervid and fearless preaching of the Rev. Rowland Hill amused me. I deemed his sermons waking dreams, that, as to a man asleep, his imaginings were to him realities, and that he was an honest enthusiast. Now and then some of his remarks startled me, but my secret unbelief stifled my conscience, and my alarms disappeared with the day.

It is remarkable that I had a vague, undefined pleasure in listening to sermons and joining in the prayers and singing. I both wished and dreaded to be religious. I had no fear or hope of futurity, no soul, or spirit to depart ; no hope but to live, no fear but to die ; no fear of death, but as the end of life.

It was my will to have as much pleasure as I could get—my means were limited, my desires boundless. I soon found my capacity for enjoyment was also limited, and I was, of necessity, pleased to be a little rational.

I began to think when all this would end, and fell into fruitless musings. I willed to be as happy as my Father—but this was impossible. I concluded that he was happy because he was ignorant. He knew nothing of literature, never read a newspaper, and it was difficult to obtain his attention for more than a few minutes to news or details of great public events —wholly destitute of learning, and of that worldly wisdom called *tact*, he lived by faith and prayer.

By the term *ignorant*, I do not wish to imply that my Father was misinformed ; but that *I* considered him so, because his information was not so varied as my own. It had been acquired in a different way, and from other sources. I had sought mine in the frivolities of worldly life, and in books, of which some had ensnared and deluded me.

My Father had read the only books of *Truth*—the *Bible* and the *Works of the Great Creator*. Thus he had become intimately conversant with the economy of the animal kingdom ; their usefulness to man, their diseases and their cures. From habitual and accurate observation he could recognise the particular sheep of a flock, by its distinctive countenance, as we recognise each other ; and by their habits and those of other animals and of insects he judged correctly of weather —its changes for wind, rain, or other atmospheric variations.

His gentle kindness to all animals was known for miles away from his dwelling. Of earth's productions, he knew the many grasses, grains, herbs, plants, and forest trees ; their construction, qualities, and different uses ; nor were flowers, as objects of beauty, slighted by him, whose eye delighted in the loveliness of rural scenery, with a pure enjoyment.

He would also watch the pliant forms and graceful attitudes of children at their innocent play, with extreme pleasure, and when he came across a fine picture would view it with a critical eye, in his appreciation of correct form and colour.

He was painfully affected by the sufferings of the poor ; could he have willed it, every human being would have been in comfort and happiness. Obedience, order, and neatness were the rule of his house. A punctual observer of time, he had such a sense of justice that if he were a quarter of an hour behind he remained at his office a quarter of an hour later, or came a quarter of an hour earlier next day ; and, scrupulous in his duties to man, his Bible was not introduced at his place of business.

He was no sightseer. Except on the occasion of the King going to St. Paul's, and when he took me to see the Royal Exchange, I have no recollection of such indulgences. Not that he was indifferent to performance of public duties—of which sightseeing was not one. Humility and patience were his practice. Temperate in personal requirements, and plain in dress, he often pointed out the Quakers as examples of uprightness in gait and in mind. I could fill a volume with anecdotes of his virtues, and do not know that he had a single vice, for vice instinctively shrank from him.

Sometimes I wished that I, too, had been ignorant—ignorant of the book which had caused me to doubt, and to believe that death was annihilation. I began to question whether my knowledge was of any use. It gave liberty to do as I would, but not the power. I desired to make every human being happy and virtuous, but I saw that if I could diffuse all the wealth in the world that its inhabitants could not be *happy* with my knowledge, and I was *sure* they would not be virtuous.

I continued to attend on Sundays at Surrey Chapel. In July, 1800, I married Sarah, the daughter of my landlady, Mrs. Johnson. I opened a circulating library in Lambeth, with stationery and books for sale. My wife's good mother, who enjoyed a respectable income, lived with us for a year or two, and my attendance at Surrey Chapel was pretty regular.

Now and then I was seriously impressed by the preaching of the Rev. W. Jay, of Bath ; and with so much advantage that I went, alone, to his Wednesday evening Lectures.

No other minister had ever interested me to that extent. One of those Lectures so seriously affected me that on the Thursday or Friday after I sought an interview with Mr. Jay, at Mr. Hill's residence. The servant told me he was much engaged, and could not be spoken with by any one. I desired to be allowed to wait his leisure, and I finally succeeded in getting to him, and telling him I wished to disclose the state of my mind. He said he could not possibly enter upon the subject with me in private ; he assured me his time was wholly appropriated, but that if I would be at the Chapel on Sunday, when he proposed to preach his last sermon before leaving London, he would then mention what would apply to me, and to others who felt as I did.

I anxiously listened to him ; he seemed to have me in his thoughts, and to have understood the particulars of my case, although I had not disclosed them ; and he exhorted with much earnestness and force. My convictions at the time were very strong, but they gradually declined.

*   *   *   *   *

Here the Autobiography, as originally set down, comes to an end. There is appended the following summary of the chief activities of his subsequent years, with a sort of apologia for his life's mistakes—it is almost the revelation of a soul in revulsion from its blind heretical lapses. At the end of this summary, written in 1838, there is a note added three years later of a reverential pilgrimage he made to the soil in which his ancestry was rooted.

(*Written 20th Dec., 1838.*) I have been a lover of the world and its pleasures, a curious observer of men and manners ; an insatiable reader in search of truth ; an anxious inquirer after happiness.

For a short time, in my early years, I was a believer in all unbelief. To efface this I read the Bible, and I sincerely reverenced its moral teachings. Utter unbelief became impossible, and I had commenced to arrange what I called " Ethics of the Bible," when I published some " Parodies " on portions of the Book of Common Prayer. These " Parodies " I suddenly suppressed in deference to the feelings of my Father and others.

Two months after their suppression I was arrested for having published them, and committed by the judges to the King's Bench. While there I continued my "Extracts from the Bible." Upon my liberation I completed the Bible Extracts, and had arranged them for publication, when I received notices of my forthcoming trial for the "Parodies." I defended myself ; and after obtaining verdicts of acquittal, I immediately inserted in every London paper a letter, disclaiming all intention of republishing the "Parodies," or of publishing any others, and admonishing others to the same abstinence.

Upon my Trials I really believed I knew Christianity —I declared myself to be a Christian. I afterwards commenced a critical examination of the New Testament, and by criticising and rationalising I made out a pleasing, but perplexing, rational Christianity. It was pleasing as a thing to admire, but as Religion it was perplexing. There was a glimmering of light to the understanding, but it imparted no warmth to my heart ; there was something in it to please me, but nothing I could *love*. I tried to be happy, and could not.

The 18th, 19th, and 20th of December, 1817, are memorable dates in my wayward life, for those days gave my name publicity. Their anniversaries might perhaps have been kept in rejoicing by me and my family, but they have annually passed unheeded, save by a casual remark that these were the days . . .

Now, however, all in the house but myself having retired to rest for the night of this 20th of December, 1838, and I being thus left in quiet loneliness, recollections arise of the hurries of that evening one and twenty years ago, and I find myself pondering on the multitude of events which have since transpired ; on the rapid flight of time ; and especially on a circumstance of more importance to me personally, and to society, through me, as one of its members, than any other connected with my existence.

Explanation to the public has long been due from me, and I no longer defer, in the hope of more leisure, to give it ; but seizing on the departing minutes of this anniversary, as though they were my last moments, I proceed to an explicit disclosure which it is my purpose and hope to continue, at brief intervals, until it be complete.

After my " Trials " (which I published in 1818), the public befriended me ; and from 1819 to 1824 I wrote political pamphlets for its amusement, which sold extensively, besides other pieces—literary, antiquarian, and controversial, of less notoriety.

Elsewhere I have related with what motives, under what circumstances, and in what manner I executed and published in 1820 a volume, the " Apocryphal New Testament." And here I desire to state that I have long felt deep remorse for having produced that work. I have lived to experience that it is justly offensive to pious minds, and so is detestable to my own. Its apocryphal gospels are contemptible forgeries.

Throughout 1825 and 1826 my time was wholly occupied in writing and conducting " The Every-Day Book " ; and in 1827, " The Table Book." In 1828 I merely edited a reprint of the late Mr. Strutt's " Sports and Pastimes of the People of England." In 1829 my pen was idle, nor was it busied in 1830, except for a few weeks upon an ephemeral " History of the Three Days' Revolution in France," undertaken much against my will, at the instigation of the publisher, who had become the proprietor of the " Every-Day Book " and " Table Book," and for whom I employed the year 1831 in writing and compiling " The Year Book."

Since 1831 I have written nothing for the public except two antiquarian articles in the *Times* of October the 17th or 18th and 21st, 1834, on the late " Houses of Parliament " ; another in that journal of November the 1st on " Tallies," and in the same journal of November the 14th a brief notice of Oberlin, the pastor of Waldbach, claiming for him and excellent Louisa Sheppler the reputation due to them as the *first institutors of Infant Schools*.

(*Tottenham, 1841.*) In July, 1840, I went with my dear wife from our then residence in London to Richmond ; while there for a few days we visited Ripley and saw Homewood Farm, where my Father was born in 1755.

The Rev. Mr. Onslow, the minister, Bonsey, the parish clerk, and other elders of the parish still remembered him. I had never been in the village before ; it was to me lovely, from its peaceful aspect, and especially endeared by the occasion of our visit to it, and was animated to my mind's eye, by my Father's fancied form in farm dress when a child ; as he had, more than half a century before, described himself to me—who was then also a child.

Now he was no more, and I, the only one in England of his descendants, had become old. I have only one dear brother—he is a barrister, holding various offices in Tasmania.

Chantrey's statue of James Watt, in Westminster Abbey, is an inimitable likeness of my Father, and the attitude is as strikingly characteristic as if he had actually sat for the great sculptor.

III

EARLY STRUGGLES

THE Autobiography extends only to a short time after his twentieth year, when he assumed a double responsibility—he married and entered into business. With a hundred pounds from his mother-in-law he purchased stationery, started a circulating library, and added his own books for sale.

Hone's first shop was at his mother-in-law's in Lambeth Walk, the highway to Town from Vauxhall and other villages. It was surrounded by gardens, and verged on the open country.

To his stock of books he soon added prints ; he attended auctions ; by assiduous study he acquired a knowledge of the different schools of design and styles of engraving, acquainted himself with works of art and artists, and read chiefly to that end.

For many years his life was a series of failures, aggravated by the responsibilities and cares of wedlock and paternity. Episodes of philanthropy and social reform, as we shall see—such as an abortive effort to establish a savings bank and an equally laudable attempt to mitigate the horrors of lunatic asylums—mark a career more interesting and successful.

He was not long in discovering that book and print buyers were somewhat rare in the locality of Lambeth Walk, though his ingenuity had devised the novel form of attracting attention by affixing descriptive labels to the book covers, an innovation which enticed a few stray customers and originated that custom of old book-sellers which prevailed before the days of elaborate catalogues.

An episode of this period illustrates that impulsive humanity which was so marked a feature in William Hone's character. His benevolent nature would perhaps have better befitted one who possessed a larger share of this world's goods ; in him it sometimes led to awkward situations.

Returning home from the City one winter night, he came upon the watchman, in whose rough custody he was astonished to see an infant in arms. The little waif had been left on a doorstep, and the watchman was not unnaturally perplexed what to do with it. "The poor little thing," said he, " will be starved if I keep it in the watchhouse till morning. Nobody will take it in. And I dare not go so far away from my beat to take it to the workhouse." Here was a pitiful plight for a forlorn and helpless infant—just the thing to go straight to the tender heart of a man like Hone, who in his characteristic way settled the difficulty, after due consideration, by taking the poor little waif to the house of his mother-in-law, Mrs. Johnson, who was easily prevailed upon to give it shelter till the morrow ; which was all very satisfactory, even though it left Hone open afterwards to the jocular sallies of his friends.

Shortly afterwards he removed with his wife and child to St. Martin's Lane, where he became acquainted with Mr. Charles Townley and many other men of learning, who highly esteemed him for his great natural talent and conversational ability.

Charles Townley, who died in 1805, was a con-noisseur, who had lived much in Rome. His collection of ancient statuary, medals, &c., was purchased by the British Museum for £28,000.

The premises in St. Martin's Lane were more favour-able for business, but unfortunately he was compelled to leave them. He had been induced to take the shop for a short term by the promise of a long lease to follow. The owner now broke faith, and another removal was necessary. But scarcely had Hone settled in this new abode, with his wife and two young children, than the giving way of a party wall necessitated their prompt removal to yet another home. And so they returned to Lambeth, which he had already proved to be anything but a centre of commercial activity, and occupied a house belonging to his mother-in-law.

In 1804 Hone compiled what he put forth as " Millington's Cookery," on which his Chatham friend John Venning wrote :—

" DEAR MILLINGTON,—It appears to me unaccountable how such a subject ever popped into your head. I should have wandered over the wide field of literature and stooped to cull many fairer flowers in preference to going near the hedge to pick gross herbs and aromatic plants for real use."

Here, with the mention of Venning, it may be found advantageous to become retrospective for a brief space, in order to introduce some of the friendships Hone had formed while living at Chatham, a few notes on which will prove helpful towards the better understanding of our subject.

It was purely on account of the democratic principles, of which he had so freely imbibed, through his connection with the London Corresponding Society, that at the age of sixteen young Hone had been sent away to Chatham. It was deemed advisable, both by his father and his employer, that he should be removed from an influence to which he, as they believed, had surrendered his better judgment.

During the two years or more that William Hone was in Chatham he formed a number of pleasant intimacies and friendships, which were kept up long after his return to London.

Extracts selected from his correspondence with these Chatham friends will throw some further light on the character of the man, or at least will prove of interest from the local and topical allusions they contain.

One friend, C. Few, writing under date September, 1797, remarks—

" that you are ' an original ' cannot be denied and that you are sometimes ' leadeny ' must also be admitted, and in the letter or note I am now answering I have a specimen of it. Oh! Hone, Hone, thou surely art somewhat confused in thy upper stories."

After this gentle piece of raillery the writer betrays his appreciation of the man, and the value of his friendship, in a later sentence :—

" To be at variance with such a worthy fellow as W. H. would give me no small share of anxiety."

From this correspondent we obtain valuable insight.

His " affectionate friend, C. Townson," writing May 13, 1799, shows an even more intimate acquaintance with Hone and his idiosyncrasies :—

" As I have just returned from a visit to friend Seaton, you may naturally conclude that I shall not sympathise with you in your hypochondriac affections. . . . Laugh ! laugh, you dog, 'tis the best cure in the world for the hyps. . . . You appear when you wrote to be under the influence of one of those melancholy moods which the soul is sometimes betrayed into. If the cause should proceed from some calamitous misfortune or real evil, it then stands in need of the soothing voice of consolation, or the pious breathings of religion. . . . Write soon, unbosom yourself to me, and the little comfort that I am able to give you shall be heartily at your service."

In the June of the year 1800 Hone received a visit from his " sincere friend, J. Venning," of Strood, who, upon his return home, writes his graceful acknowledgments of the hospitality he had received at the hands of that " amiable " woman, his friend's mother. The writer, although himself a bachelor, ventures in the course of his letter to give Hone some advice on the delicate subject of matrimony, into which it appears the latter was about to plunge.

Hone married, and in 1801 was blessed with a daughter, upon which occasion his friend writes in this strain :—

" Joy, joy, my good fellow, I give you joy of your young she bairn—it's the wrong sex. You say nothing of Mrs. H.—hope she is in convalescence. Does the babe show any symptoms of Honeyism? "

The same correspondent, in a letter dated from Rochester, September 24, 1802, makes the following significant allusion to Hone's interests, both spiritual and material :—

" I hope, Billy, you have met with another situation to your wishes or a greater share of business than when I last saw you. I am afraid Providence does not think itself under any obligation to bestow undeserving favours on you—You don't go to Church."

Allusion is made to Hone's business matters in another communication dated March 21, 1803 :—

" The last letter I received from you informed me that I should hear again when you had taken possession of your house in St. Martin's Lane, which I suppose you have long since done. . . . I hope you push on prosperously in your new situation, and meet with all the encouragement you deserve. . . . No doubt ere this you have bought some experience to enable you to act on a steady principle, and to judge of things more by their intrinsic worth than from appearances, as you commonly used to do."

The last two extracts from the same writer's epistles are dated 1804, and both have reference to Hone's wielding of the pen, first as a correspondent :—

" I cannot help noting with what facility you adopt the fusty old-fashioned and precise terms of *thee* and *thou* on all occasions in your prose correspondence. . . ."

Then with regard to his writing for publication :—

" I am informed that you are about to commence a new scene of Life and to acquire Fame by a glorious display of those powers of mind which you should thank your Creator for—it is worthy and laudable so skilful a character should employ himself so advantageously for the public good."

In after-years considerable correspondence continued to pass between Venning and Hone in relation to bookselling transactions.

In August of the same year another letter contains a remittance of £10, in two banknotes, in part payment for a number of books consigned through Venning to various purchasers. In 1812 Venning, having then taken the Parsonage House at Rainham, near Chatham, for " an Academy for the education of youths," is still writing to Hone respecting their book-dealing transactions, which appear to have been numerous and extensive. And here we may leave the Chatham associations and resume the thread of our narrative.

From being a bookseller William Hone became a student of books, and developed into what may be better described as a bookman—a tradesman who handles his literary wares with tender, loving hands,

with whom the effecting of sales is as a man parting
with his treasures, and to whom the making of a profit
is almost a sacrilege.

Like Michael Johnson of Lichfield, he was a bookseller of the old school, of that ideal type which it is
the delight of the fictionist to adopt for a character—
one who is always far more intimately acquainted with
the insides of the books on his shelves than with those
of the ledger on his desk.   As a rule, these are the
booksellers who do not wax fat and grow rich, but
who inspire the confidence of their customers, whose
shops are a centre of influence upon the culture and
intellectuality of the neighbourhood.   Where, in any
way, Hone fell short of this ideal was that, owing to
the severe buffetings he received at the hands of the
world throughout his life, his establishment lacked the
very desirable quality of permanence.

On the congenial topic of " old booksellers," Hone
himself is entitled to be heard.   In an article written
later in life he says :—

" From the time I could read and use a pen, I have
been a lover of books and addicted to writing.   My
pursuits led me frequently among the booksellers, and
I had a knowledge, more or less, of many of them now
no more.   I think I may call the late John Nichols
the father of the trade.   He was an eminent printer,
and the biographer of his friend and predecessor,
Bowyer, and the annalist of our literature during the
greater part of the two last centuries, a work for
which his connection with literary men supplied him
with abundant materials.   He had been contemporary
with Dr. Johnson and George Stevens and Edward
Malone, and intimate with most of the writers of that
school.   The whole Society of Antiquarians, of which
he was a member, were personally familiar with him.
He wrote a topographical account of his native parish
in Leicestershire, and became the able historian of
his native county, and author of many other antiquarian
works.

" Old Carter, the indefatigable draftsman of our Gothic antiquities, and Gough of Enfield, co-author with King of the sepulchral antiquities, and the laborious editor of Camden, were his friends, and he was a friend to many a humble dependant on the pen for subsistence. He was a Tory, yet he kept poor Bingley, after he had been persecuted and imprisoned and ruined for publishing the celebrated No. 45 of the *North Briton*. Wilkes had neglected Bingley, who had stoutly contested, and to the last moment firmly denied the right of the Court of King's Bench to imprison him. Mr. Nichols gave employment to the unfortunate man, and maintained him when he was past labour, and at his death, buried him.

" The Chamberlainship of the City had been obtained by Wilkes, who was as profligate in politics as in morals, and Mr. Nichols, being a member of the Corporation, and being both literary, they were intimate. I remember Wilkes. He was the last wearer of scarlet and gold in the streets, and in withered old age, with that dress, a cocked hat, a horrible squint, a satyr-like lubricity of mouth, and his tongue flopping in and out, his appearance was shocking.

" Mr. Nichols, until his death was, as his portraits exactly represent, a stout cheerful-looking man, with spectacles, remarkably active in mind and person, mild in speech and manner. His amenity was visible in the pages of the *Gentleman's Magazine*, of which he was the proprietor and editor. The manner in which he conducted this work enabled him to command local information on subjects connected with his pursuits from all parts of the Kingdom.

" Every person who met with an old ring, an ancient seal, a relique of by-gone times, or a similar custom which he required to be explained, sent an account of it to ' Sylvanus Urban,' and in this way in the course of a century, during more than which period the *Gentleman's Magazine* existed, rendered that Miscellany an immense storehouse of antiquarian facts. It was an especial favourite with quiet old country Clergymen, and favoured by all zealous antiquarian inquirers, among whom, I believe, I may reckon myself. My propensity that way procured me, now and then, a pleasurable chat with old Mr. Nichols at his Printing Office in Red Lion Court, which was afterwards Mr. Valfrey's, and is now the office of the well-known Mr. Richard Taylor, printer and learned Saxon Antiquary. Here Mr. Nichols kept his immense literary collections stored away, and accurately arranged, in old-fashioned book-cases and presses, and here he politely received every person who came to him on business, or who was, or aspired to be, an antiquary. I condescend only a smile to the sneers of witlings at the labours of such persons of whom many, surrounded by their books, can afford to say :—

> " ' Friends and companions get you gone
> 'Tis my desire to be alone,
> Ne'er well but when my thoughts and I
> Do domineer in privacy.
> No gem, no treasure, like to this,
> 'Tis my delight, my crown, my bliss—
> All my joys to this are folly,
> Nought so sweet as melancholy.'

" So in the beginning of his ' Anatomie of Melancholy,' sings or says old Burton, who, by the by, while praising the pleasures derived from ' great tomes ' and ' those studies of antiquity,' slips his pen aside, and adds inoriginally, and withal quaintly, ' As in travelling the rest go forward and look before, an antiquary alone looks round about him, seeing things past, and hath a compleat horizon, James Bifrons.' Mr. Nichols' studies and his large business as a printer proceeded together. He was printer of the Votes of the House of Commons ; sole publisher of an immense number of topographical and antiquarian works which he had printed for their authors, or on his own account, besides his own numerous productions ; and partner in the Copyright of almost every important work published for the Booksellers."

These allusions of Hone to Nichols of the *Gentleman's Magazine*, and the other literary celebrities of his time, are not without some little value.

In 1805 the vicissitudes of fortune led William Hone into another walk of life. He engaged himself as book-keeper to Mr. E. Lowton, a hop factor in Southwark. His new employer's affairs proved to be seriously involved ; he became a bankrupt, and shortly after-wards died. Hone was retained by the assignees to manage the settlement of the bankrupt's affairs, in the course of which business a characteristic little episode occurred. He found hidden away in the office a stencil plate of the " Kentish Horse " ; divining the use of this to have been the conversion of Sussex hops into the more famous Kentish brand, and feeling an unutterable contempt for such fraudulent dealings, he took the plate away with him that night, and on his way home flung it over the bridge into the Thames.

Always industrious, his spare hours at home during this period were occupied in the use of his pen. His output in 1806 included an edition of " Shaw's Gardener," and a compiled work on " Farriery." Work of this kind, and even of a more laborious nature, such as indexing a new edition of Berners's " Translation of Froissart," varied the next few years of his life, in which he was twice bankrupt. For a tradesman whose busi-ness was as yet in the making, he undoubtedly spent too much of his time upon public affairs. No busi-ness needs more constant personal attention than bookselling.

About this time Hone, true to his nature, was attracted by the tenets being promulgated by a Dutch-man named John Bone, who had escaped from the horrors of the Bastille and taken refuge in England. The two men became intimate in studying together the principles of Savings Banks, and the great national advantages to be derived from the establishment of such institutions.

With his friend Bone he established an institution which with laudable optimism they styled " Tranquillity," in Albion Place, Blackfriars Bridge, combining the features of a savings bank, an insurance office, and an employment registry office. Sir William Stirling and other persons of substance acted as trustees, but, like Hone's other philanthropic and commercial schemes, the concern soon failed.

If these two men did not become the pioneers of the savings bank as a working institution, they at least deserve some credit for the missionary work they accomplished in clearing the field for those who entered it subsequently. For any real hope of success in the establishment of so gigantic a scheme as they proposed, it was essential that they should receive the approval, and if possible the tangible support, of His Majesty's Ministers. The Government was then in the hands of a Whig administration ; Mr. Fox was in power, and the Hon. George Rose [1] granted Hone several interviews in connection with his philanthropic proposals. But though the countenance of the Government was not directly denied, no actual support was ever forthcoming, and the project fell to the ground, as already stated.

---

[1] George Rose, a statesman of some note in his day, held many offices, including those of Vice-President of the Board of Trade, and Paymaster-General. Though a placeman of whom Cobbett did not fail to make a butt, he was a man of high personal character, amiable and benevolent, and really rendered valuable services to the nation. He certainly did much to forward the foundation of savings banks, and promoted legislation securing the prosperity of Friendly Societies. Therefore the satirist who wrote the following lines must be discounted :—

> " No rogue that goes
> Is like that rose,
> Or scatters such deceit."

This appears to have been the way in which the abortive scheme took shape. Hone, as Secretary to "Tranquillity," used his influence with Stirling and other men of standing to get up a meeting to found a proposed "Society for the Gradual Abolition of the Poor's Rate." A meeting was held at the Horn Tavern, Doctors' Commons, April 23, 1806. A manifesto issued on that occasion, and signed " W. Hone," deplores the wretched condition of the " lower orders," declares the Poor Law system to have failed to ameliorate their lot, and proposes the application of entirely new principles towards that end. The poor were to be taught not to depend upon " charity," but to rely upon their own exertions.

As a means to that very desirable end, the proposed " Society " was to be linked up with the institution already founded under the alluring name of " Tranquillity," and " every respectable person was invited to become a member," pay a guinea at admission, and subscribe one guinea to its funds annually. The secretary of " Tranquillity " was to act also as secretary to the " Society." The objects of the promoters cannot be described more tersely than in the seventh resolution passed at the meeting on the date above mentioned :—

" That every one who in the time of youth and vigour treasures up all he can spare to provide for the season of Age and Infirmity, has performed the utmost duty that Society in that respect can require of him ; and if after these endeavours he has been incapable of providing what is sufficient to furnish him with Necessaries and Comforts, Society is unjust if it does not make up the deficiency, not as a matter of Charity but of right."

Do we not find an echo of contemporary effort in the terms of this manifesto? Here was " Lloyd George legislation " foreshadowed long in advance of its time. The nation was not found ripe for it by upwards of a century at least.

One of his faithful Chatham friends whose views on " necessary class distinctions " are perfectly typical of the period, wrote to him on the subject as follows :—

> " CHATHAM, 8*th June*, 1806.
>
> " DEAR HONE,—You sent Charles a small political work written by a friend of yours, and a copy of the Resolutions of the Society ' For the Gradual Abolition of the Poor's Rate ' with your name subscribed as Secretary. By having read and heard more of the plan of this Institution from Mr. Bone's publication, I have conceived the highest opinion of the system and think that it does credit to those who are now labouring to do away the corrupted establishments and inefficient measures which have for such a length of time been borne for the maintenance and keep of the poor in this country ; yet I am persuaded that old prejudices are difficult to be done away. But, my good fellow, I do not prejudice your endeavours ; my only anxiety is that as you have a wife and family to support and a reputation of talent and industry to sustain, they may perhaps suffer by your attention to this institution whilst other opportunities of improving your fortune may slip from under you, and you at length fall into a distressed and impoverished state of living.
>
> " Yours most sincerely,
>
> " J. VENNING."

Mr. Venning's fears were but too well grounded, for shortly the office of " Tranquillity " at Albion Place, Blackfriars (the site of which is now covered by the railway bridge), was closed ; the few deposits were returned, and the subscribed funds being insufficient to meet expenses, the unfortunate secretary lost his furniture under a distraint for rent, and his wife and family went to her mother, whose home was the customary refuge in their distresses. The deposits were placed in the custody of a banker in the Strand.

The home life of William Hone at this period, when his children were young, reveals him as an

exemplary father and husband. The intense love of
Nature which he manifested and which he so carefully inculcated in his children, has given to the
religious views of his early manhood a tinge of
pantheism.

Hone, like his father before him, passed through that
period of religious doubt which is incidental to the lives
of most men who are given to serious reflection. The
course taken in each of these gropings after Divine truth
differed according to the period ; that of the father (an
ardent Evangelical) was tinged with the intensity of
religious fervour characteristic of the Wesleyan Methodist
revival ; that of the son was unmistakably influenced
by the spirit of the French Revolution—we find him
at this period of his life still cherishing the doctrines
of a deistic rationalism. Hence his care for the moral
training of his children. A man who is irreligious
cannot afford to be immoral. William Hone, however,
was entirely without that mysticism in which his father
had indulged himself. Still, he was swayed by the
forces of heredity, and more so by those of training.

Hone's extraordinary industry was often impeded
by serious spells of illness. Throughout the winter of
1808 he was prostrated with rheumatic fever, one result
of which was to maim his right hand, and for months
he wrote only with his left, contributing his usual
serial articles while labouring under this disadvantage.

Indeed, the indomitableness of his industry was
manifested by the never-flagging pursuit of his literary
labours under every possible form of distraction,
whether mental anguish which was sometimes caused
by his domestic afflictions or the more persistent worry
of monetary embarrassments which so constantly beset
him. Whatever his private cares, his brave heart never
quailed at the call of duty, and every engagement
undertaken by him was fulfilled to the utmost so long
as the physical strength remained wherewith to accom-
plish it. At least distraction from present care, if

not consolation, was to be found in assiduous and unremitting labour.

Repeatedly do we find Hone embarking upon commercial enterprises without sufficient capital. He was constantly in a maelstrom of debt, struggling against heavy rents and grievous taxation, against the excessive cost of all necessaries of life incidental to war times and particularly burdensome to one with an increasing family. At length, in partnership with Mr. Bone, he took the business of Messrs. Jordan & Maxwell, " Old and Curious Booksellers," in the Strand. •

Towards the end of 1810, a year of severe commercial depression, the names of Bone and Hone were gazetted in an unusually long list of bankrupts. Mr. Bone, free from domestic ties, took a shop in May's Buildings, while his partner was glad to become clerk and cataloguer to Mr. R. Saunders, book auctioneer. Presently this employer succumbed to the general depression, and Hone's family had once more to find shelter with his wife's mother. Getting together a small stock of books, he opened a shop at High Street, Bloomsbury, and managed to eke out a living with his pen.

His second bankruptcy occurred when Hone was trade auctioneer, a post to which he was preferred in 1811 on the retirement of John Walker, by the goodwill of his bookselling brethren. He had his countinghouse in Ivy Lane, and took his brother as his clerk and assistant. His auction-rooms were at 45, Ludgate Hill, where a number of fine libraries were dispersed under his hammer, the sales of some of the collections lasting for ten or twelve days. His first large sale was at the Albion Tavern, and the results of this and the succeeding sales were satisfactory to both buyers and sellers ; but they were too far between to supply the necessities of a family of seven children. With William Hone, however, business ventures succeeded and failed with the regularity of a see-saw. To the hour of his death his life was one unsuccessful struggle. But he was not the man to be beaten down by private misfortune, and at this very time he was devoting his energies to the affair of the Burdett procession (p. 87).

With this family of seven children he lived in humble lodgings in the Old Bailey, and supported them by stray contributions to the *Critical Review* and the *British Lady's Magazine*. His letter-writing was always extensive.

It is to be feared that Hone and his family suffered privation in the times of his misfortune. Even in his later years, when his fame as a writer was established, the property which resulted from his talent—the extensive sales of his " Every-Day Book " and " Year Book," for instance—served only to provide the necessities of the hour.

IV

A BOOKMAN'S ACQUAINTANCES

AT home, as well as abroad, it will be seen, Hone was brought into contact with quite a number of public characters and people of note in his day. A bookseller's shop generally being a common meeting-ground for persons of culture may account for a number of the acquaintances he thus formed ; but many of them were political, and some few of the intimacies may indubitably be traced to that sympathetic nature, that readiness to advise and assist, which so strongly characterised the proprietor of the establishment.

In 1810 Hone published a fine engraving of Napoleon and Josephine, who were divorced that year. His personal opinion, delivered in connection with this event, was, " Napoleon has thrown away his best friend. Mark ! he will fall ! " On the question of female capacity generally, at a period when most people so grossly underrated it, he used to say : " Never despise the opinion of sensible women ; their judgment upon subjects on which they are fairly informed is in most instances correct ; they have quicker instinctive perceptions than men."

Another unhappy woman of the period with whom Hone sympathised was one of his customers. This was the Lady Augusta Murray, consort of the Duke of Sussex, the excellence of whose character, combined with her misfortune, naturally commended her to the public sympathy. The Duke of Sussex shared with the

Duke of Kent the affections of the English people, but he had married without his father's consent, and George III. had no compunction in annulling the marriage. The people, all the same, insisted upon calling her the " Duchess," and according her the dignity of " Highness."

She was the second daughter of the Earl of Dunmore, and the Duke had met her at Rome, in 1792. She was several years older than the Prince, and when he proposed marriage to her she at first declined, but in the end they pledged eternal constancy to each other, and signed a written contract. They then went through the marriage ceremony, performed by a clergyman of the Church of England, in Rome— a ceremony they repeated a few months later at St. George's Church, Hanover Square, under disguised names. All this availed but little, as the marriage was void under the Royal Marriages Act of 1772.

Two children were born of the union, and they took the name of D'Este. The Prince for some years set the decree of his father's Court at defiance, but in 1809 he applied for the custody of the children.

We now quote from Mrs. Burn's MS. Memoranda :—

" Lady Augusta came frequently, accompanied by her young son and daughter, and her sister, a slender lady of gentle bearing. The drawing-room floor used to be kept in readiness for her reception, where she would look over the books she selected. She derived much pleasure in conversing with my father, often talked of the Duke in terms of deep affection, and would weep over the cruelty of their separation. Her carefully cultured, highly improved mind attracted the admiration of the literary and other talented persons of the day. Of an amiable, generous disposition, she often brought presents of comfits, dainty sweetmeats, &c. (indulgences much rarer than in the present day), and would have the children, as she said, ' to entertain' ; her own, who were several years older, joining

6

in their play ; she would herself roll the baby's ball, and was at all times affable and kindly ; ever graciously recognising the attentions our mother was happy in affording her.

"One time, when the ball rolled under her chair, she fancied her cotton stockings attracted our notice, her sister's being silk, whereupon she laughed merrily, and said : 'My dears, I cannot afford the luxury of silk stockings as my sister can ; she is richer than I am '—an assertion that very much astonished us. Her carriage was always sent away after setting her down, as she feared that if she was known to frequent company adverse to Court politics, the security of her pension might be endangered."

Her two children who played about Hone's drawing-room grew up and succeeded in life. The daughter became the wife of a Lord Chancellor, as Lady Truro ; the son, known as Sir Augustus D'Este, filed a bill in Chancery and strove by every means to get his mother's marriage legitimatised, but always without success.

"Another regular visitor" (continues Mrs. Burn) "was Sir Lumley Skeffington, who would exclaim, as he turned over the portfolios and came upon the portrait of a handsome woman, 'The loveliest of the lovely ! ' or, perhaps, 'An angel ! ' Sir Lumley was seen many years later, attired still in the costume of his earlier days : the amply plaited shirt frill, pointed tail coat, chimney-pot hat of the old shape, shin 'pumps' tied with large bows, and white silk stockings. He walked slowly and feebly, his eccentric appearance attracting much attention, of which the venerable gentleman seemed to be totally unconscious."

Sir Lumley Skeffington was a dandy and a playwright—does not Byron allude to his "skirtless coats and skeletons of plays"? He was an intimate of the Carlton House circle, and invented for the Prince Regent a new colour, known as the "Skeffington brown." His own dress for many years comprised a dark blue coat with gilt buttons, a yellow waistcoat, white cord inexpressibles, with a large bunch of white ribbons at the knees, and short top boots. Gillray once caricatured him dancing in an exquisite attitude and attire, labelling him " Skeffy Skipt-on."

" Mr. Thomas Coram, a descendant of Captain Thomas Coram, the founder of the Foundling Hospital " (continues Mrs. Burn) " was another friend of my father's, and when a fire destroyed all his property and he received serious injuries from molten lead which poured upon him while making an ineffectual effort to rescue his two kittens, he came to our home, and stayed until his wounds were healed, and his arrangements for the future could be made.

" Soon after the revolt in St. Domingo, a coloured boy was fêted in London, by the Liberal party, as the son of Toussaint L'Ouverture. Active and intelligent, he was in great danger of being ruined by ' hero worship.' Perceiving this danger, my father pitied the lad, and rescued him by bringing him home. He interested some friends in the case, and money was subscribed to meet the expense of sending the boy to school, after he had passed some few months in our family.

" It eventually transpired that he was not a son of L'Ouverture, but my father's interest in him continued, just the same, as will be shown by the following letter.

" ' 331 STRAND
" ' *Tuesday 23rd. Octr.* 1810.

" ' MY DEAR JOHN,—I send you enclosed in this Letter " La Feuille Indicatrice des Tempéramens," and I wish you and your companions much amusement from these Temper telling Fish.

" ' Do not return them until they cease to give you pleasure and by that time my little girls will be very glad to see their old friends move about again—as you can keep them as long as you please they will be of as much use to you as if they were bought with your own money.

" ' I hope you will soon let me have the still greater pleasure of lending you some books, for from books you can gain more amusement than you can get from all the toys you have ever seen, and more instruction than you have had from all the people you have ever talked with.

" ' After you begin to read you will soon be able to understand many things which you now only wonder at, and speedily be convinced of this grand Truth, delivered by one of our greatest Philosophers, that " Knowledge is Power."

" ' I told Mr. Mercier to-day I was going to write to you, and he wished me to tell you that he was very glad to hear of your progress at Mr. Dalton's. Mr. Bone and all friends beg to be remembered to you, and we all most certainly send you the best of good wishes for your health and improvement.

" ' I am, Dear John,
" ' Your true Friend,
" ' WILLIAM HONE.
" ' John Toussaint L'Ouverture.'

" John Toussaint was at Grandmother's, Lambeth Walk, weeks or months. Fanny and Fids were there at the same time, about 1809 or '10. He used to ' climb the large pear tree like a cat, and Dads my life, Fan was up after him in a jiffy.' Those were dear Granny's words in telling of these exploits, at which you may be sure our father was highly amused. Toussaint was a handsome, perfectly black boy—I used to wonder where he slept, but never ventured to dive into the mystery. We were all sorry when he left us."

The tragic story of Toussaint L'Ouverture has been told by Harriet Martineau in " The Hour and the Man."

Mrs. Burn introduces us to another noted character of the period :—

" The soi-disant Princess Olive repeatedly requested my Father to inspect the documents which, she said, proved her claim to royal kinship. His own native desire for information prompting compliance, he went to her house, and thus describes the interview : ' I was ushered into an upstairs apartment, where, after the briefest of visiting courtesies, the Princess, in a rather excited manner, introduced me to a round table covered with papers, at which I was only permitted to look as the Princess selected or read to me. This went on for some time, when, by degrees, as the papers were scattered, her Highness edged her chair, so that I had to move mine. Then she would insist on my reading with her ' a most important paper '—another edging of the chair—another retreat—and so on until we had fairly circled the table. With the prospect of other rounds in view, I started up, seized my hat and escaped, never more to examine the proofs of the Princess Olive's title to Royalty."

The person who called herself the Princess Olive of Cumberland was a Mrs. Olivia Serres, born at Warwick in the year 1772, and educated by her uncle, Dr. James Wilmot, Rector of Barton-on-Heath, Warwickshire. She married her drawing-master, John Thomas Serres, a marine painter of some ability ; the union proving unhappy, she parted from her husband, and occupied herself with painting. Obtaining an introduction to the Royal Family, she was in 1806 appointed landscape painter to the Prince of Wales.

In 1809 she began an incoherent correspondence with the Prince, offering to lend his Royal Highness £20,000, at the same time begging for pecuniary assistance. She also tried her hand at literature, wrote a novel, some poems, and other works.

In 1817 she made her first claim to be the daughter of Henry Frederick, Duke of Cumberland, and in a petition to George III. alleged she was the daughter of the Duke by Mrs. Payne, a sister of the Rev. Dr. Wilmot, and the wife of a captain in the Navy.

These claims she later amplified, asserting herself to be the legitimate daughter of the Duke of Cumberland, and in a memorial to George IV. (1820)

assumed the title of Princess Olive of Cumberland. A newspaper called the *British Luminary* took up her cause, and a wonderful pedigree was invented for her. When arrested for debt in 1821 she claimed the royal privilege of exemption. In 1823 Sir Gerald Noel, who had long interested himself in Mrs. Serres's pretensions, presented a petition to Parliament, and moved that it should be referred to a Select Committee. Joseph Hume seconded, but the motion was negatived, Sir Robert Peel, the Home Secretary, declaring the lady's claims to be entirely baseless. Mrs. Serres spent the rest of her life in difficulties, dying in 1834 within the rules of the King's Bench. There is good reason for believing that she had a hand in writing the scandalous "Secret History of the Court of England, by Lady Anne Hamilton."

A time of great popular excitement was coming over the land. Sir Francis Burdett (the father of that estimable lady the late Lady Burdett-Coutts), at that time Member for Westminster, who had long been a champion of popular rights, in 1810 became the centre of a great turmoil in London. He had published in Cobbett's paper, the *Political Register*, a letter to his constituents, declaring the conduct of the House of Commons illegal in imprisoning a Radical orator. It appears that John Gale Jones, the manager of a debating society (one of those pioneer institutions of reform which marked the awakening of England at that time), had issued a handbill against the enforcement of the Standing Order for the exclusion of strangers from the House during the inquiry into the ill-starred Walcheren expedition. In the handbill he had declared the enforcement to be "an insidious and ill-timed attack on the liberty of the Press, and tending to aggravate the discontents of the people." Jones was incontinently committed to Newgate as guilty of "a breach of privilege."

Burdett having made an unsuccessful motion for the

discharge of Jones, wrote his " open letter," which in its turn was brought before the House, and declared to be a scandalous libel on the rights of that august assembly. For two nights an angry debate was waged in the Commons, with no little violence of language, and at half-past seven o'clock on the morning of April 5th it was determined by 190 votes to 152 to commit Sir Francis to the Tower on a breach of privilege.

When the Speaker's warrant was issued for the apprehension of the popular idol the tumult began, the populace breaking the windows of the Members who had voted against their favourite. Sir Francis resisted the warrant for his committal, and barricaded his house in Piccadilly. The Riot Act was read, and when the Guards were called out a number of the rioters sustained injuries. On Monday, the 9th, the house was broken into, and Sir Francis was conveyed to the Tower under a strong escort. On their return the troops were attacked by a furious mob and the soldiers compelled to fire ; in fighting their way through Eastcheap a number of persons were killed.

Lengthy proceedings in the courts of law ensued, Sir Francis bringing actions against the Speaker and the Sergeant in the Court of King's Bench for redress. The case was ultimately carried to the House of Lords, but in the end the authority of the House of Commons was fully vindicated : everything had been done according to ancient usage and established precedent.

When Parliament was prorogued on June 22nd the imprisonment of Sir Francis came to an end. A procession was announced to convey him home in triumph, but he departed secretly by water, and the mob followed an empty car to Piccadilly.

Foremost among those who organised this procession was William Hone. All London appeared to be out of doors that day, and every one sported the " true blue " colours. The streets along the line of route were decorated, and the windows crowded with spectators. Those at Hone's windows included Lady Augusta Murray and her sister—he was then living at 45, Ludgate Hill, on a site now occupied by the railway bridge.

When the unwelcome tidings came that Sir Francis had returned by water the disappointed people tore off their colours.

" Lady Augusta and her sister," writes Mrs. Burn, " gave theirs to our baby brother. My father indignantly tossed his out of the window, and they condoled with each other over the defection of the people's favourite. Later in the day a report was circulated that Sir Francis, whose health had suffered from his confinement, had been too ill to encounter the fatigue of a public ovation."

" Old Glory," as Sir Francis was nicknamed, was not a man to be relied on.

It may be readily understood that Hone, so sincere and enthusiastic himself, would be proportionately disappointed and mortified that the baronet, after sanctioning, or at least permitting, those public manifestations of rejoicing at his liberation, should slink away, and leave his friends to return with their flags and banners, and the decorated carriage without the golden calf.

An anecdote relating to this processional affair will show the temper of many parties at that time. Lady Augusta Murray, with her sister, son, and daughter, were at Hone's to testify their sympathy with the popular cause ; but that their presence might not be generally known they had the drawing-room to themselves—" For, you know," said Lady Augusta, " I must be careful lest I pay for my patriotism with my pension."

Among Hone's papers is a letter from Sir Richard Phillips, dated May 7, 1817, addressed to " Mr. F. Place, Woollen Draper, Charing Cross (it was evidently called forth by Hone's case, which was then exciting all London), in which he lays down that an arrest upon *ex-officio* information is so contrary to existing statutes that it constitutes an assault, and that detention under it is false imprisonment. This authority was a Radical, a vegetarian, an author, a publisher of cheap miscellaneous literature, and many other things ; he was a man of original opinions on matters of science and literature, of whom Mrs. Burn has left this note :—

" Sir Richard Phillips was a frequent ' dropper in ' and ' gatherer by the way.' He gleaned a store of information during his gossips. One day, looking over some papers with us, my Father came upon a wrapper containing some relating to Sir Richard, one being a list of about 20 titles for works. ' Sir Richard,' said he, ' once asked me to give him some subjects to work out for publication, and said if he selected any he would. pay me for the suggestions. I gave him this list, which he afterwards returned, saying there was nothing that suited him . . . now here are prospectuses and notices of various works since published by him . . . giving evidence of the use made of my list. This is how men with money will rob men without money of their brains.' "

Christopher North dubs Phillips "a dirty little Jacobin."

Sir Richard Phillips in 1823, after a life devoted to the diffusion of knowledge, and after writing, editing, and supervising innumerable books, all tending to make the next generation wiser than the last, disposed of a third share of his literary property, and retired to Brighton. At this time he was superintending the completion of the publication of a collection of " Celebrated Trials and Remarkable Cases of Criminal Jurisprudence." The work was in part compiled by George Borrow, afterwards the popular writer of gipsy lore, who was at this time doing hack work for Phillips.

Francis Place, who also has just been mentioned, was a friend of Jeremy Bentham, and with him believed in the doctrine of " the greatest happiness of the greatest number." Brought up as a breeches-maker, he, in 1799, opened a tailor's shop in Charing Cross, where his business prospered ; his name, however, has come down to us as one of the most earnest and active of the Radical reformers of the time. The library behind his shop, in which he had gathered a splendid collection of books, was the resort of reformers and all who held advanced views in politics.

V

POLITICAL ACTIVITIES

IT will be necessary here to leave Hone for the moment in the peaceful quietude of his domestic circle, and go abroad into the public life of the time to test the political atmosphere he had to breathe whenever his profound sense of citizenship impelled him to leave the bosom of his family and take his due share in the business of the State.

The acts of a Ministry uniformly opposed to the wishes and aspirations of the people were arousing a widespread spirit of resistance ; and when the leaders of that movement were met with personal oppression a rankling sense of wrong easily converted passive resistance into an active antagonism.

Hone associated himself with the Liberal party, but not to the thoughtless neglect of his business, because wherever he was engaged on an election committee he generally found his customers there too. He was a fine reader, and of a morning would hurry over his light breakfast of tea and toast to declaim the "Debate," his rare power of mimicry enabling him to reproduce to the life the mannerisms of each speaker. To these readings his children were always attentive listeners ; they traced their acquisition and cultivation of literary tastes to their enjoyment of the father's dramatic renderings, always given with the proper emphasis and modulated intonation which was necessary to interpret the eloquence in the political speeches of Fox and Pitt, Sheridan and Burdett.

In 1814 a public question which engaged Hone's attention even more than his own private affairs was that of the condition of lunatic asylums, the conduct of which was rife with the most awful abuses. In this episode we are introduced to two new acquaintances, Alderman Waithman and George Cruikshank the artist.

The maltreatment of the insane in private as well as in public asylums was a crying evil of the day, and one to which he had devoted much deliberate thought ; his knowledge of the internal arrangements of some asylums convinced him that a salutary reform in the treatment of patients could not be effected in buildings constructed as were those in existence. The Retreat of York, instituted by the Society of Friends, was the model on which he aspired to work out a plan for the foundation of a similar establishment near the Metropolis, and he had projected several schemes toward the fulfilment of that purpose, when an incident occurred which seemed opportunely favourable to his views, and led to the " Investigation of Lunatic Asylums."

He said : " I was at a Coffee Shop in Fleet Street, sitting next to Alderman Waithman, when James Bevans came in. We talked on the subject of mad-houses ; I, of the abuses and cruelty to the patients, and he (an architect) of the buildings. We walked to his house in Bunhill Row, where he showed us some of his drawings, and he was much interested in the facts I then related to him.

" I proposed forming a committee to investigate, and wrote to Edward Wakefield in the country, who came to London. Subsequently, at a meeting held at Fry's in the Poultry, Basil Montague proposed that we should not bring matters to an issue until a sub-committee should have inspected the Lunatic Asylums, and named to that intent Edward Wakefield, William Hone, and James Bevans.

" Thus self-authorised, we knocked at the door of one Asylum after another. The evidence of Wakefield is correct, and was founded upon our joint notes. I was unable to appear, myself, owing to a severe attack of quinsy and a prolonged illness which increased my pecuniary difficulties ; and he never mentioned my name in connection with the report. James Bevans he also threw overboard."

To Hone's unwearied efforts may be attributed, to a great extent, the steady advance of humane treatment of the mentally afflicted ; for though through a combination of adverse circumstances and unworthy motives his name was kept in the background, his views were embodied in the improved conditions which contrast so strikingly with the horrors of the " old Bethlem " and of many of the private madhouses of that period.

The Report, which contains the notorious description of the condition in which William Norris was confined, was in the handwriting of William Hone ; subsequently he published etchings by George Cruikshank of the unfortunate man as he was kept chained to a bar in his cell in Bethlem.

The printed Report of the Sub-Committee of the " Intended London Asylum for the Care and Cure of the Insane," appointed at the City of London Tavern, on March 2, 1814, is an interesting document, whoever prepared it ; as to the nature of the revelations it contained one extract will suffice :—

" In one of the cells of the lower gallery, the Committee saw William Norris. He stated himself to be 55 years of age, and that he had been confined about fourteen years ; that in consequence of attempting to defend himself from what he conceived the improper treatment of his Keeper, he was fastened by a long chain, which passing through a partition, enabled the keeper, by going into the next cell, to draw him close to the wall at pleasure ; that, to prevent this, Norris muffled the chain with straw, so as to hinder its passing through the wall ; that he afterwards was confined in the manner the Committee saw him ; namely—A stout iron ring was riveted round his neck, from which a short chain passed to a ring, made to slide upwards or downwards on an upright massive iron bar, more than six feet high, inserted into the wall ; round his body, a strong iron bar, about two inches wide, was riveted ; on each side the bar was a circular projection, which being fashioned to, and enclosing each of his arms, pinioned them close to his sides ; this waist-bar was secured by two similar bars, which passing over his shoulders, were riveted to the waist-bar, both before and behind ; the iron ring round his neck was connected to the bars on his shoulders by a double link ; from each of these bars another short chain passed to the ring on the upright iron bar. We were informed he was enabled to raise himself, so as to stand against the wall, on the pillow of his bed, in the trough-bed in which he lay ; but it is impossible for him to advance from the wall in which the iron bar is soldered, on account of the shortness of his chains, which were only twelve inches long. It is conceived equally out of his power to repose in any other position than on his back ; the projections, which, on each side of the waist-bar, enclosed his arms, rendering it impossible for him to lie on his side, even if the length of the chains from his neck and shoulders would permit it. His right leg was chained to the trough, in which he had remained thus encaged and chained more than twelve years. To prove the unnecessary restraint inflicted on this unfortunate man, he informed the Committee that he had for some years been able to withdraw his arms from the manacles which encompassed them. He then withdrew one of them, and observing an expression of surprise, he said, that when his arms were withdrawn, he was compelled to rest them on the edges of the circular projections, which was more painful than keeping them within. His position, we were informed, was mostly lying down, and that, as it was inconvenient to raise himself and stand upright, he very seldom did so ; that he read

WILLIAM NORRIS, AS HE WAS CONFINED IN BETHLEM

Figure B.

a great deal ; books of all kinds ; history, lives, or any thing that the keepers could get him ; the newspaper every day ; and conversed perfectly coherently on the passing topics and the events of the war, in which he felt particular interest."

An accompanying paper, prepared by Edward Wakefield, prints the remarks submitted to the Right Hon. George Rose, M.P., and various other Members of the House of Commons for the regulation of Houses for the Reception of the Insane.

The exposures of this voluntary sub-committee, on which Hone served, led to gradual improvement in the treatment of lunatics, and at last to the total abolition of mechanical restraints, first at Lincoln, in 1837, and at Hanwell and other enlightened establishments shortly after.

The illustration is a copy of that

" Printed for William Hone, No. 55 Fleet Street, London. Sketched from the life in Bethlem by G. Arnald, Esq. A.R.A. and etched by G. Cruikshank from the original drawing exhibited in evidence to the Select Committee of the House of Commons, 1815. (Price One Shilling)—

A WHOLE LENGTH PORTRAIT OF WILLIAM NORRIS, an Insane American riveted alive in Iron and for many years confined in that state, by chains 12 inches long, to an upright massive bar in a Cell in Bethlem."

As a prelude to the next public episode which interests us, here are Hone's private notes of the state of the political atmosphere at that time :—

" The history of the first quarter of the nineteenth century teems with instances of the profligate violence that marked the progress of oppression by a corrupt and persecuting Ministry. Discord reigned at Court and in the City.

" From 1812 to 1817 the Government Spy System
prevailed, and added to oppressions of the people.
' Blood Money Spies '—Vaughan, the celebrated Detec-
tive proved to be one.

" Political prosecutions—Ex-officio Inditements—
Daniel J. Eaton prosecuted 8 times for printing Paine's
' Age of Reason '—Corn Bill Riots."

The particular episode which agitated the political
barometer and engaged the energies of Hone was the
remarkable case of Lord Cochrane, afterwards the
famous Earl of Dundonald.

As a sailor Cochrane had already rendered his
country valiant services ; but as a Member of Parliament he had made himself a number of powerful
enemies by his unsparing attacks on the many naval
abuses of the time. In 1814 he was arrested on a
charge of fraud. A rumour of Napoleon's overthrow
had sent up the funds, and he, with two others, was
tried for propagating it and selling out upwards of a
million sterling at a gross profit of £10,000.

Thomas, Lord Cochrane, knew nothing of expediency,
and made enemies at every step through life ; and, in
the second place, he lived in times when the Admiralty
not only neglected but actually crushed those naval
officers who had fallen under its displeasure. At the
very outset of his career in the Royal Navy Lord
Cochrane contrived to make himself objectionable to
the officials in Whitehall, and he has left upon record
a solemn statement of his conviction that the charge on
which he appeared in the dock, of having conspired with
two others to " rig " the Stock Market, was got up
" by Admiralty malice " and pressed to extremity by
official virulence. The conclusion of the trial was that,
after a summing-up by Lord Ellenborough, which is
one of the greatest stains upon that Judge's fair repute,
Lord Cochrane was found guilty, and sentenced to
stand in the pillory at the entrance of the Royal
Exchange, to a year's imprisonment in the King's Bench

prison, and to a fine of £1,000. The first part of his sentence it was found impossible to execute. Sir Francis Burdett, who was at that time Lord Cochrane's colleague as Member for Westminster, immediately avowed his intention of standing by his colleague's side in the pillory if any such indignity were inflicted upon him. The Government of Lord Liverpool was already so unpopular that it dared not face the storm of indignation to which the very sight of Lord Cochrane in the streets of London would have given rise. But, in other respects, the malignity of his persecutors had full swing. He was confined in the King's Bench prison, and escaped from it only to be again led back to prison, after putting in a somewhat melodramatic appearance in the House of Commons, from which he had been expelled by a vote of its Members, but to which he was instantly re-elected by his constituents in Westminster. When he left prison his fine of £1,000 was raised by public "penny subscriptions," in the collection of which Hone took a prominent part. Mrs. Burn makes an interesting note on the method of Cochrane's escape. She says :—

"He was not dungeoned, but had the parole of the Prison Yard or airing ground, from which he managed to make his escape.

"Many were the surmises as to how it had been effected. A sofa had been taken out of the Prison at one time, a press bedstead at another. It was concluded that he must have been secreted in one of these. His Lordship's height and peculiar figure were opposed to any supposition of his having walked out, and it long remained an unsolved mystery.

"His Lordship thus related the manner of his escape. A medical gentleman going home one night, found a person lying on the ground who, on being questioned, said he was much hurt. The gentleman offered his assistance, said he lived near, and would get a conveyance. The injured person begged he would not,

7

and said if the other would assist him, he would prefer to walk. He helped the injured man to rise, and in the dimness of night recognised him as Lord Cochrane, who said, ' I have fallen from the wall, you will not betray me? ' ' Certainly not,' replied the other, and supported him to his house.

" Lord Cochrane was severely bruised and remained there, under care, and in the enjoyment of home comforts, until the payment of his fine released him from concealment, whereupon he immediately took the oath and his seat in Parliament."

In the year following the Cochrane affair, having recovered his health, Hone took an intense interest in the case of Eliza Fenning, a poor innocent servant-girl who was hanged for a supposed attempt to poison her master, a law stationer, in Chancery Lane. Her case has often been cited as one showing the danger of acting on purely circumstantial evidence.

As stated by Sir Samuel Romilly, this poor girl was tried at the Old Bailey in April, 1815, before the Recorder of London, for administering poison to her master and mistress and her master's father. The only evidence to affect the prisoner was circumstantial. The poison was contained in dumplings made by her ; but then, she had eaten of them herself, and been as ill as any of the persons whom she was supposed to have intended to kill, and her eating of them could not be ascribed to art or to an attempt to conceal her crime, for she made no effort whatever to remove the strongest evidence of guilt—if guilt there was. She had left the dish unwashed, and the proof that arsenic was mixed in it was furnished by its being found in the kitchen the next day, exactly in the state in which it had been brought from table. No motive, moreover, could be found for so atrocious an act. Her mistress had reproved her about three weeks before for some indiscretion, and had given her warning, but had afterwards consented to retain her in her service.

ELIZABETH FENNING,

Executed 26 July 1815, on a charge of

POISONING THE FAMILY OF MR TURNER,

taken from the Life in Newgate.

The Autograph *Elizabeth Fenning*

Hand Signed by Mr W. Hone, 55 Fleet St.

To face p. 94.

This was the only provocation for murdering, not her mistress only but her master and her master's father.

A crime of such enormity produced by so very slight a cause has probably never occurred in the history of human depravity. The Recorder, however, appeared to have conceived a strong prejudice against the prisoner. In summing up the evidence he made some very unjust remarks and unfounded observations to her disadvantage, and she was convicted.

The victim was given a public funeral, which at once advertised her presumed innocence and appealed to popular sympathy. Not less than ten thousand persons assembled in and around the churchyard of St. George the Martyr to see her buried. Hone published " An Authentic Report of the Trial " ; and Charles Phillips wrote a brilliant rhapsody on " the fate of one so young, so fair, so innocent, cut down in early morn, with all life's brightness only at its dawn." " Little," said that facile writer, " did it profit thee that a city mourned over thy early grave, and that the most eloquent of men—Curran, a fellow-countryman—did justice to thy memory."

The singularity of the trial attracted the notice of many persons to her case, and they interested themselves in her favour, Hone being one who worked hard to obtain signatures to a petition in which they applied to the Crown for mercy. The master of the girl was requested to sign a petition on her behalf, but at the instance of the Recorder he refused. Every effort was unavailing ; the sentence was executed, and the girl died, apparently under a strong sense of the truths of religion, and solemnly protesting her innocence.

Hone thus relates the scene of her execution :—

" I was going down Newgate Street on some business of my own. I got into an immense crowd that carried me along with them against my will ; at

length I found myself under the gallows where Eliza
Fenning was to be hanged.   I had the greatest horror
of witnessing an execution, and of this in particular ;
a young girl of whose guilt I had grave doubts.   But
I could not help myself ;   I was closely wedged in ;
she was brought out.   I saw nothing, but I heard
all.   I heard her protesting her innocence—I heard
the   prayer—I   could   hear   no   more.   I   stopped
my ears, and knew nothing else till I found myself
in the   dispersing   crowd,   and   far   from   the   dreadful spot.   I made my way to the house of a bookseller with whom I was very intimate ;   I asked him
for a glass of water ;   I sat down and told him where
I had been, and that people were saying the unhappy
girl had ' died with a lie in her mouth.'   ' Friend
Hone,' said he, ' she is with her Almighty Father ;
I have visited her in prison, so have many of my
friends, and we are satisfied of her innocence.'   I
was up immediately.   ' Why, then, was she executed? '
' We made every possible exertion to save her life,'
replied he, ' but we were not listened to.'   ' The public
must be roused about it,' said I.   My friend replied,
' You are the man to do it, and I will print what you
write."

Hone continues :—

" I took lodgings away from my family, for I could
do nothing among them, and for three weeks I was
wholly engrossed on the case of Eliza Fenning.   On
the   fourth Saturday   evening   my   wife   came   to   ask
me for money—but I had none.   I told my wife to
go home, and that I would bring her the money, but
I had no idea where to get it ;   I had not sixpence.   I
went off to my friend the bookseller, and charged him
with having made me neglect my family, asking him
for the loan of a few pounds.   Having obtained this,
I walked through the turnstile into Lincoln's Inn Fields,
and on, until a play-bill stuck up in large letters
caught   my   eye :   ' The   Maid   and   the   Magpie,
repeated   with   unbounded   applause   to   overflowing

houses.' An idea flashed upon my mind. I changed one of my notes and went to the play, in the pit, and saw ' The Maid and the Magpie.'

" I went home and said to my wife, ' Give me a pair of candles and snuffers upstairs, and send for George Cruikshank.' He came ; I said, ' Make me a cut of a Magpie hung by the neck to the gallows '— and I put my head on one side, and looked as like a dying Magpie as I could.

" I walked to my printers, and by six o'clock in the morning ' The Maid and the Magpie ' was completed— and a thousand struck off. Cruikshank was ready with the frontispiece ; and my wife sewed them. When the coaches drove up for the newspapers, we were ready with our pamphlets. ' Will you have this? '—' How many? '—' Half a hundred '—' A hundred.' So we effectually roused the public as to the case of Eliza Fenning, and I and my family lived for four months on ' The Maid and the Magpie.' "

That the case excited a great amount of public interest is evident from the amount of " literature " which grew out of it. Hone, then at 55, Fleet Street (a small shop where he was twice robbed), published two works having rather formidable titles. One, at five shillings, was—

" The Important Results of an Elaborate Investigation into the Mysterious Case of Elizabeth Fenning : being a detail of Extraordinary Facts discovered since her Execution, including the Official Report of her Singular Trial . . . also a Memorial to H.R.H. The Prince Regent ; and Strictures on a late Pamphlet of the Prosecutors' Apothecary ; by John Watkins, LL.D." ;

The other, published at eighteenpence, was entitled—

" Thirty Original and Interesting Letters written by the late Elizabeth Fenning whilst in prison and under sentence of Death, Declaratory of her Innocence . . .

Containing an Exposure of the Fabrications of the 'Observer' Newspaper, and other Falsehoods respecting the Case."

Hone also published a portrait of the poor girl, drawn by Isaac R. Cruikshank, father of George Cruikshank ; while in the columns of the *Traveller* newspaper his pen was constantly busy in her defence.

Wherever there was trouble there William Hone seems to have been found, if only to give publicity to the wrongs of those whom his sympathetic nature looked upon as victims or sufferers in any sense—we find him as a witness at inquests held upon two persons shot during the Corn Riots on March 7th, before the house of Mr. Robinson, in Old Burlington Street ; and, of course, he published reports of both these inquiries.

With all his Radicalism and ardent advocacy of political reform, Hone, as might be expected of "so mild a mannered man," was always opposed to the employment of physical force. In December, 1816, occurred the Spa Fields Riots, when the shops of the gunsmiths were attacked for arms. Apprehensive that the movement if accompanied by violence would prejudice the causes he had so much at heart, Hone printed placards, which he had widely posted, calling on the people to preserve their own liberties by keeping the peace and becoming the custodians of them. He exhorted the populace not to confound agitation with rioting, and, like the good citizen he was, used every influence he possessed to restore public order.

At the same time, he never slackened in his attacks on the Government with his vitriolic pen ; he regarded himself as the mouthpiece of the people, and on their behalf kept up the fight for the free expression of opinion.

VI

AN ALERT PUBLISHER

HONE at this period, it will be observed, was publishing two classes of works, in both of which he had (at the outset, certainly) more than a commercial interest—his political satires, in which he advocated his views on public polity, and a number of opportune sensational tracts and broadsheets, on those topics of the day which were exciting the greatest amount of public attention. The earlier ones of the latter class, such as those relating to William Norris and Eliza Fenning, were no doubt genuinely inspired by Hone's humanitarian sympathies with the victims of injustice and wrong. But as much cannot be said for some of his later cheap tracts and booklets. He was a struggling tradesman with a young family to maintain ; he was indefatigably industrious ; he was alert, and had a keen eye for what would sell.

In 1815 he was brought up before the Wardmote Inquest of St. Dunstan's for placarding his shop on Sundays, and for carrying on a retail trade as bookseller and stationer, not being a freeman.

It was in 1813 the famous Catnach Press was founded in Monmouth Court, off Little Earl Street, St. Giles's, for the publication of ballads, broadsides, " last dying speeches," and every other kind of gutter literature, which the public bought with avidity in the days of dear newspapers. During the time Hone was in Fleet Street he did not disdain to emulate this class

of publication. A good specimen of this trumpery
stuff, issued by him in 1815, is a sixpenny tract,
entitled " The Power of Conscience." It is of the
" catchpenny " type, consisting of eighteen pages of
sensational stuff, which includes the confession of
Thomas Bedworth, delivered at Newgate September 18, 1815, for the murder of Elizabeth Beesmore
in Drury Lane, relating, among other things, his
horrible sufferings occasioned by constant supernatural
visitations of the murdered woman and other dreadful
apparitions—all of it, of course, " from the original
paper now in the possession of the publisher."

Although misfortune seems to have pursued William
Hone with a relentlessness that would have broken
the spirit of some men—once he was burnt out, and
twice was his Fleet Street shop broken into and
plundered—nothing could repress the elasticity of his
cheerful and hopeful nature. In 1815 we find him the
publisher of the *Traveller* newspaper, afterwards
amalgamated with the *Globe*. A year or so afterwards he issued the *Reformist's Register*, which ran
a feverish career of a few months only. Then, in conjunction with George Cruikshank, he commenced the
publication of a series of political satires which achieved
an immense success ; one of them, " The Political
House that Jack Built," passed through fifty editions.

In some of the political pamphlets—not regarding
the Church of England liturgy with the same veneration as the Bible—he parodied portions of the Prayer
Book, an indiscretion which landed him within the
meshes of the law, though the law had to be strained
on purpose to entangle him. Hone emphatically
asserted that he never had any intention to bring
religion into ridicule. But ridicule, if a powerful
weapon, is a dangerous one, especially with which to
attack a corrupt and an unscrupulous Ministry—a
Government that would not hesitate to strain or even
alter the law to meet its own ends, and that would

certainly have no compunction in construing an alleged political libel as a blasphemy, if that were deemed safer ground on which to prosecute. That Hone was really prosecuted for the alleged libels contained in his pamphlets, because of their obnoxious satires on the Government of the day, there never has been a shadow of a doubt. The public, both before and after his trials, felt that had they been on the other side of the question, written in defence of the Ministry instead of in ridicule of it, no notice would have been taken.

It was in this matter that Hone was forced into the unenviable position of the defender of the freedom of the Press ; that he suddenly found himself the object of a Government prosecution ; that, in fact, he became a public, an historic character. He was not unaware of the terrors of which he stood in danger.

Lady Morgan, a contemporary novelist, though not always wise in what she wrote, has this to say :—

" Ridicule derives its efficacy from the responsive sympathies of the audience addressed.

" The ridicule of unknown persons excites no emotion. The ridicule of a known person for qualities which he notoriously does not possess, is equally impotent.

" When Hone represented the British Constitution by an inverted pyramid, resting on the crown at its apex, and supported by bayonets, the sensible image of instability he presented found a prompt reflection in the public mind. He advanced, however, no novel statement. If a conviction had not pre-existed in public opinion of ' something rotten in the state of Denmark,' his humour would not have told. Had he supported the tottering edifice with a printing press, instead of a bayonet, the misrepresentation would have been rejected with scorn."

One of the sixpenny tracts published in 1816, and bearing Hone's two addresses—55, Fleet Street, and

67, Old Bailey—was a "genuine" edition of "The Eloquent Speech on the Dethronement of Napoleon, the State of Ireland, the Dangers of England, and the Necessity of Immediate Parliamentary Reform, delivered by Charles Phillips, Esq., at a Public Dinner given to him at Liverpool, on 31st October, 1816."

One brief extract will convey a fair notion of the contents :—

" There is now scarce an object but industry in rags, and patience in despair—the merchant without a ledger —the fields without a harvest—the shops without a customer—the Exchange deserted, and the *Gazette* crowded. . . . Here in England, after all her vanity and all her victories, surrounded by desolation, like one of the pyramids of Egypt, amid the grandeur of the desert—full of magnificence and death—at once a trophy and a tomb."

Although somewhat obscured by the flowers of rhetoric, the description of England's condition is a telling one.

France, and the movement of public events there, naturally interested a publicist like Hone, at a time when French politics acted and reacted on the affairs of this country.

Concerning the work entitled " Louis XVIII. climbing the Mat de Cocagne," an interesting prosecution occurred which throws considerable light on the publishing amenities of those times. A printseller, named Sidebotham, of the Strand, applied to Hone for impressions of this caricature at less than cost price, threatening that if Hone did not accede to his request he would pirate the picture. On Hone's refusal, Sidebotham applied to Cruikshank to make him a copy, and, on receiving a second refusal, actually got the work effected elsewhere. Not contented with this, the pirate publisher had the effrontery to send his errand-boy with six of the spurious prints with the mild request that Hone would exchange six of his genuine prints for them. The exasperated Hone simply tore up the offending pictures, and sent them back by the boy as the only answer he would make to his master. Sidebotham promptly summoned the outraged publisher for the damage, and the case came before the Court of Requests at the Guildhall. The newspaper report ends very satisfactorily with this sentence :—

" The Court conceiving that Mr. Hone had received great provocation, as well as sustained serious injury by the plaintiff's piracy, dismissed the summons."

Phillips, having made a name by his florid oratory, engaged in literature. The business relationships between Phillips and Hone were pleasant enough, although the advantage seems to have been on the side of the former, whose " blarney " easily vanquished the susceptible Hone. The publisher not only regularly paid the author in cash as it became due, but we find him, characteristically enough, making the insinuating Irishman a present of a silver snuff-box, engraved with a complimentary inscription.

Charles Phillips was familiarly known as " Napoleon Phillips," on account of an oration in which he celebrated the downfall of the Corsican conqueror, a passage from which, long preserved as a familiar quotation, was—

" Grand, gloomy, and peculiar, he sat upon the throne, a sceptred hermit, wrapt in the solitude of his own originality."

Lord Brougham was an admirer of Phillips, who, in later years, engaged himself heartily in the struggle for Catholic emancipation. His daughter married Augustus, youngest brother of Charles Dickens, and the original of " Boz."

To a topical writer so alert and eager as William Hone—" the ever-watchful Hone "—the death of the Princess Charlotte in November, 1816, afforded a fund of excellent material upon which his ready pen was not slow to seize. He published, from 67, Old Bailey, four booklets at sixpence each ; these were—

> " Life of the late Lamented Princess Charlotte ; the order of succession ; the chance of Jerome Napoleon becoming King, &c., &c. .With engravings."
>
> " Authentic Particulars of the Death of the Princess Charlotte and Her Infant ; with engravings."
>
> " Funeral of the Princess Charlotte ; with a folding plate of the Grand Burial Procession in St. George's Chapel, Windsor, and an illustrative vignette."
>
> " Memoirs of Prince Leopold ; with Portraits."

These were not all he had published on the subject of the Princess. Earlier had appeared :—

> " Hone's authentic Account of the Royal Marriage, consisting of original memoirs of Prince Leopold and Princess Charlotte. . . . A great variety of Anecdotes of His Serene Highness. . . . Details of the Marriage Ceremonial . . . with an Appendix containing the Acts for naturalising Prince Leopold," &c.
>
> " Authentic Memoirs of the Life of the Late Lamented Princess Charlotte—with clear statements —showing the succession to the Crown and the probability of the wife of Jerome Buonaparte becoming Queen, and her son Jerome Napoleon being Prince of Wales, and afterwards King of these realms."

This latter was a striking, if a lengthy and somewhat cumbrous title. Doubtless at a period when " Buonapartephobia " (which is the title of another of Hone's topical publications) was rife, the pamphlet sold readily enough. It contains only sixteen pages, and the following extract, in the substance of which Hone is historically and legally correct, is taken from it :—

" The first wife of Frederick, King of Wurtemberg, was Caroline of Brunswick. Their daughters, the Princess Catherine and the late Princess Charlotte of .Wales, were of like kin to Frederick, Prince of Wales, the father of his present majesty, both being his great-grandchildren. The Princess Catherine was married to Jerome Buonaparte, King of Westphalia, and had a son by him. If the male line of succession to the Crown of Great Britain should fail, by the Prince Regent and the Royal Dukes dying without issue, then the sovereignty would vest in the female line ; and in that case, as by the Act of Settlement of 11 and 12 William III. c. 3, the heirs of the Princess Sophia, being Protestants, are entitled to the Crown in succession, the succession would be thus :—

First, the Duke of Brunswick, son of the Duchess, and if he had no issue

Secondly, to the Prince of .Wurtemburgh [sic], grandson of the Duchess ; and if he had no issue

Thirdly, to the wife of Jerome Buonaparte, the Princess Catherine, as great grandchild of Frederick, Prince of Wales ; who would, by the Act of Settlement, be Queen Regnant, and her son, young Jerome Buonaparte, be Prince of .Wales. Thus, after his mother's death, and professing the Protestant religion, he would claim the throne by hereditary right, being as near akin by the female line to the reigning family, as any other claimant, he having descended from Frederick, the common ancestor to all the claimants of the Crown.

Thus it appears, unless Parliament interferes, the line of Guelph failing, the British Throne may be filled in succession by the line of Buonaparte."

As a printseller and publisher of political portraits, Hone appears to have done quite a brisk trade from 1815 to 1817.; and after several trials at authorship he founded the *Reformist's Register*, the aim of which is indicated by its title, but which, it may be added, attacked the doctrines of Robert Owen. He continued to issue also his series of political squibs, illustrated with great force and spirit by George Cruikshank, then a young and unknown man ; and their success was undoubted. Not content with these, however, he published his famous " Parodies," which quickly brought him within the meshes of the law, as then administered.

Hone's *Reformist's Register* was an octavo of sixteen pages, published every Saturday at the price of twopence, as a weekly commentary on current events, and intended to constitute a history of the parliamentary reform movement. The subjects dealt with in the opening numbers included Universal Suffrage, Annual Parliaments, Suspension of the Habeas Corpus Act, and so forth.

The general feeling of discontent among the lower classes, says the historian Hume, and an outrage committed upon the Prince Regent, the windows of whose carriage were broken as he was returning from opening the Parliament, January 28, 1817, led to the suspension of the Habeas Corpus Act on February 21st.

" At the same time the execution of the law was severely pressed, and numerous *ex-officio* informations were filed against political writers, not the least remarkable of which were those against the well-known Radical and Reformist bookseller, William Hone. It is difficult to imagine a more degraded and dangerous position than that in which every political writer was liable to be placed in the year 1817."

He might be apprehended on a warrant, imprisoned upon suspicion, held to heavy bail or kept in prison, and prosecuted by the Attorney-General on *ex-officio* information. It is even said that the Government's instructions issued to Lords-Lieutenant directed that the magistrates should only admit to heavy bail in

SKETCH SUPPOSED TO BE BY GEORGE CRUIKSHANK, OF HIMSELF
AT THE AGE OF 20.

To face p. 116.

these cases of "blasphemous and seditious pamphlets." The proceeding has been stigmatised by another historian as the most daring invasion of public liberty attempted since the time of the Stuarts.

The law was being directed in particular against the press, and at this time William Hone was publishing and selling very largely political parodies, founded on the style and phraseology of the English Liturgy, which the Government were not slow to pounce upon as profane publications. One was modelled on the Catechism, one on the Litany, and one on the Creed. The famous parodies were three in number, and were published sharply one after the other.

A distinction might perhaps be made between bringing Holy Writ into ridicule and the parodying of Creeds and Catechisms. That the reader may form his own estimate, a few samples of the parodist's efforts are presented.

In the January of 1817 had appeared :—

The late
JOHN WILKES'S
CATECHISM
of a
MINISTERIAL MEMBER
Taken
From an Original Manuscript in Mr. Wilkes's Handwriting, never before printed, and adapted to the present Occasion.
With Permission
LONDON :
Printed for one of the Candidates for the Office of Printer to the King's Most Excellent Majesty, and Sold by William Hone, 55 Fleet Street, and 67 Old Bailey. Three doors from Ludgate Hill. 1817. Price Two-pence.

The pamphlet was a close parody of the Church Catechism, supposed to be "an instruction, to be learned of every Person before he be brought to be confirmed as Placeman or Pensioner by the Minister," the copy of which reached Hone through the post, and was supposed to have been '" written by the late Mr. Wilkes." It opened thus :—

" *Question*. What is your Name?
" *Answer*. Lick Spittle.
" *Question*. Who gave you this Name?
" *Answer*. My Sureties to the Ministry, in my Political Change, wherein I was made a Member of the Majority, the Child of Corruption, and a Locust to devour the things of this Kingdom.
" *Question*. What did your Sureties then for you?
" *Answer*. They did promise and vow three things in my Name. First, that I should renounce the Reformists and all their Works, the pomps and vanity of Popular Favour, and all the sinful lusts of Independence. Secondly, that I should believe all the Articles of the Court Faith. And thirdly, that I should keep the Minister's sole Will and Commandments, and walk in the same all the days of my life.
" *Question*. Dost thou not think that thou art bound to believe and to do as they have promised for thee?
" *Answer*. Yes verily, and for my own sake so I will ; and I heartily thank our heaven-born Ministry that they have called me to this state of elevation, through my own flattery, cringing, and bribery ; and I shall pray to their successors to give me their assistance, that I may continue the same unto my life's end.
" *Question*. Rehearse the Articles of thy Belief.
" *Answer*. I believe in George, the Regent Almighty, Maker of New Streets and Knights of the Bath."

Following closely the lines of the Liturgy, it presently came to the Ten Commandments. To quote the travesty it made of six of them will suffice :—

" IV. Remember that thou attend the Minister's Levee day ; on other days thou shalt speak for him in the House, and fetch and carry, and do all that he commandeth thee to do ; but the Levee day is for the glorification of the Minister thy Lord. In it thou shalt do no work in the House, but shall wait upon him, thou, and thy daughter, and thy wife, and the Members that are within his influence ; for on other days the Minister is inaccessible, but delighteth in the Levee day, wherefore the Minister appointed the Levee day, and chatteth thereon familiarly, and is amused with it.

" V. Honour the Regent and the helmets of the Life Guards, that thy stay may be long in the Place, which thy Lord the Minister giveth thee.

" VI. Thou shalt not call starving to death murder.

" VII. Thou shalt not call Royal gallivanting adultery.

" VIII. Thou shalt not say that to rob the public is to steal.

" IX. Thou shalt bear false witness against the People."

On a later page the parody grates worse :—

" Our Lord, who art in the Treasury, whatsoever be thy name, thy power be prolonged, thy will be done throughout the empire, as it is in each session. Give us our usual sops, and forgive us our occasional absences on divisions ; as we promise not to forgive them that divide against thee. Turn us not out of our Places ; but keep us in the House of Commons, the Land of Pensions and Plenty ; and deliver us from the People. Amen."

And so on to the end of the Catechism, the portion relating to the Sacraments being thus burlesqued :—

" *Question*. How many Tests hath the Minister ordained?

" *Answer*. Two only, as generally necessary to elevation ; (that is to say) Passive Obedience and Bribery.

" *Question*. What meanest thou by this word Test?

" *Answer*. I mean an outward visible sign of an inward intellectual meanness, ordained by the Minister himself as a pledge to assure him thereof.

8

" *Question*. How many parts are there in this Test?

" *Answer*. Two ; the outward visible sign and the inward intellectual meanness.

" *Question*. What is the outward visible sign or form of Passive Obedience?

" *Answer*. Dangling at the Minister's heels, whereby the person is degraded beneath the baseness of a slave, in the character of a Pensioner, Placeman, Expectant Parasite, Toadeater, or Lord of the Bedchamber.

" *Question*. What is the inward and intellectual meanness?

" *Answer*. A death unto Freedom, a subjection unto perpetual Thraldom ; for being by nature born free, and the children of independence, we are hereby made children of Slavery."

This was the kind of " twopenny trash " which brought William Hone into national notoriety.

The second parody was " The Political Litany," " to be said or sung until the appointed change come." It commenced with invocations in this strain :—

" O Prince, ruler of the people, have mercy upon us, thy miserable subjects.

" *O Prince, Ruler, &c.*

" O House of Lords, hereditary legislators, have mercy upon us, pension-paying subjects.

" *O House of Lords, &c.*

" O House of Commons, proceeding from corrupt borough-mongers, have mercy upon us, your should-be constituents.

" *O House of Commons, &c.*"

One deprecation will suffice :—

" From an unnational debt ; from unmerited pensions and sinecure places ; from an extravagant civil list ; and from utter starvation,

" *Good Prince, deliver us !* "

The few obsecrations here given are a very fair sample of the whole :—

"That it may please ye to place within the bounds of economy the expenditure of all the Royal Family ;
"*We beseech ye to hear us, O Rulers!*
"That it may please ye to deprive the Lords of the Council, and all the Nobility, of all money paid out of the taxes, which they have not earned ;
"*We beseech ye to hear us, O Rulers!*
"That it may please ye to bless all the people with equal representation, and to keep them safe from borough-mongering factions ;
"*We beseech ye to hear us, O Rulers.*"

The third parody was "The Sinecurist's Creed," modelled on that of St. Athanasius. It begins :—

"Whosoever will be a Sinecurist : before all things it is necessary to hold a Place of profit."

The conclusion of this parody is so remote from the original model, that it is all but unintelligible :—

"And Coleridge shall have a Jew's Harp, and a Rabbinical Talmud, and a Roman Missal ; and Wordsworth shall have a Psalter, and a Primer, and a Reading Easy ; and unto Southey's Sack-but shall be duly added ; and with Harp, Sack-but, and Psaltery, they shall make merry, and discover themselves before Derry Down Triangle, and Hum his most gracious Master, whose Kingdom shall have no end.
"This is the Sinecurist's duty, from doing more than which except he abstain faithfully, he cannot be a Sinecurist.
"Glory be to Old Bags, and to Derry Down Triangle, and to the Doctor.[1]
"As it was in the Beginning, is now, and ever shall be, if such *things* be, without end. Amen."

---

[1] See pp. 218 and 221 for identification of these.

On February 22nd Hone stopped the sale of these pamphlets, for which there was a brisk demand at that time. Immediately they were suppressed the demand for them increased, and wherever they were to be had enhanced prices were freely given for them. To complicate matters, Hone had no sooner withdrawn them from sale than they were reprinted and sold by another Radical publisher, namely—

" by R. Carlile, at the Republican Office, No. 183 Fleet Street, and sold by all who are not afraid of incurring the Displeasure of His Majesty's Ministers, their Spies and Informers, or Public Plunderers of any denomination. 1817. Price Two-pence."

As one instinctively gathers from such an imprint, this reissue was directly contrary to the wishes of Hone, who wrote this note to Carlile :—

" 67 OLD BAILEY
" 8th. August 1817.

" SIR,—I shall be very glad of a call from you as soon as possible—Now if you can make it convenient—at any rate before you publish the Parodies, which Mrs. Hone tells me you have just informed her you are about to do.

" I am, Sir,
" Yours Obedly,
" W. HONE."

The appeal to Carlile was without avail. On May 20th a Portsea printer was apprehended under a warrant from Lord Ellenborough for printing Hone's Parodies on the Litany, Creed, &c. He was admitted to bail.

Richard Carlile not only reprinted Hone's Parodies, but wrote a series of imitations of them, for which he got eighteen weeks' imprisonment. He was an avowed

Freethinker, a courageous champion of the Press, the publisher of a Radical paper called the *Black Dwarf*, a great friend of George Jacob Holyoake, and altogether a very remarkable man, a proof of which is that for the sake of his opinions he spent an aggregate of nine years and four months in prison.

VII

IMPENDING PROSECUTION

FOR three successive years, immediately after the close of the great war—namely, in 1816, 1817, and 1818—there were bad harvests. If a shortage of food supplies followed thus closely on the heels of an exhausting war, is there any wonder that the land was filled with murmuring and discontent? And whenever was there general discontent that did not find expression through some of the bolder spirits of the time?

Instead of remedial legislation, instead of seeking to remove the causes at the root of the national discontent, an Administration working on traditional lines had no panacea to offer other than repression. It was always repression. The people asked for parliamentary reform, and the Government switched off their liberties.

The suspension of the Habeas Corpus Act in 1817 was aimed at the popular agitation for reform ; to the side of the governing class had rallied the propertied classes, and all who viewed with vague and apprehensive fear any movement of the common people towards general freedom and advancement.

The bitter cry of a starving and over-burdened population was to be interpreted as sedition, and to meet this new domestic difficulty the liberties of the nation were suspended with as little compunction as they had previously been for wars and rumours of wars. Neither Whig nor Tory had any clear conception of popular rights ; both parties were equally devoid of sympathy with the growing aspirations of the masses. Any concession to the demands of the reformers was regarded as nothing but an invitation to a feast of revolution.

The Government of the day had little or no hesitation in straining the law in every way possible, to meet their own purposes ; and to make the way of transgressors hard, the judges who were entrusted with the carrying out of the law were appointed undisguisedly on political grounds. In the approaching struggle for political freedom, what quarter reformers and agitators like William Hone and William Cobbett were likely to get may easily be imagined. Yet it was in 1817 that the spell of despotism was first broken, and a brighter horizon began to open out than had prevailed during the dismal period of the war, when the prosecution of Horne Tooke, of the *Times*, the *Chronicle*, and the *Examiner*, had marked the darkest days of the English terrorism.

The first incident which brought Hone into disfavour with the Court was the alleged insult to the Prince Regent. The Prince opened Parliament on January 28th, and the speech from the throne expressed in ominous terms the resolution of the Ministry " to omit no precaution for preserving the public peace, and for counteracting the designs of the disaffected." Yet on his way from Parliament the crowd expressed their decided disapprobation of the threat, by hissings and groanings loud and deep, and, as it is alleged by some, by overt acts of violence. Such an outrage on so exalted a personage was not to be tolerated.

In the same month William Hone had issued two numbers of a serial entitled *Hone's Weekly Commentary*, which he had now discontinued or, as was stated in the advertisement, merged in the *Reformist's Register*. The price of the *Commentary* had been sixpence, that of the *Register* was only twopence.

In the January of 1817 *Cobbett's Register*, having been reduced in price to twopence, this " twopenny trash "—as its enemies scornfully dubbed it—was being sold at the rate of 50,000 copies a week. At this juncture Francis Place came forward to assist William Hone in the publication of a similar paper.

The first number of the *Reformist's Register* was published on February 1st, in time to report the incident of the " insult." The editor of the *Register* turned the alleged outrage into ridicule ; in a vigorous article bristling with notes of exclamation, with a profusion of italicised passages, and closely dotted with capitals— most of Hone's political writings are wonderful to behold in this respect—he asked for evidence of any " outrage." The editor was satisfied, after examining all the available evidence, that the noble lord who made the allegation was too frightened to distinguish between a stone and a bullet—he shrewdly opines that gentle- man would scarcely have thrust his hat into a broken carriage window to keep out missiles from a firearm.

Hone's view of the matter was no doubt the correct one ; but that his journal dared to reflect public opinion and public feeling in the true light was vexatious to the Court party. The sycophantic spirit of that party is well exemplified by the form of solemn thanks- giving which was drawn up for the occasion, to be used through the convenient medium of the State Church : —

" Almighty God, &c., who in compassion to a sinful nation, hast defeated the designs of desperate men, and hast protected from the base assaults of a lawless multitude the Regent of the United Kingdom . . . shield him from . . . the madness of the people."

The people who asked for the rights of citizenship were mad, and the Ruler who lived in luxury and licentiousness was to move the grateful heart of the nation.

FRANCIS PLACE.

Author of "The Principle of Population."

To face p. 120.

The second number of Hone's *Register*, issued February 8th that year, contained Francis Place's reply to Brougham, entitled " Universal Suffrage and Annual Parliaments against Mr. Brougham and the Whigs." On the 17th of the month was published a special fourth number of this little paper, with the title of *The Register Extraordinary*. It was produced in the attempt to get that statesman to desist from attacking the Reformers, and contained the report of a speech delivered by him at the City of London Tavern, in June, 1814, at a time when he expected to become the Reform candidate for Westminster. This publication had only the effect of exasperating Brougham, and making him attack the Reform party more fiercely than ever.

While petitions for parliamentary reform were pouring into the House of Commons, the Government was concerning itself only with the methods whereby the aspirations of the people could be most effectively quenched. In Hone's *Register* of March 1st appears the significant passage : —

" To my utter astonishment last Saturday morning it appears, that the night before, whilst I was at the printer's correcting the proof of my *Register* for publication, His Majesty's Secretary of State for the Home Department, Lord Sidmouth, was actually causing a Bill to be read in the House of Lords, for suspending the Habeas Corpus Act ; when it was read a first time without opposition, and ordered to be read a second time on Monday ; when the noble Lord passed it through the two remaining stages."

More than this, and touching him personally, Hone discovered that his " Parodies on the Scriptures and the Church Liturgy " had been specially referred to as requiring the notice of the Government—along with other dangerous agencies, such as political clubs, secret meetings, and outspoken Radical newspapers.

It was tolerably certain that the Government had determined to strike a blow, and that the blow would not improbably fall upon William Hone. Yet his conduct, in view of such contingency, seems to have been extremely maladroit. To have shown contempt for Lords Sidmouth and Castlereagh might have been consistent with a courageous and independent spirit ; but to alienate Whig friends like Lord Holland and Mr. Waithman was scarcely prudent under the circumstances, and particularly in the case of a man who had a profound dread of imprisonment. It was certain he would need all the friends he could muster, and all the support they could afford him. But William Hone was never worldly-wise.

The oligarchical Government had set its teeth in a grim determination to uproot all forms and phases of sedition ; the people's demand for reform it had laughed out of the High Court of Parliament. And Hone, knowing full well he would be too poor to employ counsel should the need arise, and profoundly convinced that in a law-court he would be no match against Sir William Garrow, the Attorney-General, nor able to withstand the fierce sarcasms and thundering denunciations of the Lord Chief Justice, Ellenborough—Hone, fully cognisant of all this, still went on with his big capital letters and italics, the prolific use of which was intended to intensify the fierceness of his language, attacking friends and foes alike when they fell short of the standard of reform he had set up in his *Register*.

Hone, who was no physical-force reformer and had nothing to do with secret societies or suspicious combinations of any kind, was marked out for prosecution simply because it was possible to construe his " Parodies " as blasphemies ; and the authorities hugged to themselves the knowledge that when charges of sedition had failed to convict a man, a conviction for blasphemy had been secured from the most public-spirited juries. All sensitive minds shrink from the ridiculing of sacred subjects, and the average man, whatsoever his creed, resents it as an unpardonable liberty ; it would, therefore, be comparatively easy to fasten the blasphemy on Hone, if the charge against him were so preferred as to keep the sedition in the background.

Lord Sidmouth, in moving the suspension of the Habeas Corpus Act, declared that libellous and blasphemous publications were scattered over the country, and that many of them had been selected for prosecution ; that ignorant people were pointed to defects in the Constitution as the cure for distresses, and grievances ; that there had been riots in London, and that even the sacred life of the Regent had been threatened. Lord Grey, on the other side, declared the suspension of the people's liberties to be entirely uncalled for, and Lord Holland held similar views. In spite of Government spies and Government agents inciting to sedition and treason, not the slightest sign of insurrection had been discerned in any quarter. The subscription to the Spa Fields Riot in the December of the previous year had amounted to only £10 ; the ammunition-wagon had contained fifty balls and a few pounds of powder, and these had not yet been paid for. The whole affair was more of an uproar than a riot, the outcome of hunger, misery, and the depression in trade.

In the Commons, Lord Castlereagh made much of the alleged attack on the Regent, and sounded the note of alarm against tumultuous assemblies, debating societies, secret oaths, and political organisations with " fraternised branches " in various parts of the country. Sir Francis Burdett promptly avowed himself a member of a number of clubs, one of the so-called " traitors ", ; but he denied that to speak of constitutional reform was treason. Other speeches on the same side tended to show that William Hone was a little mistaken as to the attitude of some of the Whig statesmen.

The Government pressed forward their measure at high speed, their ignoble policy also including a Seditious Meetings Bill, a Treasonable Practices Bill, and an Army and Navy Seduction Bill. The Habeas Corpus Suspension Act became law on March 4th, and other Bills followed. The year 1817 was a memorable one in the history of the struggle for constitutional liberty.

William Hone had been watching events with a keen eye, and recording them with a critical pen. He was a man who courted publicity, and therefore the breathing out of threats and slaughterings against secret assemblies had no terrors for him. But the Government net was purposely cast wide to take in seditious writings also, and it was here he stood within the peril.

On March 27th Lord Sidmouth dispatched his famous circular to the Lords-Lieutenant of counties, in which he declared that in the opinion of the Government the justices of the peace might issue a warrant to apprehend any person charged before them on oath with the publication of blasphemous or seditious libels, and compel him to give bail to answer the charge.

Now, considering the jealousy with which any political interference with the liberty of the Press was regarded, and that by Fox's Libel Bill even the judges were held unfit to decide on the character of a libel, which was to be left to the decision of a jury, it is difficult to conceive a more high-handed procedure than that of the Home Secretary. It was palpably a scandalous interference with constitutional privileges.

Considerable use was made of these instructions, yet on the whole with so little success that the Government secured but a single conviction. The trials of William Hone were the most important of the series, and the failure of the Government in these must have shown how odious and useless were these attempts to stifle the free expression of opinion. The Tory policy, dictated by fear and a dread of popular violence, though it temporarily hushed the agitation for reform, was gradually alienating all classes, and giving rise to hopefulness for the future in the breasts of the optimistic and far-seeing.

Five numbers of Hone's *Register* were written by Francis Place. He was conducting a considerable business at this time, and was therefore unable to find the leisure necessary to continue the work.

"My other avocations," he states, "would not permit me to write *Weekly Registers* and I was obliged to desist. . . . The crisis was now past. . . . The Whigs were scoffed at by Ministers and despised by the people ; I had put *Hone's Register* on its legs ; the profits were considerable, and I was in hopes he would be able to continue it, and by its means have found a maintenance for his family ; to this he was unequal—the sale soon declined. The work lingered on till October 25th and then expired." (See " Life of Francis Place," by Graham Wallas.)

It may not be without interest to the present-day politician to recall the kind of abuse the *Register* had to expose in the struggle then being made for parliamentary reform. In borough-mongering no more glaring example could be found than that of Gatton, in Surrey, a borough of six houses, where the franchise was vested in the freeholders, and in the inhabitants paying scot and lot. The main facts of this particular case were amusingly set forth by Hone, in his issue of August 9th, in an article suggesting that the Prince Regent might usefully make a tour of observation through the country to instruct himself at first hand how the people of England were really represented in Parliament. On his arrival at Gatton, for instance, he might be received by Sir Mark Wood, who had recently purchased the property, and then been made a baronet ; " not because he was a borough-proprietor " —oh, no ! but on account of some subtle merit discovered in him by a discerning Administration. The

interview, says the *Register*, would proceed somewhat
on these lines : —

" ' You are the proprietor of this borough, Sir
Mark? '—' I am, may it please your Royal Highness.'—
' How many members does it send to Parliament? '—
' Two, Sir.'—' Who are they? '—' Myself and my son.'
—' You are much beloved, then, in the borough, Sir
Mark? '—' There are not many tell me otherwise, your
Royal Highness.'—' Were there any opposition candidates? '—' None, Sir.'—' What is the qualification for
an elector? '—' Being an inhabitant and paying scot
and lot.'—' Only six electors, then? for I see you
have only six houses in the place? '—' Only one elector,
please your Royal Highness.'—' What ! one elector,
and return two members ; how is that? But what
becomes of the other five householders? '—' By buying
the borough, I am the freeholder of the six houses ;
I let five by the week, pay the taxes myself, live in the
other ; and thus, being the only elector, return myself
and my son as members at the election."

With telling illustrations such as this did the pamphleteer enliven and enforce his preachment to the people
of England—or as many of them as subscribed to
the *Reformist's Register*.

William Cobbett, having two or three years previously suffered a sentence of imprisonment in Newgate,
in addition to the imposition of a heavy fine, for his
violent political utterances, fled to America on the
suspension of the *Habeas Corpus*. Hone, as if he
were Cobbett's accredited representative, immediately
began to address the latter's readers in vindication of
the fugitive. " Fellow-countrymen," he wrote, " every
one of us who feels he has a country now feels his
mind distressed, his heart heavy, his courage fail
him." Was it to be wondered at, after this, he
asked, if Cobbett should seek the protection of the
American flag? that Mrs. Cobbett and their two
daughters should prepare to follow him? Staunchly

Hone promised to make his *Register* the vehicle for Cobbett's thoughts ; Cobbett's patrons should now become his subscribers. Conscious that in literary power his appeal might be less effective than that of the " exile," he doubtless hoped to make good any deficiencies of style by the sincerity of his advocacy.

In all this we seem to have first-hand evidence that Cobbett's principles were Hone's principles, and that their thoughts ran in the same groove—indeed, that Hone had become a hero-worshipper, and that Cobbett was his hero.

" The last time I saw Mr. Cobbett," he writes, " was on Saturday, March 15th, at his house in Catherine Street. I seem to have the sound of his voice in my ear. I see his very attitude, as he sat in his chair when I left him by his fireside in Catherine Street. I cannot get these little incidents out of my head. We attach importance to such trifles when they are connected with recollections of those whom we esteem and admire, and whom we shall perhaps see no more."

Surely there is the ring of sincerity in all this.

Cobbett's *Register* was partly suspended ; Hone's had just come into being. It cannot be conceived that Cobbett contemplated or suggested that he would write in safety in America, and send his writings for Hone to publish in a terrorised England. If Cobbett held, as it is declared, that no man was bound to sacrifice himself and his family for the general good, he may be credited with applying the principle to others as well as to himself. This line of argument is induced by the very different complexion which is placed upon the subsequent relationships of the two men by the private papers which have been preserved by the Hone family. If Hone himself ever admired Cobbett, it is evident his family did not share in that admiration — their dislike of the man is apparent everywhere in the papers alluded to.

According to these documents, the estrangement of Hone and Cobbett had actually commenced before the date of the friendly meeting in Catherine Street ; and it was clinched by an incident occurring three years later, which—if true, and not the distorted impression of a jaundiced imagination—it would be difficult to describe in adequate terms of reprehension. It is given here for what it is worth—and in estimating the relative values of the two men, the independence of Cobbett's life will always stand out in contrast to the dependence of Hone's.

In 1816 Hone announced the publication of " The Life of William Cobbett, Author of the Political Register, written by himself " ; the authorship of which, however, that writer almost immediately repudiated, and stigmatised as a fraud on the public, alleging it to be full of errors, omissions, and suppressions. Cobbett objected to Hone, as a rival " reform " publisher, offering this work, " containing as much as a half-crown pamphlet " at a low price of fourpence. How well it sold at this price is evidenced by the number of editions through which it quickly ran ; and the quarrel it bred may be realised by Hone's challenge to Cobbett printed on the advertisement to the seventh edition—a challenge full of sound and fury, asseverating the authenticity and genuineness of his fourpenny publication. With two copies of *Cobbett's Weekly Political Register*, dated respectively October 12th and October 19th of that year, found among Hone's papers, there is a memorandum in his (the latter's) handwriting, to the effect that they were brought to him for an estimate of cheap printing, which he gave, but afterwards heard no more about, though he discovered subsequent issues were being cheaply produced. " Then I published Cobbett's Life, by himself," says the memorandum. So that the estrangement between the two has all the appearance of originating in a business disagreement.

But (as the family papers disclose) Hone was scarcely the kind of man to fraternise with Cobbett. He was never a man of violent principles, and often expressed his dislike to Cobbett's violent writings. The two men did not meet more than two or three times, and in each case it was Cobbett who sought the interview. Two of these meetings, if the family papers may be relied upon, seem to bear a sinister significance.

In the early part of 1817, while the *ex-officio* informations were pending, William Cobbett, accompanied by a person who was a stranger to Hone, called at his house and discoursed very freely on the iniquitous prosecutions which were then hanging over him, suggested the prudence of his seeking safety by quitting the country, and entered on the persuasive detail of funds that were ready to effect his immediate departure to America.

The fugitive's wife and family were to be cared for, and quickly follow him. Hone calmly told Cobbett he never entered on any important business without discussing the question with his wife, and he had an idea that she would never be favourable to the proposal. Mrs. Hone opportunely entered the room at that moment, and Cobbett reiterated his suggestions to her, in his usual plausible manner. " What shall we do, my dear? " said her husband. " Stay where we are," was her reply ; and turning to Cobbett, she continued: " You don't know my husband if you imagine he is the coward to desert a cause he believes to be right ; but if he determines that he ought to go, whenever it may be, Mr. Cobbett, we all go together ; there will be no following."

There was nothing hesitating or indecisive about this, and so ended Cobbett's mission to Hone. As we know, while the latter faced his prosecution, Cobbett fled to America rather than stand a similar trial. His *Political Register* appeared again on July 12th, and from that date was regularly published in London under the supervision of his son, Cobbett contributing some of the articles from America.

Mrs. Burn, upon whose testimony alone this episode rests, writes : —

" The last occasion on which he saw Mr. Cobbett, was when he called one afternoon and pressingly invited my father to accompany him to a meeting of politicians at the ' Hole in the Wall ' in Barbican. My father declined, and on Mr. Cobbett still urging him to go, my mother, who had reason for distrusting the man, said : ' No, Mr. Cobbett, Mr. Hone and I have not spent an evening together since his Trials ; all our young people are on a visit, and he has promised that we shall take tea together this evening ; I cannot let him forego that promise.' Cobbett stayed and took tea with them and later in the evening my father, went to Newgate, to see John Cam Hobhouse, who was imprisoned for his pamphlet ' A Trifling Mistake.' "

There would have been nothing very extraordinary in Cobbett's calling and trying to prevail upon William Hone to attend a meeting of Liberals, had it not occurred on the 23rd of February, 1820 ; but on that evening, from Barbican, the meeting—not of Liberals or Radicals, but a band of miserable cut-throats and incendiaries—adjourned to a loft in Cato Street, hired for them by their instigator, the miscreant Edwards, a Government Spy. Here they were captured, with the exception of their leader, Thistlewood, by a posse of Bow Street officers aided by Foot Guards. As the officers ascended to the loft, the foremost, Smithers, received a sword thrust through the heart from Thistle-wood, who leaped out of a back window, and escaped to a friend's house, where he was captured in bed the next morning, by the Bow Street officers.

Mrs. Burn continues : —

" My mother's belief that Cobbett was ' a dangerous bad man ' was fortified by the fact of his having endeavoured to persuade my father to associate himself with such a gang as had been gathered together in Barbican. My father and Cobbett never met again.

" In the course of his last illness, while conversing with his family, the name of Cobbett turned up. He remarked, ' Cobbett was a bad man ; he once endeavoured to persuade me to adopt a course which I knew would be wrong, urging the necessity of a man studying the interests of himself and his family before that of the public, and he said he should not mind seeing London knee-deep in blood, if it served his family.' "

VIII

THE ARREST

THE gradual decline of the English labourer had marked the course of the great French War, and after Waterloo the impoverished state of the country was deplorable. Tens of thousands were out of work ; and though their fierce cries for bread rent the air, the fashionable preachment of the clergy and those superior persons who did not even faintly realise all that was involved in a patient endurance of the miseries of semi-famine was resignation and the cultivation of a spirit of contentment. A ballad by that " searcher after happiness," Hannah More, was hawked about London, inculcating this comfortable doctrine. The village labourer, whose children were perishing for food, was expected to put aside these trivialities of life and sing, like some merry villager of the mimic stage, to the lilt of " The Cobbler there was and he lived in a Stall " :—

" The parliament men, altho' great is their power
Yet they cannot contrive us a bit of a shower ;
And I never yet heard, though our rulers are wise,
That they knew very well how to manage the skies ;
For the best of them all, as they found to their cost,
Were not able to hinder last winter's hard frost."

There is plenty more in this strain, but the quoting of one other couplet will amply suffice :—

" So I'll work the whole day, and on Sundays I'll seek
At church how to bear all the wants of the week."

.When the people cried for bread this was the kind of stone offered them. Platitudinous philosophy of this description was well calculated to rouse the ire of a man like William Hone, and he was railing his loudest at the ineptitude of the ruling powers—the subject engaging his pen at the particular moment was Political Priestcraft—when his arrest was determined upon. It was never discovered how offensive satire was till a humble individual like Hone used it with sledge-hammer ferocity. As a polished weapon in the hands of a statesman, or a dignitary of the Crown, as used by Bolingbroke and Canning, or by Swift, it was endurable. But an obscure bookseller daring to set his pen and tilt at exalted and mighty personages from his shabby little shop, " 63, Old Bailey, three doors from Ludgate Hill," must be made an example of.

The power of *ex-officio* information had been extended so as to compel bail by an Act of 1808 ; but from 1808 to 1811, during which forty such informations were laid, only one person was held to bail. It was under this Act that William Hone was arrested, May 3, 1817, and committed to prison on three separate charges, the misdemeanours set down against him being the " printing and publishing certain impious, profane, and scandalous libels." Of course the truth of the matter was that the prosecution was really for its satire on the Ministers and Government of the day.

These arbitrary *ex-officio* informations were laid at the suit of the King, by his Attorney-General, without application to the court wherein they were filed for leave, and without giving the defendant any opportunity to show cause why they should not be filed.

Similar were the proceedings which had been taken against William Cobbett, who promptly fled to America (March 28th), suspending the publication of his *Register* for four months.

The first victim of Sir William Garrow was at least

able to reach his friends and sympathisers—through the medium of his paper.

" I wrote my last *Register* at home in the midst of my family. Since then the Reign of Terror has commenced, and I now write from prison."

Very circumstantially he then recounts the incidents of his arrest :—

" He [Sir William Garrow] has filed three criminal informations against me, and, assisted by the Court of King's Bench, put me into confinement. The reader shall be circumstantially informed how this has been effected. On Saturday last, in the afternoon, not having been out during the whole of the day, I left home about half-past four o'clock. On my return I purchased two articles from the catalogue of Mr. Major, bookseller, in Skinner Street, one of them written by Samuel Johnson, in the year 1692, entitled ' An Argument, proving—First, That the People of England did actually Abrogate or Dethrone King James II. for Misgovernment, and Promoted the Prince of Orange in his stead ; Secondly, That this proceeding of theirs was according to the English Constitution, and Prescribed by it.' Just before I got to Fleet Lane in the Old Bailey, walking towards my own door, I opened this pamphlet to look at it. At the corner of the lane, two men rushed upon me, and one taking hold of me, said, ' You are my prisoner. I have a judge's warrant against you.' I was at that moment reading these words in the pamphlet—' Shall a poor pickpocket or a highwayman be hanged for a little loose money, and these wholesale thieves, who strip a nation of their lives, liberties, and estates, and all they have, not be looked after? ' I shut to the pamphlet, and putting my finger between the leaves that I might not lose the place, said to the man :—

" ' Very well, walk home with me, and I will go with you.'

" *Officer*. ' No, I shall not suffer you to go home.'

" *Myself*. ' We are going past the door. You will surely step in with me, and let me speak to my wife? '

" *Officer*. ' No, you must go with me.'

" *Myself*. ' Why did you not call upon me at home? Why take me in the street? '

" *Officer*. ' I did not expect to find you at home.'

" *Myself*. ' I am almost constantly at home. I am very seldom out ; I have not been out the whole of the day, till lately.'

" *Officer*. ' I did not call, I tell you, because I did not expect to find you.'

" *Myself*. ' Well, I am willing to go with you ; but I, of course, wish to apprise my family of what has happened.'

" *Officer*. ' I tell you I shall not let you go home. The bail is very large ; you must not go home at all.'

" *Myself*. ' What has the bail to do with my going home or not going home? Go along with me ; I shall not detain you, or run away from you.'

" *Officer*. ' It does not signify ; you shall not go home.'

" *Myself*. ' Very well. Do as you please. I am in your power. Where are you taking me to? '

" *Officer*. ' Here is the judge's warrant—Lord Ellenborough's warrant. Read it.'

" *Myself*. ' No, not here. I will read it at the place you take me to.'

" *Officer*. ' No, read it at once—here it is.'

" *Myself*. ' There is no necessity for it now, in the street.'

" *Officer*. ' Yes—you had better read it here.'

" *Myself*. ' Very well.' (I stood against a post and having read the warrant, returned it to him. It was dated April 28th, five days before, and signed Ellenborough.)

" *Officer*. ' There, now go with me.'

" *Myself*. ' By all means. Where are you taking me to? ' (We now crossed the way toward Newgate Street.)

" *Officer*. ' To a lock-up house.'

" *Myself*. ' Whose? ' (The officer named one or two

near the Bank. I objected to going to a lock-up house in that direction ; telling him I preferred Hopwood's, in Chancery Lane, or some other towards Temple Bar, it being nearer my friends.)

"*Officer.* 'I will take you to the Compter, if you do not choose to go where I tell you.'

"*Myself.* 'I am in your power, and therefore you will do with me as you please.' (A coach being called, I got in, and the officer followed.) "

The prisoner was driven to a house of detention in the neighbourhood, and there found he was precluded by the form of warrant from obtaining bail without forty-eight hours' notice. He could not have read it carefully in the street, and why he was taken to a sponging-house is not quite clear.

Arrested on Saturday, May 3rd, Hone was called upon the following Monday in the Court of King's Bench to plead to a criminal information for printing and publishing a certain blasphemous libel, entitled a " Parody on the Catechism in the Book of Common Prayer " ; and also two other blasphemous libels, the one being a " Parody on the Prayer of Our Lord Jesus Christ, entitled the Lord's Prayer," and the other being a " Parody on the Ten Commandments in the Book of Common Prayer, aforesaid."

Before the information was read the defendant took a primary objection that having been taken into custody only on Saturday, he had not had an opportunity of consulting with any one as to the course he should take. He complained that he was illegally detained.

The Attorney-General said the course before the defendant was simple—he could plead either guilty or not guilty. Lord Ellenborough said that any application to the court upon the subject of his apprehension the defendant could make after the reading of the information. To Hone's request that he might be permitted to sit during the reading of the information, owing to his indisposition, Lord Ellenborough sharply said " No ! "

The first count was now read, and when the Master of the Court came to that part reciting the " Parody on the Lord's Prayer " the Attorney-General apologised to the court for its being necessary to offend their ears by repeating such blasphemy.

Hone declined to plead till he had been supplied with a copy of the information. The court stated that there were no funds with which to supply the copies asked for. The defendant replied that he had no funds for such purpose. He pleaded that it was impossible to carry all the contents of the information in his mind—there were several counts, to part of which he might think it right to plead guilty. The court remained obdurate on the ground of precedent and custom. Hone persisted after each of the other charges that he could not conscientiously plead without the informations before him to peruse.

In the end the Attorney-General moved that the defendant be committed till the first day of the next term. Hone was then informed that he might be at large upon giving notice of bail on all informations ; for each of the first two on personal recognisances of £200 and two sureties of £100 each, and for the last in similar bail for half the amount in each case.

When brought up on Monday, the 19th, he complained of the impossibility of giving the forty-eight hours' notice of bail, and recounted the circumstances of his arbitrary arrest, thirty yards from his own house, and the officer's refusal to let him go home to speak to his wife ; how he threatened that he would be taken to the Compter, was then immediately taken to Serjeant's Inn Coffee House, and thence to Hemp's Lock-up House ; and how he was subjected to other exceptional and uncalled-for severities at the hands of the tipstaff. After some sharp passages between Lord Ellenborough and the defendant, who pleaded his ignorance of judicial forms, the latter said his motion was that he should be discharged out of the custody of the Marshal of the Marshalsea, on the ground that his commitment did not truly state the reason of his committal—he had *not* prayed a further day to plead. Lord Ellenborough told the prisoner his refusal to plead legally amounted to this, and remanded him in custody.

He found in a fellow-prisoner named Wooler another sufferer in the same cause, with whom he was in close sympathy.

Thomas Jonathan Wooler was a Radical journalist who had succeeded Cobbett as editor of the *Statesman*, and on the collapse of that journal appealed to a larger public in the *Black Dwarf*, which was published by him every Sunday morning. For a particularly pungent attack on the Ministry in the tenth number of this paper he was prosecuted for libel. The case was tried before Mr. Justice Abbott and a special jury on June 5, 1817. On a second count Wooler was found innocent of libel, and on the first was granted a new trial, in which he defended himself so ably he again came off victorious. On his release he attacked the special jury system vigorously, and for many years afterwards took a very active part in politics. In Cruikshank's caricature of George IV. as Coriolanus, Wooler (who was really tall of stature) is depicted as a " black dwarf " by the side of the gigantic Cobbett.

Wooler's advocacy of his own cause and ultimate acquittal, in the earlier part of the year, may have inspired Hone to undertake his own defence and prompted him in making the elaborate preparations to answer the charge against him.

His intercourse with Wooler certainly induced him to review the working of the Government spy system.

The *Reformist's Register* of June 28, 1817, charges the Government with fomenting public excitement as a pretext for the subvention of constitutional rights and liberties. An exposure is made of the treacherous working of the Government spy system :—

" I shall relate one or two facts in support of this opinion. Mr. Wooler, who is here in confinement with me, in a letter which appeared in the *Morning Chronicle*, stated that Oliver, the Informer, called on him shortly after his commitment to this prison, to induce him to put in bail and go down into the country in order to further insurrectionary movements, and next, to obtain him to print bills for the same purpose, in both which objects he failed.

" From the description Mr. Wooler gives of this man, I am persuaded he visited me about the same time. I was confined to my bed from illness, in the King's Bench, when a person entered my room expressing sorrow at my situation. He said he came from the country, that everything was in a very bad state, the people greatly distressed, the whole population of some districts ripe for anything ; that with leaders and proper encouragement they would inevitably overwhelm the Government. He strongly recommended persons who were objects of persecution or likely to become so, to turn round on the Government at once and crush it. I told him that however distress might prevail, there was an increase of knowledge diffused throughout the country, and I was assured that patience and right thinking would induce those who felt the most pressure to attempt constitutional means only, for redressing their grievances.

" He replied by urging the necessity of immediate action, and that it was an opportunity not to be missed, and he particularly represented that it could do no harm to encourage the people a little to come to London in bodies, and show their strength. He asked me if I had ever been at Birmingham, or other manufacturing towns where the workmen were unemployed? I told him, no. He then inquired if I knew anybody at Birmingham, or Liverpool or Leeds, as he was going to make a journey, and would be glad to take letters for me, or visit any of my friends at either place. To this I observed that he was a stranger to me, that I could not think of troubling him with mere letters of business, which I was then too ill to write ; that I never had any secrets or entertained sentiments beyond those which I had frequently expressed in print, and I deprecated all attempts to further incite or goad the people to acts which would endanger the public safety.

" He attempted with much ingenuity and suavity to reason down what he called my scruples, and want of confidence, which he said prevented public men from uniting to obtain a complete victory over the Government. I was then obliged to tell him that he had mistaken his man, and that he would be no friend to the people or to me who recommended such measures. He continued to prolong the conversation a considerable time, very dexterously feeling his way, and returning to his points, interlarding his remarks with praise and flattery ; I at length informed him I was too ill to talk much, which he met by saying that though I did not know him, he would soon satisfy me who he was ; that he knew several of my friends, and would convince me that when he called again I might trust him, and said he was going to call on Mr. Wooler in an adjoining staircase, and inquired if I knew him.

" He further inquired if I was generally alone. I ended by telling him I had no friends who would act in the way he described, and that if he called again, I should have a third person present. He took his leave with great civility and many professions of regard, and I saw him no more. As I related before, he fully answered Mr. Wooler's description of Oliver. I forgot to mention that he told me he wanted several thousand political bills printed, which he said I should do. I wholly declined the offer, or even to look at the MS., which he said was not quite finished.

" Previous to my confinement, I had several strangers call on me, who used violent language, and who I am well persuaded were emissaries to entrap me. I always manifested my displeasure to such persons, and desired them to withdraw. I have received bushels of manuscript of very dangerous tendency, which I have destroyed as soon as I received them, sometimes much to the displeasure of those who afterwards claimed them.

" One manuscript was of so peculiar a description that I shall show how it came into my hands, what it was, and how I disposed of it. It is not my fault that it is not in the green bag now lying on the Table of the House. If it is, I hope means have been taken by the Suspension Committee to discover the author.

" On Saturday the 22nd of March, about 8 in the evening, I received a letter by the two-penny post, signed with initials. It stated the necessity of immediately adopting measures to show the Government the strength of the people, for which purpose it requested that I would cause several thousand copies of a bill, the MS. of which was enclosed, to be printed immediately as a poster or Placard. I was assured that I should receive liberal payment, and was directed to send them off by different conveyances, so that they might reach every part of the Kingdom on the same day.

" It mentioned particular towns to which they should most especially be sent. They were to be forwarded to every person throughout the country who I might know, or suppose to be likely to dispose of them as directed, and where names could not be collected, it was requested they might be forwarded to Bookvendors, Blacking, or other agents of small wares, or persons keeping similar shops in every town. Each of these persons was to be requested to take charge of the bills, and post them up before sunrise on a day named. The Posting Bill was an Address to the People, acquainting them that the whole nation would be in arms on the same day, namely, the 7th of April, by each Parish meeting in its Churchyard on that day, armed with a rake and a small sword or dagger (most minute instructions for making which instruments were given in the bill) and thus armed, every man was required to remain at the place of meeting for one hour, and then return home. Figures of the arms were very neatly drawn in the MS. and required to be engraved on wood, to be inserted in the bill.

"This bill and the instructions to myself were circumstantially drawn up at great length, and copied in a neat law hand. Conceiving as I still do, that this communication was a wicked plan to entrap me, I put the papers in my pocket, and immediately went down to the Office of the Secretary of State at the Treasury. No officer of the establishment was in attendance, but I was informed that Mr. Beckett, the Under Secretary, lived in Great George Street, where I went, but finding him at dinner, I retired to Ireson's Hotel until 10 o'clock, when his servant said he would leave the dinner-table. At that hour I sent in a signed note to Mr. Beckett, requesting to see him, and he received me in the parlour, saying, ' What business can you have with me, Mr. Hone? ' I told him I had just before received a letter by the two-penny post, enclosing a paper which I considered dangerous to possess, and desired to put both letter and paper into his keeping. He read each of them deliberately ; as soon as he had done so, I departed, no further conversation taking place. Having thus presented the papers to the Under Secretary of State, which, if found in my possession might have subjected me to I know not what suspicion, imprisonment, and punishment, I was surprised to find that the attempts of this same instigator were renewed upon other persons.

"On the 17th of April, ten days after that, when according to the before-named bill, the nation was to have been in arms, Messrs. Hay & Turner, Printers, of Newcastle Street, Strand, received a bill of like import, appointing the arming of the nation for Sunday, the 4th of May. Their bill was much shorter than mine, and without diagrams or figures. The letter of Messrs. Hay & Turner differs from that to me, as it directs them to forward the bills to a Mr. Nicholls, an Attorney, 29 Bennet St., Stamford St., Blackfriars Road.

" On receiving the letter and bills, Messrs. Hay & Turner addressed a note to Mr. Nicholls, designedly to acquaint him they had an order for bills to be addressed to him, and requesting the £10 to be remitted previous to their proceeding to print. Hearing nothing from Mr. Nicholls, they had almost forgotten the matter, until nearly a week afterwards, when it occurred to them that it was perhaps dangerous to hold such a paper, and they went to Sir N. Conant, at Bow Street, who recommended such an application to Mr. Nicholls as they had already made, and sent them to the Secretary of State's, where they were introduced to Mr. Noble, one of the senior clerks, who took charge of the papers, and said they should see Lord Sidmouth. He left them in an ante-chamber. About ten minutes afterwards a person entered the room and sat down with Messrs. Hay & Turner, in silence. This person was presently familiarly beckoned into another room, by a servant in waiting, and was immediately closeted with Lord Sidmouth.

" Messrs. Hay & Turner waited upwards of an hour for him to come out, and from other engagements were obliged to leave the office without seeing his Lordship. To their astonishment, they afterwards discovered this person to be Mr. Nicholls, the Attorney, to whom they were to have sent the bills.

" Letters and posting-bills to the like effect were also received by Mr. Harvey, a Printer of Blackfriars Road ; by Mr. Molineux, a Printer of Bream's Buildings, Chancery Lane, and by several other printers. They were to be sent to the same Mr. Nicholls, whom Messrs. Hay & Turner left closeted with Lord Sidmouth, His Majesty's principal Secretary of State for the Home Department.

" There appears to have been a deliberate plan to ensnare persons connected with the press, because these papers affected to announce risings on the 7th of April and on the 4th of May ; whereas the Reports of the two Houses which notice various intended risings do not mention either to have been designed to take place on those days. Is it possible that the employment of spies and informers, now unblushingly avowed, has subjected us to such dreadful machinations as these? Having escaped the insidious and horrible attacks of concealed assassins, surely in a prison, and under three Government prosecutions, men might suppose themselves secure from further persecution, and yet Oliver's attempt to entrap Mr. Wooler and, I believe myself, shows the unrelenting earnestness with which these wretches prosecute their cruel purposes. Surely we have a right to supplicate for vengeance.

"WILLIAM HONE."

That Hone's suspicions were not unwarranted appears from the fact that Edwards, the notorious Fleet Street spy, took lodgings opposite the shop of Richard Carlile, professing to be a sculptor, an art for which he had some talent, in a plot to entrap that daring publisher, a piece of villainy which happily failed.

That the wretch Oliver was really fomenting sedition in various parts of the country, as indicated in the *Reformist's Register*, and doing so with the knowledge, if not the connivance, of Lords Sidmouth, Liverpool, and Castlereagh, is tolerably clear from an exposure which appeared in the *Morning Chronicle* of July 12, 1817. The seditious bill sent to the printers to which allusion has been made affords an interesting commentary on the state of public feeling at that time:—

" BRITONS !

" Petitioning avails you nothing ! The Ministers say you are disaffected, and that the Meetings to petition for Reform have been under pretext for treasonable purposes. You were unarmed, and obeyed the laws ; yet your liberties are at an end. There is now only one way left you, and that is, to show them with arms in your hands, that you can be obedient to the laws. The whole nation will assemble on Sunday, the 4th May, at five minutes past nine in the morning, each parish at its own Church Yard, armed as follows :—

"ARMS.

"Take a stick like a broom handle, nine feet long; bore a hole at the top, and fill it with rosin; take the blade of a strong dinner knife, heat the shaft of it, and put it in the hole; when cool it will be fixed, the same as in a knife handle, and make an excellent pike; the knife must be pointed. Each man should have a belt, and a good sized carving knife therein, as a sword. Being armed thus, meet as above; and exactly as the clock strikes ten, disperse, and go quietly home. You will be surprised the effect this proceeding will have; but should it fail in effect, our countrymen will hear further from us."

Hone's correspondence at this time also indicates, like a political barometer, the actual state of public feeling, the temperature of which would not improbably affect his position.

Here is a letter from Mr. Robert Ogle (of Ogle, Duncum and Cockrane, Holborn) to Hone soon after his apprehension in May, 1817 :—

"DEAR HONE,

"I just called in to hear after your welfare and am glad to find that Mrs. Hone and you are both in good spirits. I find on enquiry that we may see you, which I did not know was permitted. So do not think that I am one of your sunshine friends, or afraid to visit you, although there are many timid people about, ready to take alarm at their own shadows.

"Now for the Parodies—there is an Article in the 'Bible Magazine' respecting a parody on a Psalm which we Christians allow to be applicable only to Christ and to the Church. In this version it is applied to 'Old George'; was there ever any thing more in point? I engage to furnish you with the name of the writer of this Article, who I believe is a clergyman of the Established Church, whom you may subpœna as a

10

witness, and if you have not a Jury of the most base hirelings of corruption that ever crawled, you *must* be acquitted.

" Things look very bad all over the world—slavery and despotism are triumphant—but I doubt not God will ere long confound their devices in a way we least think of.

" I think you should have said a few words in exculpation of the charge of blasphemy, in your ' Reformist's Register.' The Catechism, Litany, St. Athanasius Creed, and so on, are not part of Scripture. A Presbyterian would as soon learn his child an Ave Maria as the Athanasian Creed. The Catechism was John Wilkes', I understand, and as for the Litany and the Creed, they are no part of the Holy Writ, but a composition of men.

" Yours very truly,
" R. OGLE."

About the same date the following letter came from Francis Place :—

" About a dozen of the Whigs are to dine at the Crown and Anchor on the 23rd at the Anniversary of Burdett's Election ; among them Brougham—who has again committed himself in writing. Something might be said in the ' Register ' in praise of Burdett, and introductory to his motion on the 20th.

" The *Dwarf* has taken up your defense on the right point, and so far as he has gone has done it remarkably well.

" I have just now heard that Brougham intends on the 20th to speak ' right out ' in favour of Annual Parliaments, and is determined to go as far as any one on the 23rd—we shall see.

" Let me have all the references you can find to Parodies on Holy Writ, and on Creeds, &c., for the purpose of a good row which will be made respecting them and you in Parliament by Brougham and others."

The monotony of prison life was relieved by much letter-writing. The twopenny post brought him, on

May 26th, a letter from another political friend, Major Cartwright, founder of the Hampden Club, and author of " A Plan of Radical Reform," in which the prisoner is kept well informed of the proceedings of Parliament, particularly with reference to *ex-officio* informations.

The case, being one of great political significance, was brought up in Parliament.

On May 12th Earl Grey mentioned in the House of Lords that a Mr. Hone, a pamphleteer who recently had so much amused them, was proceeded against for publishing some blasphemous parody ; but he had read one of the same nature written, printed, and published some years ago by other people without any notice having been officially taken of it. The parody to which Earl Grey alluded, and a portion of which he recited, was Canning's famous parody, " Praise Lepaux " ; and he asked whether the authors, be they in the Cabinet or in any other place, would also be found out and visited with the penalties of the law.

This hint to the obscure publisher against whom these *ex-officio* informations had been filed for blasphemous and seditious parodies was effectually worked out by him in the solitude of his prison and in the poor dwelling where he had surrounded himself, as he had done from his earliest years, with a collection of old and curious books.

From these he had gathered an abundance of knowledge that was destined to perplex the technical acquirements of the Attorney-General, to whom the sword and buckler of his precedents would be wholly useless, and to change the determination of the boldest judge in the land to convict, at any rate, into the prostration of helpless despair. Altogether, the three trials of William Hone are amongst the most remarkable in our constitutional history. They produced more distinct effect upon the temper of the country than any public proceedings of that time. They taught the Government a lesson which has never been forgotten, and to which, as much as to any other cause, we owe the prodigious improvement as to the law of libel itself, and the use of the law, in our own day—an improvement which leaves what is dangerous in the Press to be corrected by the remedial power of the Press itself, and which, instead of lamenting over the newly acquired ability of the masses to read seditious and irreligious works, depends upon the general diffusion of this ability as the surest corrective of the evils that are incident even to the best gift of Heaven—that of knowledge.

The apt illustration quoted by Lord Grey was a parody of the " Benedicite," which had appeared in the *Anti-Jacobin* in 1798. It was supposed to be a " brilliant satire," in which Canning had gibbeted his Republican opponents for their worship of Lepaux and other French revolutionary demigods: —

" All creeping creatures, venomous and low,
　　Paine, .Williams, Godwin, Holcroft, praise Lepaux."

Whether this was satire or profanity, it showed the difficulty and danger of leaving to a magistrate the deciding of when or when not to prefer a charge of blasphemy, as had been required by Lord Sidmouth's outrageous circular letter to the justices.

The case of Hone is not without its ludicrous aspect. Here was a poor bookseller who spent his life in the quest of rare and curious books, and in the accumulation of more knowledge than wealth, challenged to a duel with the Government because his Parodies had made the Administration the laughing-stock of the world.

IX

THE FIRST TRIAL

IT may not have been altogether a surprise to Hone to find himself in the position of a prisoner placed on trial for what was practically sedition. His early association with the London Corresponding Society, from which he undoubtedly absorbed his democratic principles, may have prepared him for this culmination. The French Revolution had kindled an ardent love for political justice in the breasts of thousands of thoughtful Englishmen.

The London Corresponding Society, in the early days of the great French upheaval, held great public meetings on the fields near Copenhagen House, Highbury, at which the Government were alarmed and the Tories trembled with fear and rage. The most threatening of these meetings was held on October 26, 1795, when Thelwall and other sympathisers with France and the cause of liberty addressed a concourse of forty thousand persons, throwing out hints that the mob should surround Westminster on the 29th, when the King would go to the Houses of Parliament. The hint was taken, and on that day the King was shot at, but escaped unhurt.

In 1794 many members of the Corresponding Society, including Thelwall, Hardy, Holcroft, and Horne Tooke, were tried for high treason in connection with the doings of the Society, but were all acquitted.

Even so grave a matter as a trial for treason could

not repress Horne Tooke's jocularity. As he was
returning from the Old Bailey to Newgate one cold
night a lady placed a silk handkerchief round his
neck, upon which he gaily said, " Take care, madam,
what you are about, for I'm rather ticklish about the
neck just now." While the trial was proceeding, Tooke
one day expressed a wish to speak in his own defence,
and sent a message to that effect to Erskine, saying,
" I'll be hanged if I don't," to which Erskine wrote
back, " You'll be hanged if you do." After his acquittal
Tooke remarked to a friend that if a certain song exhibited at the trial of Hardy had been produced against
him, he would have sung it to the jury, that, as there
was no treason in the words, they might judge if there
was any in the music.

William Hone, though so very different from these
men—having neither the stern determination of the
author of " Political Justice " nor the levity of his
fellow-admirer of John Wilkes—could not have flung
himself into the stream of active politics without some
dim foreboding of what might possibly be in store
for him from a Government that was still fearful and
suspicious of every manifestation of a popular movement towards liberty.

Brought into court again on Thursday, June 19th,
Hone was informed that if he still refused to plead
to the indictment he would be brought up in a few
days to receive judgment. Forced to it, he then
pleaded Not Guilty, and asked for permission to go
to the Crown Office to make copies of the information,
which was peremptorily refused. He thereupon pro-
tested that the proceeding of the Attorney-General was
illegal and unconstitutional. Lord Ellenborough rejoined, " Well, protest " ; and after being informed
that he would be tried at " Sittings after this Term,"
at Guildhall, he was removed in custody.

On June 27th Hone preferred the request that he
might be liberated from the King's Bench Prison on

his own recognisances to any amount, in order to have the opportunity to provide for the maintenance of his seven children, concerning whose welfare he was naturally anxious.

He wrote from his prison to the Crown Office at the same time to protest against the jurors nominated to try his issue, challenging the legality of the whole proceedings. The correspondence certainly discloses more than a suspicion that the selection of the special jurors, from the lists furnished by the sheriffs, had been anything but impartial ; indeed, there was unmistakable evidence of a secret intention on the part of the law officers of the Crown to secure a conviction by means of an incompetent or partial jury. A reply was obtained from the solicitor for the prosecution waiving the nomination of the special jurors.

That ancient institution, Trial by Jury, was in danger, for there had been discovered a precious art of making the jury-lists to carry only certain classes of names, from whence by the same high art special juries were selected. When the fierce laws of 1817 enhanced the dangers of this pernicious system, it had to be fought in the interests of justice generally, and in the case of Hone particularly. Mr. Charles Pearson, a city solicitor, and a friend of Hone, took an active part in this struggle.

" When I went to the Crown Office," he said, " with Mr. Hone to strike the Jury, and endeavour to abolish that system which has sent many persons as innocent as he to dungeons and death, I found there the ostlers of the Augean stable, with the hacks of the court in waiting, and the Jehus of the law ready mounted to ride over the liberties of the people. They said, ' Gentlemen, there shall be no selection—there shall be an indiscriminate taking ; you may proceed to any part of the stable,' well knowing that the sorry jades in that stable, almost worn out in the service of corruption, were ready to give us the long trot the moment they were employed. I was fortunate enough to produce an opposition to that system. I stated my determination to attack in every way a system detested by good men in all times, a system reprobated on the trial of Mr. Horne Tooke, a system, the principle of which those who have been the victims of it never took on themselves to investigate, because they felt so many strong prejudices embarked in favour of what appeared to be a fair jury. We, however, sent their hackneys back to the stable, and I am happy to say I have now secured stable and all, I have them in my possession."

When, in November, the court was forced to admit openly that the " jury-lists had been illegally, improperly, and partially prepared," the battle was virtually won.

It may be mentioned that a year or two later the Common Council of London instituted an inquiry into the state of the Jury Lists, and the report disclosed the existence of an alarming and most discreditable state of things. Although many citizens were qualified, by the possession of £100 worth of property, to serve as special jurors, very few names got upon the lists, and these lists were left with the Master of the Crown Office for weeks on purpose to give him the opportunity of learning the politics of the persons whose names were on—in fact, when the question was put whether the Crown Office had made the alleged inquiries into the politics of these jurymen, no direct denial was forthcoming, the witness resorting to the miserable subterfuge that he had " no recollection " of such inquiries being made, whereupon the *Examiner* caustically remarked that *Non mi ricordo* was far from being exclusively Italian. Another journal was equally wrathful on the subject. The *Morning Chronicle* argued that the prevailing method of selecting jurors was absolutely destructive of the purity of trial by jury, and made it a mockery to talk of the freedom of the Press under the Blasphemous and Seditious Libel Act, especially in the presence of a body which had just sprung into existence, calling itself the Constitutional Association for the Prosecution of Seditious and Blasphemous Libels. A libel, said the *Chronicle*, is anything that twelve jurymen can be induced to call such, and all depends on the nomination of the jurors. " Who does not know, for instance, that twelve Tory jurymen would, without a moment's hesitation, pronounce a publication containing Whiggish sentiments libellous that twelve Whig jurymen would consider deserving of praise? "

Returning to Hone's case, a series of events of much personal and political interest during the next few months are to be gleaned from the pages of the *Reformist's Register*.

In the issue of July 5, 1817, Hone writes: " I am now at home. I was this morning released from prison, after being confined from May 3rd. The Crown abandons its Special Juries."

He and his fellow-prisoner, Wooler, had been enlarged upon their own recognisances.

In the final number of the *Reformist's Register* Hone refers to the sad case of Mr. Evans and his son (a mere youth, but twenty years of age), who had been imprisoned under the suspension of the Habeas Corpus Act, for nearly three years without trial.

" When taken before the Privy Council, they were simply asked whether they knew Mr. Thistlewood and Dr. Watson? and this accident of personal acquaintance with these individuals has been the only cause ever hinted for their arrest and continued imprisonment."

Mrs. Evans being in great pecuniary distress, Hone strongly appeals in his columns for friends to come to her assistance. The proprietor-editor concludes : " I now take a very unwilling leave of my readers. This is the last *Register* I shall publish." It appears he had suffered for some time both from bad health and from the dishonesty of country agents, who received large weekly consignments of *Registers* and other goods but never remitted a sixpence to him.

" This is the death-throe of the *Register*, and with pain I bid my readers farewell.   67 Old Bailey, 23rd Oct. 1817.

"WILLIAM HONE."

This journal had only been running from February 1st of that fateful year.

Finally he adds, " I shall now return to my business as publisher "—having no suspicion that in the following month he was to receive notice of trial for the Parodies, which he had suppressed in the February, almost immediately after their publication.

In Hone's copy of the *Reformist's Register* is found, written in some unknown hand:—

" This is a very valuable, but painfully interesting Work, containing much of the Personal History of Mr. Hone, and the cruel persecution and suffering he underwent during the period of its Publication.

" If ever England shall have—what has never yet appeared—an honest Historian—he will here find ample materials for a narrative of events of 1817, in the bold and unflinching exposure of Plots and the Spy System, Special Jury abuses, *ex-officio* Informations, Police and Blood Money Villany, Arbitrary Proceedings of Parson Hay and other Manchester Justices, The Overbearing insolence of Chief Justice Ellenborough, the bullying barefaced profligacy of Brougham, the unabashed mendacity of Castlereagh, *et cum multis aliis*."

The day appointed for the trial arrived.   Here we quote Charles Knight—

" On the morning of the 18th of December there is a considerable crowd round the avenues of

Guildhall.   An obscure bookseller, a man of no
substance in worldly eyes, is to be tried for libel.
He vends his wares in a little shop in the Old
Bailey, where there are, strangely mingled, twopenny
political pamphlets, and old harmless folios that the
poor publisher keeps for his especial reading as he sits
in his dingy back parlour.   The door-keepers and
officers of the court scarcely know what is going to
happen ; for the table within the bar has not the usual
covering of crimson bags, but ever and anon a shabby,
boy arrives with an armful of books of all ages and
sizes, and the whole table is strewed with dusty and
tattered volumes that the ushers are quite sure have
no law within their mouldy covers.

" A middle-aged man—a bland and smiling man—
with a half-sad, half-merry twinkle in his eye—a seedy
man, to use an expressive word, whose black coat is
wondrous brown and threadbare—takes his place at
the table, and begins with the aid of his young brother
to arrange and turn over the books which were his
heralds.   Sir Samuel Shepherd, the Attorney-General,
takes his seat, and looks compassionately, as was his
nature to do, at the pale man in threadbare black." (Sir
William Garrow had resigned the Attorney-Generalship
on May 5th, the day Hone had been first brought up.)
" Mr. Justice Abbott arrives in due time ; a special jury
is   sworn ;   the   pleadings   are   opened ;   and   the
Attorney-General states the case against William Hone,
for printing and publishing an impious and profane
libel upon the Catechism, the Lord's Prayer, and the
Ten Commandments, thereby bringing into contempt
the Christian religion.   ' It may be said,' argued the
Attorney-General, ' that the defendant's object was not
to produce this effect.'   I believe that he meant it, in
one sense, as a political squib, but his responsibility
is not the less."

As the Attorney-General proceeded to read passages
from the parody upon the Catechism, the crowd in
court laughed ; the Bench was indignant, and the
Attorney-General said the laugh was the fullest proof

of the baneful effect of the defendant's publication. And so the trial went on in the smoothest way, and the case for the prosecution was closed.

Then the pale man in black rose, and with a faltering voice set forth the difficulty he had in addressing the court, and how his poverty prevented his obtaining counsel. And now he began to warm in the recital of what he thought his wrongs, his commitments, his hurried calls to plead, the expense of copies of the information against him, and, as Mr. Justice Abbott, with perfect gentleness, but with his cold formality, interrupted him, the timid man, who all thought would have mumbled forth a hasty defence, grew bolder and bolder, and in a short time had possession of his audience as if he were " some well-graced actor," who was there to receive the tribute of popular admiration.

They were not to inquire whether he were a member of the Established Church or a Dissenter ; it was enough that he professed himself to be a Christian ; and he would be bold to say that he made that profession with a reverence for the doctrines of Christianity which could not be exceeded by any person in that court. He had his books about him, and it was from them that he must draw his defence. They had been the solace of his life. He was too much attached to his books to part with them. As to parodies, they were as old at least as the invention of printing, and he never heard of a prosecution for parody, either religious or any other. There were two kinds of parodies ; one in which a man might convey ludicrous or ridiculous ideas relative to some other subject ; the other, where it was meant to ridicule the thing parodied. This latter was not the case here, and therefore he had not brought religion into contempt. This was the gist of William Hone's defence.

To show fully how this argument was worked, with what readiness, what coolness, what courage, would be

to transcribe the whole proceedings of the three days.
It was in vain that the Attorney-General urged that
to bring forward any previous parody was the same
thing as if a person charged with obscenity should
produce obscene volumes in his defence. It was in
vain that Mr. Justice Abbott repeated his wish that
the defendant would not read such things. On he went,
till interruption was held to be in vain. It was worse
than vain, it was unjust. Truly did Hone reply to
Mr. Justice Abbott: —

" My Lord, your Lordship's observation is in the
very spirit of what Pope Leo the Tenth said to Martin
Luther—' For God's sake, don't say a word about the
indulgences and the monasteries, and I'll give you a
living,' thus precluding him from mentioning the very
thing in dispute. I must go on with these parodies,
or I cannot go on with my defence."

Undauntedly he went on, from the current literature
of the time, such as grave lawyers read in their few
hours of recreation, to the forgotten volumes of old
theology and polemical controversy, that the said
grave lawyers of modern days are accustomed to regard
as useless lumber. The editor of *Blackwood's
Magazine* was a parodist—he parodied a chapter of
Ezekiel ; Martin Luther was a parodist—he parodied
the First Psalm ; Bishop Latimer was a parodist, and
so was Dr. Boys, Dean of Canterbury ; the author
of the " Rolliad " was a parodist, and so was Mr.
Canning. Passage after passage did Mr. Hone read
from author after author. He thought it was pretty
clear that Martin Luther did not mean to ridicule the
Lord's Prayer ; that Mr. Canning did not mean to
ridicule the Scriptures. Why, then, should it be presumed that he had such an intention?

As soon as he found that his parodies had been
deemed offensive, he had suppressed them, and that
he had done long before his prosecution. It was in

vain that the Attorney-General replied that Martin Luther was a libeller, and Dr. Boys was a libeller. The judge charged the jury in vain. William Hone was acquitted after a quarter of an hour's deliberation.

To the slowest perception it was clear that the Bench was influenced by a spirit of tyranny, revenge, and persecution. That parodies intended to advance the cause of Reform could be interpreted as part of a great conspiracy against the Throne and Constitution was more than the plain, honest citizen was prepared to admit.

Immediately on a declaration of a verdict of Not Guilty the court rang with acclamations of "Long live the honest jury!" and when order was again restored Mr. Justice Abbott delivered a stern reprimand, desiring those who felt called upon to rejoice at the decision to reserve their expressions of satisfaction for a fitter place and opportunity. Accordingly the crowd surged forth into the streets with their jubilations.

The trial of the information against William Hone for a parody on the Litany was ordered by the court to come on the next morning at half-past nine o'clock.

X

CLOSE OF THE TRIALS

THE announcement having been made by the Attorney-General at the close of the first day's proceedings that he intended to persevere in the trial of the second information against William Hone, public curiosity was roused to an extraordinary pitch, not only by the importance of the case, but far more by the triumphant defence the accused had made to the first charge against him.

Consequently, at a very early hour on Friday, December 19th, all the avenues of the court were literally blocked up by a multitude of spectators, anxious to become auditors of the proceedings ; and when the doors of the court were opened, not one-twentieth part of the multitude could find standing accommodation.

It was very generally supposed that Hone having been acquitted on one of the informations, the Attorney-General would not proceed against him on either of the others. It appeared, however, that any such supposition was unwarranted, and at a quarter after nine the accused entered the court, followed by several large bundles of books, all carefully tied up. He took his station at the end of the court table, and having untied his books, he ranged them before him, covering nearly a fourth of the table.

At twenty minutes before ten Lord Ellenborough entered the court and took his seat on the bench.

His lordship's appearance was unexpected, it being generally supposed that Mr. Justice Abbott, who was afterwards Lord Tenterden, having conducted the first trial, would have presided at any subsequent proceedings in the cause.

Mr. Justice Abbott, on his way home after the first trial, called on Lord Ellenborough, who expressed his surprise that the whole day had been occupied by the one trial of Hone. " Well ! and the verdict? " asked his lordship.

" An acquittal ! " was the reply.

" An acquittal ! " angrily exclaimed the judge. " Why ! how did you charge? "

" How did I charge? Constitutionally, my lord ! "

" I'll go to him myself to-morrow."

Can there be any doubt that political passion was influencing the judgment-seat? The severity of the Lord Chief Justice to the reforming Member for Westminster, Lord Cochrane, must not be forgotten.

When the morrow arrived, notwithstanding that it was a foggy morning, the Lord Chief Justice, enfeebled with illness as he was, doggedly rose from his bed and of set purpose proceeded to the Guildhall, to prostitute his great talents as a partisan. He had been deeply mortified by the acquittal of a man named Watson for high treason ; he was now resolved that the political libeller should not escape punishment. He swore, says Lord Campbell, that at whatever cost he would himself preside in court that day, that a conviction might be made certain and the law vindicated.

With lowering brow Lord Ellenborough took his place in the judgment-seat which he deemed had been too mercifully filled on the previous day. The mild firmness of the poor publisher, and his gentlemanly sense of the absence of harshness in the conduct of his first trial, had won for him something like respect ; and when on one occasion Mr. Justice Abbott asked him to forbear reading a particular parody, and the defendant said, " Your lordship and I understand each other, and we have gone on so good-humouredly hitherto that I will not break in upon our harmony," it became clear that the puisne judge was not the man to enforce a verdict of guilty on the second trial.

Hone was this day indicted for publishing an impious and profane libel called " The Litany, or General Supplication."

Again the Attorney-General affirmed that whatever might be the object of the defendant the publication had the effect of scoffing at the public service of the Church.   Again the defendant essayed to read from his books, which course he contended was essentially necessary for his defence.   Then began a contest which is perhaps unparalleled in an English court of justice. Upon Mr. Fox's Libel Bill, upon *ex-officio* informations, upon his right to copies of the indictment without extravagant charges the defendant battled with his judge —imperfect in his law, no doubt, but with a firmness and moderation that rode over every attempt to put him down.   Parody after parody was again produced, and especially those parodies of the Litany which the Cavaliers employed so frequently as vehicles of satire upon the Roundheads and Puritans.   Hour after hour his argument never failed ; the defendant never faltered to the end, though his relevancy was often in doubt— one man against all the power of a Government, and his poor knowledge of the law opposed to that of a " legal lion."

The Lord Chief Justice at length gathered up his exhausted strength for his charge, and concluded in a strain that left but little hope for the defendant.

" He would deliver the jury his solemn opinion, as he was required by Act of Parliament to do ; and under the authority of that Act, and still more in obedience to his conscience and his God, he pronounced

11

this to be a most impious and profane libel. Believing and hoping that they, the jury, were Christians, he had not any doubt that they would be of the same opinion."

The jury in an hour and a half returned a verdict of Not Guilty.

It might have been expected that these prosecutions would have here ended. But the chance of a conviction from a third jury upon a third indictment was to be risked. On December 20th Lord Ellenborough again took his seat on the bench, and the exhausted defendant came late into court, pale and agitated.

The Attorney-General remarked upon his appearance, and offered to postpone the proceedings. The courageous man made his election to go on. This third indictment was for publishing a parody on the Creed of St. Athanasius, called "The Sinecurist's Creed." After the Attorney-General had finished his address Hone asked for five minutes' delay to arrange the few thoughts he had been committing to paper. The judge refused the small concession, but said that he would postpone the proceedings to another day if the defendant would request the court to do so. The scene which ensued was thoroughly dramatic.

"No! I make no such request. My lord, I am very glad to see your lordship to-day, because I feel I sustained an injury from your lordship yesterday—an injury which I did not expect to sustain. . . .

"If your lordship should think proper, on this trial to-day, to deliver your opinion, I hope that opinion will be coolly and dispassionately expressed by your lordship. . . . My lord, I think it necessary to make a stand here. I cannot say what your lordship may consider to be necessary interruption ; but your lordship interrupted me a great many times yesterday, and then said you would interrupt me no more, and yet your lordship did interrupt me afterwards ten times as much. . . . Gentlemen, it is you who are trying me to-day. His lordship is no judge of me. You are my judges, and you only are my judges. His lordship sits there to receive your verdict. . . . I will not say what his lordship did yesterday ; but I trust his lordship to-day will give his opinion coolly and dispassionately, without using either expression or gesture which can be construed as conveying an entreaty to the jury to think as he does. I hope the jury will not be beseeched into a verdict of guilty."

When Hone began to repeat his speech of the two previous days and to allude to the parodies published by others he was interrupted by the judge, who said :—

" I think it necessary thus early to apprise you, that if you wish to show that as a sample of publications of the like tendency which have been written, or for the purpose of proving that the sacred Scriptures have been ridiculed and brought into contempt by other subjects of the realm as well as yourself, I shall not receive it. The commission of crimes, by how many soever persons they may have been committed, does not qualify the guilt of the individual committer. It is my decided purpose not to receive this in evidence : and therefore you may use your discretion, whether you shall dwell further upon a matter of evidence which I declare, judicially, to be inadmissible."

It was solemnly laid down in this case that " the Christian religion was part of the law of England."

The plea of poverty which the defendant made must have had a powerful effect upon his hearers. He humbly apologised for the shabby clothes in which he was compelled to appear before them, but what little money he had recently possessed had been swallowed up by the law ; within the last twelve months his children had been without beds to lie upon ; he could not in the imminent peril in which he stood employ counsel for his defence because he could not fee counsel ; he had been asked when he would publish

his " Trials," but he could not pay a reporter, and
at that moment he had no reporter in court. In subdued
tones he proceeded :—

" Seven or eight years ago I went into business with
a friend in the Strand.   I had then a wife and four
children, and I was separated from them by evils accumulated from endeavouring to help those who could
not help themselves.   I attempted, in conjunction with
the friend, who originated the plan, to establish something of an institution similar to the savings' banks
that are now so general.   There was a number
associated for this purpose, and I was their secretary.
Our object was to get the patronage of ministers to
our scheme.   Mr. Fox was then in power.   It was the
Whig Administration.   We hoped to throw a grain
into the earth which might become a great tree—in
other hands it has succeeded.   It was very Quixotic—
we were mad ; mad because we supposed it possible,
if an intention were good, that it would therefore be
carried into effect.   We were not immediately dis-
couraged, but we met with that trifling and delaying
of hope which makes the heart sick.   I find I am
entering into too much detail.   I meant simply to state
that I lost everything, even the furniture of my house.
With that friend I got again into business. We became
bankrupts, owing to the terms on which we commenced
it.   But, on the meeting of our creditors, the first
question was, ' Where is your certificate? '   All signed
it at once, save one, who was unintentionally the cause
of my failure two and a half years ago, when I went
into prison for debt, and was discharged by the
Insolvent Act."

And so, while arguing the justice of his cause, he
won the sympathy of his auditors.

On the case for the Crown being closed, after this
surprisingly able, novel, and animated defence on the
part of the defendant, the noble judge, who had
appeared oppressed with indisposition during the latter
part of the trial, delivered his charge to the jury,

but in so faint a tone that it was scarcely audible beyond the bench. The Chief Justice was un- mistakably ill.

The triumph of the weak over the powerful was complete. " The frame of adamant and soul of fire," as the biographer of Lord Sidmouth terms the Chief Justice, quailed before the indomitable courage of a man who was roused into energies which would seem only to belong to the master-spirits that have swayed the world. Yet this was a man who, in the ordinary business of life, was incapable of enterprise and per- severing exertion ; who lived in the nooks and corners of his antiquarianism ; who was one that even his old political opponents came to regard as a gentle and innocuous hunter after " all such reading as was never read " ; who in a few years gave up his politics altogether, and, devoting himself to his old poetry and his old divinity, passed a quarter of a century after this conflict in peace with all mankind, and died the sub-editor of a religious journal.

It was towards the close of this remarkable trial that the judge, who came eager to condemn, sued for pity to his intended victim. The defendant quoted War- burton and Tillotson as doubters of the authenticity of the Athanasian Creed. " Even his lordship's father, the Bishop of Carlisle," he believed, " took a similar view of the Creed." And then the judge solemnly said : " Whatever that opinion was, he has gone, many years ago, where he has had to account for his belief and his opinions. . . . For common delicacy forbear." " Oh ! my lord, I shall certainly forbear." Grave and temperate was the charge to the jury this day, and in twenty minutes they once more returned a verdict of Not Guilty.

There had been huzzaing in court several times during the altercations between the defendant and his oppo- nents ; the verdict evoked round upon round of cheers, and the excitement soon spread to the streets.

The Liberal, or Opposition, journals were jubilant in recording the final verdict, and popular feeling ran very high. It was estimated that twenty thousand people had been present, partly in the hall and partly in the crowded avenues.

The law officers of the Crown had strangely miscalculated the talent, the erudition, and the unflinching courage of the man they had resolved to crush ; the man who now fearlessly confronted his judges and dared to argue with " the proud Colossus who in past years by his memorable defence of Warren Hastings had poised his powerful eloquence against the lofty appeals of Burke, the impassioned oratory of Sheridan, and the sublime rhythms of Fox." For Edward Law, now the ermined Baron Ellenborough, was the triumphant advocate in the historic trial of the ex-Governor of India, Warren Hastings.

Lord Campbell has an anecdote of the Chief Justice which indicates the struggle he made against any display of his deep mortification at the issue of this prosecution :—

" Bishop Turner, who was present at the trial, and accompanied the Chief Justice home in his carriage, related that all the way he laughed at the tumultuous mob who followed him, remarking, ' that he was afraid of their saliva, not of their bite ' ; and that passing Charing Cross he pulled the check-string, and said, ' It just occurs to me that they sell the best red herrings at this shop of any in London ; buy six.' "

Lord Campbell adds :—

" The popular opinion, however, was that Lord Ellenborough was killed by Hone's trial, and he certainly never held up his head in public after."

There is a more conclusive evidence of his feelings than popular opinion. On Sunday, December 21st,

the day after this last trial, Lord Ellenborough wrote
thus to Lord Sidmouth :—

" The disgraceful events which have occurred at
Guildhall within the last three or four days have led
me, both on account of the public and myself, to consider very seriously my own sufficiency, particularly in
point of bodily health and strength, to discharge the
official duties of my station in the manner in which, at
the present critical moment, it is peculiarly necessary
they should be discharged. . . . I wish to carry my
meditated purpose of resignation into effect as soon
as the convenience of Government, in regard to the
due selection and appointment of my successor, may
allow."

After an illness of considerable duration Lord Ellenborough resigned all his judicial employments, and in
about three weeks after ceased to exist. His lordship's death occurred on Sunday, December 13, 1818,
in the seventieth year of his age, and a little less than
a year after the Hone trials.

Hone defended himself partly because he could not
afford to pay counsel and partly (he said) because he
doubted the courage of any one else to stand up against
Lord Ellenborough, while confident in his own determination not to be browbeaten by that cynically open
partisan ornament of the justice-seat. As a matter of
fact, a Mr. Williams, a banker, of Birchin Lane, had
offered to employ counsel for Hone's defence if he so
desired. As to the employment of his brother the
barrister, he felt the delicacy of the religious differences
which divided them.

When the defendant submitted himself to the court
for advice his lordship curtly replied : " The court
has too much to do to become the advisers of all
persons who conceive themselves aggrieved. . . . It
is really not our business to give such advice." He
therefore had to struggle on, making good his lack of

legal knowledge by drawing upon his vast stores of general reading.

Hone always, and not without good reason, maintained that his politics were the cause of his persecution, while irreverence to religion was merely the pretext. The juries manifestly accepted this view of the case ; and considering him the victim of a political prosecution, undertaken, perhaps, for the ridicule he had so often heaped upon the Government of the day, acquitted him of any intention to bring religion into contempt—for that was the charge brought against him by the prosecution.

On the three days he spoke, alone and unsupported, six, seven, and eight hours respectively, and it is estimated that he was heard on those occasions by an aggregate of nearly twenty thousand persons, the best feelings of whose hearts would have been naturally outraged by profane parodies, and yet who rejoiced in the success of his appeal to an English jury's sense of justice. At the conclusion of the trials the multitude broke forth into cries of " Long live an honest jury ! An honest jury for ever ! " It was a notable achievement to have fought single-handed in defence of two great constitutional rights, the Liberty of the Press and Trial by Jury.

The most noticeable result of the trials upon the man himself was that while his political principles underwent no change, and he remained to the end of his days a Radical reformer, he was utterly ashamed of ever having been charged with an offence against religion, and showed his remorse, perhaps sometimes too ostentatiously, in all his after-life.

His own account of this, the chief event of his life, written later, emphasises the point of his religious attitude at that time :—

" On the morning of the 18th of Dec. 1817, the first of three remarkable days that will never be blotted from my calendar, I rushed from my wife and children in bitter agony, leaving them sorrowing, and hopeless of seeing me repass the threshold of their home—a home no more to them, if I could not defeat the powers then gathering themselves in Guildhall for my destruction. At that moment, or at any time before, I was in no custody, and no one was under recognisances that I should appear ; but the charges were untrue, and I loved truth too well to fly from falsehood. The advocates against me were able and eloquent, and the judgment-seat was occupied by talent and experience. The archers shot at me, but I climbed beyond their reach. I stood upon truth as a rock of sure defence, and from that vantage ground I refused to be forced or enticed.

" Early in my first day's defence, I referred to the numerous pieces I had published, the greater part written by myself ; and addressing the Attorney-General, assured him that if in any one of these pieces he could lay his finger on a single sentence of a profane or irreligious nature, or tending to degrade or bring religion into contempt, I would refrain from uttering another word in defence. . . . Impressed by the most solemn feelings, ' You will not,' I observed to the Jury, ' hear me say one word that I do not utter from my heart and from perfect conviction. It is of little consequence whether I am a member of the Established Church, or dissent from it ; it is enough that I am a Christian, and I make the declaration with a reverence for Christianity not to be exceeded by any person in this Court.

" In my third day's defence, referring to the extreme depression under which I had laboured at the commencement, from illness and debility, produced by the two former days' exertions, and long previous anxiety, I could not forbear from thus expressing astonishment at the resuscitation of my faculties. ' If Providence ever interfered for the protection of the weak and the defenceless, that interference is most surely manifest in my case. It has interposed to protect me, a destitute and helpless man, from the rage and malice of my enemies. I can attribute my defence to no other agency, for I am weak and incapable, and at this moment I am a wonder to myself.' "

Hone's trials must be regarded as a landmark in the history of the public Press, taking their place with such historic struggles for the freedom of political comment as the affair of John Wilkes and his *North Briton* (1762), the prosecution of the printers of the " Letters of Junius " (1767), the trials of John and Leigh Hunt for their comparatively mild articles in the *Examiner* on the " very susceptible " Prince Regent (1812), and the nearer episode of Cobbett's heavy fine and imprisonment for a very ordinary piece of political criticism. All of these were but successive episodes in the same struggle for freedom which the public Press of this country has been compelled to wage in the past against parliamentary privilege and the law of libel.

Up till the time of James I. there was no newspaper. Such a publication made a first appearance in the days of the Star Chamber, when its conductor risked the chances of dungeons and torture. Subsequently an Act was passed to the effect that only twenty persons should be associated with a newspaper, and that no newspaper should be published except in London, at York, or the two Universities. In the days of Queen Anne a daily paper was published, but no political discussions were allowed in its pages—and those were the glorious days of such writers as Addison, Steele, Swift, and Bolingbroke. In the reigns of George I. and II. the newspaper contributors were men of the calibre of Pope, Goldsmith, Johnson, Sterne, Gray, and Fielding, whose writings sparkled with wit and satire or the polished gems of English literature ; and yet not one word of political criticism appeared till the famous " Letters of Junius " challenged the authority of the censor, and took up that defiant attitude which the House of Commons called " the scandalous licentiousness of the Press." The pillory, the prison, and the imposition of ruinous fines did their deadly work for a time, but failed in the end, as they were bound to fail, to repress the Englishman's inherent love of liberty—and the ultimate liberty of the Press was brought well within sight at Hone's trial, when Lord Ellenborough quailed before the storm of public opinion.

The proceedings of the Government in the libel matters of 1817 were signal failures. A few miserable hawkers were held to bail, or sent to prison under Lord Sidmouth's Circular ; some *ex-officio* informations were filed, with only one conviction—that of a printer in the country, who republished one of Hone's parodies, and was tried before Hone himself was tried. As to the three acquittals we have described, it is perfectly evident that three juries, consisting of respectable London merchants, would have assuredly convicted the defendant, had they not felt that the real sting of the alleged profaneness was the severity of the political satire. Although the indictment stated that these parodies were seditious as well as profane, the sedition was studiously kept in the background. Had they not been really prosecuted for their political doctrines, their unquestionable indecency and impropriety must have carried a verdict against them on the first trial. The second and third trials looked like persecution, and public opinion threw its shield over the offender. There was a feeling, moreover, that political passions were influencing the judgment-seat. The severity of the Lord Chief Justice to the reforming Member for Westminster, Lord Cochrane, was not forgotten.

Hone promptly announced a full and exhaustive account of the proceedings against him, and in January, 1818, appeared : —

" The Three Trials of William Hone for publishing Three Parodies, viz. ' The late John Wilkes's Catechism,' 'The Political Litany,' and 'The Sinecurist's Creed,' on 'Three Ex-Officio Informations,' at Guildhall, London, during Three Successive Days, December 18th, 19th, and 20th, 1817, before Three Special Juries and Justice Abbott, on the First Day, and Lord Chief Justice Ellenborough, on the last two days."

Although the price was four shillings, there was evidently a good sale for the work. In more recent years a new edition has been issued by William Tegg & Co., with Introduction and Notes by William Tegg (1876).

A dispassionate perusal of the work will leave no doubt in the reader's mind that the prosecutions were a grievous mistake, and that Hone's triumph really lay in his tact in conducting his defence as an appeal from the Law to Public Opinion.

A number of satirical cartoons belong to Hone's earlier years, published while he was in the first full stride of his political propaganda. The exuberance of his satire was not subdued by his trials, as is evidenced by the issue of: —

"Great Gobble, Gobble, Gobble, and Twit, Twittle, Twit ; or Law versus common sense—Being a Twitting Report of successive attacks on a Tom Tit, his stout defences and final victory. A new song with original music by Lay Logic, Esq."

The coloured illustration by George Cruikshank on the front page depicts a farmyard scene. On the rail of the fence sits Little Tom Tit (William Hone) twittering, "Let me remind you, gentlemen, of your own vile nonsense, Twit twittle twit, twit, twittle, twit ", ; while the Geese cackle—" O law ! O law! shocking, horrible. This twitting is most blasphemous, nay worse, illogical — cackle cackle, cackle " ; and the Turkey-cock (Lord Ellenborough) ejaculates, " This is not to be borne ! What ! are we to be twitted to our

CARTOON OF BONE AS A TOM-TIT TWITTING HIS PROSECUTORS.

faces, and must I stay here for ever, the object of profane diversion? Fellow! I charge thee! no more. Gobble, gobble, gobble!" Mr. Justice Abbott, in the guise of an Owl, flies off, with the remark, "This light is too glaring for learned eyes, I shan't stay here to be made *a butt* of."

A coloured print by George Cruikshank was published by S. W. Fores (" 50, Piccadilly, 10/1/18 "):—

"William the Conqueror, or The Game Cock of Guildhall,"

representing William Hone having fought and conquered the prostrate figures of the "Game Cocks," Sir Samuel Shepherd and Mr. Justice Abbott. William Hone has his foot planted upon "Trial by Jury."

A monochrome print is—

"Out witted at last—or, Big Wig in the Wrong Box."

This represents the Scale of Justice, with Hone and Trial by Jury, surmounted by Liberty of the Press, weighing down the Scale against Law, Rule of Court, and the Attorney-General.

The best of this series is the one entitled—

"Law versus Humanity, or a Parody on British Liberty. And the Recording Angel lets fall a tear.—*Sterne.*"

This represents Hone on the first day's trial, in great physical suffering, asking, "Pray, may I be allowed to sit?" Mr. Justice Abbott roars out such a surprisingly elongated "No-o-o-o-o-o-o-o," that it extends right across the court, and the Recording Angel drops a tear, while Hone's supporters cry, "O Loh!"

XI

AFTER THE TRIALS

CONGRATULATIONS poured in from all sorts of people and from all quarters. From his brother, Joseph, barrister-at-law, Gray's Inn, came an affectionate epistle: —

"DEAR WILLIAM,—I have already, through your family, expressed the singularly high gratification I experienced on your recent triumph.

"I rejoice the more that it should have been the result of the most firm and manly, but, above all, respectful appeals to a British Jury, that I ever heard or read of—it is in your recollection my telling you—last Sunday sennight, that, in my judgment, such a line of conduct would blunt the weapons of your adversaries, if not wrest them from their hands.

"Had the first verdict been followed by an abandonment of proceedings on the two last Informations, great as the victory would have been on your part, some degree of praise would have been due to those at whose instance they were filed ; but the subsequent measures were unworthy and disgraceful in the extreme, and obviously founded in the most persecuting spirit that could possibly have been evinced.

"It appears to me that Lord Ellenborough has placed himself in a situation somewhat novel, but not particularly enviable. He states upon his oath that your Publications were Libels, but the People of England, through their constitutional organ (the jury)—also upon their oaths—say that the Publications were *not* libellous.

LAW *versus* HUMANITY; or a *Parody on British Liberty*

LAW VERSUS HUMANITY ; OR, A PARODY ON BRITISH LIBERTY.

The Lord Chief Justice of England is therefore at issue with all Englishmen.

" You have, however, done more for your own personal character by your letter in the papers of Wednesday, than you can possibly conceive—it disarms all who would yet contend with you on the score of an impious and blasphemous intention.

" With great pleasure I hear of the intended Meeting at the London Tavern—May God Almighty incline a host of friends to rally round you for your pecuniary protection. I trust it may be the means of re-instating you in business, and of extricating you from every difficulty. My best wishes, now and for ever,

" Believe me, dear William,

" Most affectionately yours,

" J. HONE."

The relationship between the two brothers is not easy for the plain man to understand. The " affectionate " Joseph, though a qualified barrister, does not come forward to undertake the defence of his brother William in the hour of his direst need, even after the latter has proclaimed to all the world his inability to pay for professional assistance in an uneven encounter with the disciplined legions of the law. Joseph Hone, like his father, was shocked at the freethinking propensities of William—having said which, the matter may be dismissed with this observation—what a cheap way of expressing religious zeal can always be found in prosecutions for " blasphemy " ! William, on the other hand, always dealt very tenderly with Joseph. In a letter to his friend Scott (other extracts from which are given on pp. 280 and 323) he pleads : " As to my brother, poor fellow, you will oblige me by refraining from stricture upon him. He is gone out to Van Dieman's Land as Master General in the Law Courts there. We parted as brothers should, and my most affectionate regards go with him."

The attitude of his father weighed very heavily with

the offender. Mr. Howard, in his not unbiased pamphlet, writes:—

"I think it due to his memory to record a circumstance in connection with his Trials which does credit to his filial feelings, and also places the character of his father before us as a man of stern principle. Hone used to relate that when his father became acquainted with what had happened, he came to him and said, 'William, what have you done?' Seeing his father's grief, Hone promised faithfully to suppress all further issue of the Parodies. To this promise he adhered, although a very tempting offer was made to him by a bookseller, whilst under confinement, which would have put him in possession of money, of which he was sorely in need."

From Dr. William Lawrence, who continued a lasting friend, came this:—

"COLLEGE OF PHYSICIANS,
"22nd. Decr. 1817.
"I learn from the *Times* Newspaper of this day that it is proposed to call a meeting for the purpose of evincing in a more substantial form that public sympathy and approbation which your persecution and your noble resistance to it have already called forth. That you may not in the mean time suffer from that poverty and distress, in which I have this day for the first time learned that you are involved, I beg your acceptance of the inclosed; which I present also as a tribute of my admiration of your talents, your independent mind and undaunted spirit, and of gratitude for my share of that public benefit which must flow from so signal and successful an exertion in the cause of liberty.
".With unfeigned respect, believe me to be,
"Your sincere well-wisher,
".WILLIAM LAWRENCE."

Dr. Lawrence was the author of a work entitled "Lectures on Man," which contained such materialistic passages as caused him to be regarded for a time as a member of a free-thought party.

The Hones were honoured at this juncture with a last visit from Sir Philip Francis on December 23, 1817. The conversation was miscellaneous, and proved highly interesting, for care was taken that he should both lead and select the subjects. They talked of the news of the day. He was astonished at the times in which he lived ; Mr. Hone had displayed great talents in his defence ; had beaten both judge and counsel ; three different trials for three different counts of the same libel ; this was intolerable. There was a general diffusion of knowledge ; everybody wrote, and wrote well now-a-days ; he had read Wooler's productions ; Cobbett was able, but hurt his cause by his violence. And so rippled on the pleasant converse of the incomparable Junius.

The courage, learning, and mental vigour displayed by Hone in his three speeches in his own defence excited much public sympathy for him. A public meeting was held at the London Tavern, December 29th, for the promotion of a subscription for the purpose of showing some practical sympathy with the victim of a spiteful prosecution, in an appropriate and a substantial manner. It was with the aid of money thus raised that he was enabled to remove from the Old Bailey to a large shop at 45, Ludgate Hill, where he started on another period of publishing.

The prime mover in this effort was a city friend of Hone—for Hone was " a citizen of credit and renown," —in that he had always taken his share in the work of local self-government—the well-known Alderman Waithman.

Robert Waithman was a draper, his first shop standing on the site of the obelisk erected to his memory at Ludgate Circus. He was a bustling politician who had made his first speech in 1792 at

12

Founders' Hall, Lothbury, nicknamed " The Cauldron of Sedition ", ; on which occasion he and his fellow-orators put to flight the constables sent by the Lord Mayor to disperse the meeting. Four years later he was elected to the Common Council for the Ward of Farringdon Without ; he became Sheriff, and in 1823 was Lord Mayor. He was for some years one of the most prominent Radicals in London, a staunch friend of William Hone, and much hated by Cobbett, who ill-naturedly says of him that he was " illiterate and eaten up of self-conceit." No one who follows his history, however, can deny that in the cause of political reform he evinced considerable talent, and displayed a vast amount of energy.

A public meeting of the " Friends of Liberty of the Press and Trial by Jury " was held at the City of London Tavern, Monday, December 29, 1817, Mr. Robert Waithman in the chair. A full report of this meeting occupied nearly a whole page in the following day's *Times*. Among the resolutions passed were these : —

" That a hypocritical prostitution of Religion, and a pretended zeal for its defence when used by corrupt Statesmen as a mask for political persecution, must ever be held by all sincere Christians as the worst profanation of its sacred name."

" That the extensive knowledge, the varied talents, the manly intrepidity, the energy of mind, and the unshaken perseverance, which enabled Mr. William Hone so dauntlessly to resist the reiterated assaults of Ministerial persecution, entitle him to the gratitude and support of every friend of constitutional freedom."

" That a subscription be now opened, and that the money which may be subscribed be placed in the hands of a Committee, to be used in such way as shall appear to them best calculated to promote the permanent welfare of Mr. Hone and his family."

Mr. Waithman became treasurer to the fund, and Sir Francis Burdett was thanked for his spontaneous offer of co-operation.

The proprietors of several " independent " country newspapers opened " Books for Subscriptions " at their respective offices, and the movement went along briskly in many directions.

With all this burning zeal for right and justice, for constitutional liberty, and the integrity of British statesmanship, it is sad to relate that of the £3,000 raised, £1,000 was swallowed up in expenses, another £1,000 was stolen, and only a poor remnant of £1,000 ever reached Hone's hands.

The first published subscription list was a lengthy one, at the top appearing the names of the Duke of Bedford for £105, the Earl of Darlington £105, the Earl of Sefton £105, Lord Cochrane £100, " a Member of the House of Lords " £100, the Marquis of Tavistock £50, and other members of the aristocracy for varying amounts. The names of that incorrigible scandal-monger, Thomas Creevy, and many other notable personages of the time, are to be found in the list.

One of the jurymen contributed, and many of his old friends, like Sir Francis Burdett. There were donations from Manchester, Henley-in-Arden, Broadway, Cambridge, Sheffield, Stamford, Darlington, Scotland, and other distant places ; from Americans and Mussulmans ; from Reformers, friends, and admirers under no end of adopted names to express their admiration of the man and his achievement, and their detestation of his persecutors ; Samuel Parr, D.D., and a whole host of clergymen and other ministers of religion who, while disapproving the Parodies, entirely acquitted William Hone of intentional profanity.

Letters in support appeared in the papers from a number of influential and prominent personages ; sympathetic references were made in the great London papers, the Dublin *Freeman*, and various provincial journals ; meetings or committees actively promoted the cause in Liverpool, Lewes, Norwich, and other large towns. The movement to recognise Hone's efforts and achievements was national.

From Leeds, and the " Friends of Freedom " in other distant centres of population, came congratulations, together with numerous orders for copies of " The Trials " which Hone with his customary business alertness had already announced. One correspondent compares William Hone to Gilbert Wakefield (who had lain two years in Dorchester jail for a " seditious " answer to Bishop Watson) as being an equally deserving recipient of a national subscription.

Mrs. Burn has left a note on the subject of the public subscription : —

" It is difficult to realise that out of the handsome sum of £3,000, not more than a third part was secured for his use.

" Newspapers were, at that time, heavily taxed, and advertisements charged high. The subscription was extensively advertised, and the Principals of a leading Journal very kindly suggested to my father that his committee should discontinue the advertisements, otherwise the whole sum would be absorbed ; expenses already incurred having amounted, according to their computation, to at least £900.

" About ten years later, strolling one evening in the neighbourhood of Belvedere Place (my father having on his grey studio coat) we came upon a man, standing behind an open fence, about twenty yards from us. ' You see that man ? ' said my father ; ' his name is —— ; he robbed me of a thousand pounds—he acted as a collector or secretary to the Subscription Fund in 1818, and instead of paying the moneys into the hands of Alderman Waithman, the Treasurer, he went off to America with a thousand pounds which should have come to me. I could not allow Alderman Waithman, who was much harassed with other matters,

to be troubled by making the affair public.   The fellow
has come back and is now a prisoner in " The Rules."
I have learned all about him, and have several times
met him in the street, but he cannot look at me.'   My
father's reticent nature would probably never have
revealed this circumstance but for the chance meeting
with this man."

The great diminution in the capital relied upon to
set him up in business at 45, Ludgate Hill, was the
beginning of a series of embarrassments which eventually resulted in his failure, arrest, and loss of all
pecuniary interest in " The Every-Day Book," " Table
Book," &c.

The trials naturally aroused a vast amount of interest
in the country, which found expression in the Press,
and even in Parliament.

In the House of Commons one honourable Member
(Mr. W. Smith) moved for " An account of the sums
received at the Crown Office for the several Informations filed by his Majesty's Attorney-General against
William Hone, together with a statement of the
authority upon which the same were demanded and
the purposes to which the same were applied."   The
motion was too awkward for the Government, and the
Attorney-General opposed it.   Of course it was lost,
but not till it had raised an animated discussion, and
served the useful purpose of ventilating a grievance.

In the Press some of the comments were " severe,"
and not a few were " lively."   In the course of a bold
and outspoken article, attacking Mr. Wilberforce for
his aristocratic leanings, which a month or so afterwards
appeared in the columns of the *Scotsman*, occurred
this passage : —

" We are morally certain that scarcely anything
would induce him to take Mr. Hone by the hand ; but
Mr. Canning, who wrote a parody on the 143rd Psalm,

is his Right Honourable friend, and esteemed fellow-labourer in the cause of anti-jacobinism."

And if this article truthfully reflects the spirit of the times, then it becomes painfully apparent that the time had not yet arrived when the plain, honest trades-man might presume to hold, and to express, an opinion of his own on all that concerns Church and State and the government of the country.

As to those who held opposite views, Hone relates that travelling outside a coach in 1818, the conversa-tion turned on politics, when one gentleman uttered some sharp remarks on " that fellow Hone." Another said, " I expect you would not be surprised to meet him furnished with hoofs and a tail." " Well, I do not think I should," was the rejoinder. The other passengers joined in a laugh ; the remainder of the journey passed in cheerful conversation, and on parting, the first-named gentleman, presenting his card, ex-pressed a wish to " improve an acquaintance." " Per-haps you may be less desirous when you know the dangerous company you are in," said William Hone, as he gave his card in exchange. The other, astonished, stammered out his surprise and an apology, expressing regret at having so unjustly prejudged a highly informed and entertaining gentleman—and one, it must be added, with whom he afterwards long continued on terms of friendship.

This anecdote of a Satanic resemblance is the favourite story in the Hone apocrypha.

A month or so after the trial came a note of con-gratulation from a member of the Childs family, of Bungay, in Suffolk. Messrs. Childs were a large firm of printers there, and seem previously to have been unknown to Hone. But they were all ardent Radicals, and appear to have been so struck with the gallant fight which Hone had made in defence of the liberties of the Press, that they made friends with him, and remained staunch and true to him from this period to the end of his life. Here is the letter which began an acquaintanceship that ripened into a lifelong friendship: —

" 9th. Feb. 1818.

" To Mr. Hone.

" I beg to offer you my gratulations on the glorious victory you achieved over ministerial hypocrisy, and judicial tyranny—May you long live to enjoy the laurels so nobly won ; and that you may receive a liberal support from the people whose rights you so bravely supported is the sincere wish

" Of your obedient servant,

" R. Childs."

As surely as the festive season of Christmas came round, so surely did the annual present of a turkey from John Childs of Bungay make its appearance at Hone's house. The usual courtesies of correspondence were observed every year, but it is not necessary to quote all the letters which passed on such occasions. The motive which inspired the annual observance of the compliment is thus expressed in a letter which accompanied one of the many presents: —

" Believe me, it affords me the highest gratification to recur to those days when you stood before the wickedest tribunal that ever existed in this country, and were saved by the common sense of a few plain men.

" The remembrance of that day ought to be kept fresh in the memory of both old and young. My young ones shall not forget it if I can help it, for on every Christmas Day, I give them the history of your prosecutions, and give the toast, ' Mr. Hone and his jury '—which I and my eight sons drink with all the noise we can make."

Charles Phillips wrote to Hone, from Ireland (the postage on the letter was 4s.) on July 4, 1818 : —

" I assure you, my dear Sir, you only do me justice in supposing that I participate most sincerely in the triumph which all liberal men must feel at the success of such a man as Waithman. Thank God, the Ministry are likely to feel in the next Parliament, the just consequences of their profligate corruption in the last. . . .

" I saved the life of Mr. Grattan yesterday—during his chairing he was most ferociously attacked by the people, whom he has certainly treated very cavalierly of late—brickbats, clubs, and stones and every kind of missile were not spared. He took refuge in a house after having had his chair torn to shivers, and his eye almost knocked out, but I hope he will not lose it. The mob waited in thousands outside the house, when luckily I happened to catch their attention, and by some flattery and the remembrance of old times, I persuaded them to leave his life. What a thing is popularity ! A few years ago, if a man but breathed on Grattan, he would be torn to pieces."

The latter incident relates to Grattan's re-election for Dublin without opposition—the attack was made upon him as he was leaving the hustings. The " triumph " mentioned was Waithman's election, after several previous defeats, as one of the Members for the City of London.

Early in 1818 appeared Hone's full and complete account of his " Three Trials," in the Preface to which he announced his intention—conducting his bookselling business " on a more respectable footing than hitherto " —to prepare an enlarged Report in a more permanent form, and one more acceptable to the library. For this hurried production was in three parts (corresponding with the three separate trials), each issued at a shilling ; or, bound up with the Proceedings at the Public Meeting, to sell at four shillings. There was a great

Trial By Jury

TRIUMPH OF THE BRITISH PRESS

This Print is intended to Hand down to posterity
the Three Honest Juries, who so honourably acquitted

Mr HONE,

to whom this Plate is respectfully inscribed.

First Trial		**Wilkes' Catechism.**	
J. G. Bearing.	Leadenhall Street	N. Ashton	Ironmonger Lane
W. Syme	Finchurch Buildings	Samuel Brook	Old Jewry
J. Woollett	Gould Square	Jas. Hunter	Barge Yard
J. O'Brien	Broad Street Buildings	Wm. Thompson	Queen Street
Wm. Noakes	Little Eastcheap	Thos. Lewis	Queen Street
J. Gardner	Old Broad Street	Thos. Edwards	Coleman Street
	Merchants.		Merchants.

Second Trial		**Political Litany**	
Wm. Gilman	54 Broad Street	James Jones	
J. Landers	Lawrence pountney Lane	James South	
Rich. Thornton	Old Swan Passage	Joshua Thorne	
Robt. Wilson	Great Eastcheap	James Donaldson	
J. Monks	12 Botolph Street	William Hale	
Nat Black	11 Broad Street	William Green	
	Merchants.		Tradesmen.

Third Trial		**Sinecurist's Creed**	
Geo. Morewood	Pomeris Lane	Richard Lewis	
Geo. Elwall	Love Lane	Alfred Giles	
Robt. Edson	Finchurch Street	James Pearce	
Dan. Eskenstein	Cathen Hill	Frederick Simeome	
Jas. Bissey.	Cateaton Street	Anthony King Newman	
Jas. Brockbank	Bucklersbury		
William Clark	Philpot Lane	by his Obedt. Servt.	
	Merchants.	Jas. Head	Tradesman.

A MEMENTO PUBLISHED BY J. HEAD, OF 141, FETTER LANE (FEB. 6, 1818).

To face p. 185.

demand, and Hone at one time proposed to embody the result of his extensive studies in the history of parody in this volume of his Trials ; but the idea was given up for various reasons, among which were the desire to get the Trials out quickly, and more particularly the remonstrance of the Rev. Dr. Parr and others against the re-publication of any parodies other than those to which he had referred in his defence. He therefore next proposed to publish his " History of Parody " as a later volume ; between 1820 and 1824 it was advertised to appear at the price of two guineas, but the proposal at last went into limbo.

Concerning Hone's prompt publication of an authoritative account of his trials it is curious to note in the *Scotsman* a few months later, " in answer to numerous inquirers," that " a second supply of the ' Three Trials ' was shipped last week on board a London smack and is hourly expected " in Edinburgh.

In a small way quite a literature of the Hone Trials grew up. John Fairburn, of 2, Broadway, Ludgate Hill, in January, 1818, issued " The Discontented Hypocrites, a Scene from a Dramatic Entertainment lately performed with Great Applause in London." The *dramatis personæ* were Lord Sadmouth, Lord Hellborough, Old Bags, Derrydown Triangle, George Cunning, &c. Here is a sample of its quality : —

" *George Cunning:*
Well, Hone's acquittal is poor Christmas fare !
Sadly this chap has hauled me over the coals.

* * * * *

By our good luck we were, alas, forsaken ;
But needs I must declare, this crafty Hone
We ought entirely to have left alone."

Later, the same publisher got out a parody on Hone's " House that Jack Built," which was headed by a woodcut of William Hone and underneath was:—

"This is the Man who published the Parodies
Thrice he routed all his foes
And thrice he slew the slain."

Popularity is all very well for those who court it, who have a love for all the movement and excitement of public life, and who, above all, have the physical robustness to carry it through. But soon after his trials Hone became a physical wreck, and was found ere the year was out, not only broken in health and spirit but once more impoverished. The disheartening story of a year's ineffectual endeavour may be learnt from a letter to his newly-made friend :—

" 45 LUDGATE HILL
" *8th. Jan.* 1819.

" MY DEAR SIR,—On the 21st. of last month, or so soon after as conveniently could be conveyed, I received from you what, in London, we call ' an Alderman in chains '—this was reserved for our Christmas Day dinner, when we, that is my wife, and our seven young ones, played our many parts and drank your health, and carolled away till our eighth little one crowed herself so hoarse that we were obliged to adjourn our mirth. It was not forgotten that the day of the date of your note was the anniversary of the day after the Trials, which Ministers and their myrmidons designed should send me to keep Christmas in the custody of the Marshal of the Marshalsea of our sovereign Lord the King. It was not forgotten, either, that this attempt brought me acquainted with some of the best of my countrymen, who, with stout English hearts in their bodies, are unsubduable by all the powers of despotism ; nor was it forgotten that, to a contempt for tyranny and a proud hate of it, Britain is indebted for all her liberties, and I for my Christmas dinner.

" My dear Sir, my wife and I thank you heartily for
your kindness ; it was my duty to have done so before
but—(now for a civil lie)—procrastination is the thief
of time, and I put off, and put off, even unto this day,
when, finding my conscience troublesome, that is, the
burden of the reproach greater than I could bear, I
mustered courage to say ' thank ye ' with my pen—my
heart and mind having done so as often as I thought
of you.

" I have been, and am, ill—dying, but not dea'd.
Blood at the head, apoplectic affection—cupping—bleed-
ing—blistering—lowering—a fortnight at Bath, &c.—
vexation at home and habitual melancholy which
increases upon me ; all these are indications of that
sure and certain event which happeneth unto all, and
which may happen to me in an instant. I am, in fact,
in a very bad way—the Trials have given me a physical
shake which has compelled me to abandon what I
entered upon with alacrity and spirit, the sales by
Auction of Libraries &c. for which I had made
expensive and extensive arrangements and had neglected my other business to further. I have, therefore,
now to begin the world afresh nearly.

" From my bad health the Prospectus of the Trials
has been delayed—of course the Trials themselves are
not much forwarded. When the prospectus is ready
I will send you some down, knowing they will be where
they will be used. Wishing you and yours health and
happiness

" I am, My dear Sir,
" Yours faithfully,
" W. HONE.

" TO MR. CHILDS,
    " Bungay."

In apologising for non-attendance at a public dinner at
the Crown and Anchor Tavern in January, 1819, which
was held to celebrate " Mr. Ward's glorious victory
in the Court of King's Bench," he pleads ill-health,
and alludes to " alarming and frequent symptoms of
a tendency of blood to the head," which two months

previously had laid him in a dangerous condition on a sick-bed, "under the routine of blistering, cupping, and lowering," as a result of which his nervous system was demanding complete repose. He added parenthetically that he was relinquishing one department of his business, which was found to "agitate and harry" his spirits too much.

At the same time Hone protests his never-failing attachment to the principles of public liberty, and his great desire to be present at the banquet. And although he was not in the habit of attending public dinners, we find his name on the committee of the Friends of Parliamentary Reform, who arranged a similar celebration in honour of "Purity of Trial by Jury—the Palladium of British Liberty," in November, 1821, which was the twenty-seventh anniversary of the acquittals of Thomas Hardy, John Horne Tooke, and John Thelwall.

XII

THE CRUIKSHANK CONNECTION

IT was in 1818, when William Hone commenced the issue of his " Facetiæ," that the relationship between him and George Cruikshank was placed on a business footing.   There was a tradition in the Hone family that the acquaintanceship between the two had begun as far back as 1811 ; that the elder man had befriended the younger, then nineteen, on the death of his father, Isaac Cruikshank, who was also a caricaturist.   The more probable date is 1815.

Cruikshank etched several caricatures on the result of the trial as well as a series of reduced copies of some engravings by Gillray, which Hone intended to publish in a work justifying his Parodies.

Hone's first acquaintance with George Cruikshank is thus described by Mrs. Burn:—

" I think our father's first acquaintance with the artist was his wanting a plate re-touched (either Napoleon or Byron), and Cruikshank was recommended as a young artist with a light purse by (I think) Mr. Neely of Sherwood's house.   He had been finishing etchings for them of some plates his father had left incomplete.   Then he sketched Meg Merrilies, and Kean as Bertram, and afterwards the caricature ' Mat de cocagne ' (the greasy pole).—Our father took great interest in the young, and almost self-taught artist, and encouraged him to the exercise of a talent in which he was unrivalled. Caricature was one of the fashions of the time, and most were by a Jew named Marks, (I think), the coarse features delineated always betraying an Israelitish origin. Fores was the chief publisher. In time George Cruikshank eclipsed all others in that line. It was not acknowledged, I believe, but it is certain that my father first actually employed and brought him into notice. Beyond that, both our mother and father sought to draw him from the loose companionship he indulged in, by keeping him at home in the evenings, and often to sleep—he was the only one our mother ever had a bed made up for. In all the work he executed for William Hone, our father himself was a ruling spirit, conveying the motif of the design, by description in words, for George Cruikshank to carry out with his pencil."

To what intimacy the connection afterwards grew is evidenced by this letter:—

Mr. Hone to Mrs. Cruikshank.
" LUDGATE HILL,
" *8th. July* 1822.
" Whatever of kindness I entertain, and I entertain much, for your son George, has been from admiration of his talents and respect for his honourable disposition. For everything that could diminish either of those qualities, I have expressed to him not only deep regret, but remonstrated with him more severely than any one but a sincere friend, feeling deeply for his best interests and real welfare, would venture to do. If he has, as you say, left your house for three years, you must be better acquainted with the reason for his seeking a home elsewhere, than I am."

During the long intimacy with the Hone family, many of George Cruikshank's drawings were inspired or suggested by William Hone, and his artist son, Alfred, sometimes by means of rough sketches, but oftener the ideas were conveyed by verbal description. Hone's vein of pungent criticism is to be traced in much of Cruikshank's work as a political caricaturist, and perhaps sometimes as a delineator of social life and manners, in which he was akin to Hogarth. Cruikshank considered that the " great event of his artistic life " was the Bank Restriction Note, 1820, designed by him, at Hone's suggestion.

In 1819 Hone wrote his well-known " Political House that Jack Built," which soon ran through fifty-four editions. Numerous imitations were published, among them " The Dorchester Guide, or a House that Jack Built," the " Royalist's House," the " Financial House," and many others. It is generally conceded that the extraordinary popularity of the " Political House " was largely owing to the forcible woodcuts of Cruikshank, who adorned in the same style Hone's other squibs on the Regent and the various politicians whom he lampooned. Without the pictures the writing would have missed much of its piquancy, for it was the artist who gave the necessary point to the author.

On the occasion of the illuminations, November 11 to 15, 1820, " to celebrate the victory obtained by the Press for the liberties of the people, which had been assailed in the person of the queen," it was Cruikshank who painted for Hone's shop-front a transparency, engraved in the " Political Showman."

" Hone " (says W. Hamilton, a biographer of Cruikshank) " has been accused of meanness towards the artist, yet he probably paid him more than others would have done, and being engaged in a very dangerous business, he took all responsibility on himself. No slight risk, for it must be remembered that the Government frequently prosecuted him for various publications, and Hone was never at any time a rich man. Hone was at least a man of his word ; he paid Cruikshank what he agreed to pay, for he well knew how true was the advice that an opposing critic tendered him :—

" Make much of that droll dog, and feed him fat ;
    Your gains would fall off sadly in amount,
  Should he once think your letterpress too flat,
    And take to writing on his own account,
  Your libels then would sell about as quick, sir,
" As bare quack labels would without th' elixir."

If the employer was a poor man, the artist was wild and careless. " He does just what is suggested or thrown in his way," wrote Professor Wilson (in *Blackwood*) in 1823. His biographer says he always " made money enough for his pleasures, even when drawing wood blocks for Hone at ten shillings and sixpence each. He could execute two or three in the course of a day." On a later page the same authority says: " According to a reviewer of ' Three Courses and a Dessert,' in *Fraser* (June, 1830), the whole sum received by Cruikshank from Hone was £18. But this was not so."

Nor was it. A memorandum in Hone's handwriting contains a list of the blocks drawn by George Cruikshank for the " Facetiæ" ; there were seventy-eight of them, and the price paid was £60 :—

For " The House that Jack Built " ...   13 drawings.
  " Man in the Moon "   15   ,,
  " Queen's Matrimonial Ladder "   20   ,,
  " Non mi ricordo "   3   ,,
  " Political Showman "   24   ,,
  " Right Divine "   2   ,,
  " Form of Prayer "   1   ,,

There are also preserved three accommodation bills, bearing in big, bold characters that dashing signature of George Cruikshank, which even in the tiny reductions at the foot of his pictures never fails to strike the eye

AN ACCOMMODATION BILL BETWEEN AUTHOR AND ARTIST.

—bills for varying amounts and a total of forty-seven pounds, all accepted by William Hone between the years 1821 and 1824, the period in which the latter was publishing his " Facetiæ." For the twelve illustrations he supplied for the " Every-Day Book " Hone paid him £36.

The political cartoons, says Blanchard Jerrold, haunt the imagination. Then he adds: " To Cruikshank they were productive of nothing but the fame of their cleverness and the odium of their politics." With the imprimatur of the audacious Hone and the biting illustrations of George Cruikshank, there can be little doubt they did irretrievable damage to the Ministry.

It is worth quoting this biographer of the artist at length:—

" Very early in his career," says Jerrold, " George Cruikshank came into contact with Hone. Of this connection, Dr. R. Shelton Mackenzie has given an account which is stamped with the authority of the artist, since, in ' The Artist and the Author ' he cites the doctor as armed with information given by himself.

" In the year 1819, while Cruikshank was a mere youth, Mr. William Hone observed his peculiar ability, and determined to exercise it. He illustrated ' The Political House that Jack Built ' in January, 1819, at the age of 19½ years.

" At that time the political condition of this country was about as unpleasant and unsatisfactory as it could be. The people clamoured for reform, which the Government steadily and sturdily resisted. Then came the struggle between Right and Might ; and by means of what was called ' the strong arm of the law,' the right was baffled for a time, albeit not beaten. To add strength to ' the strong arm ' in question, the Habeas Corpus Act was suspended, and six Acts were passed.

" These were the enactments avowedly framed to prevent the expression of public opinion, whether at

13

public meetings or by the medium of the press. The anti-press ordinances of July, 1830, which were the means of hurling the Bourbons from the throne of France, were scarcely more tyrannical than the Gagging Acts in question. They drove Cobbett to America. We believe that they were especially levelled against him and his plain-speaking *Register.* . . . At this crisis the late Mr. William Hone, who felt warmly in politics and had a particular antipathy to Castlereagh, Canning, Sidmouth, and Wellington, determined to try what might be done by bringing the Fine Arts against the Ministry. At that time Canning was chiefly known as a flashy, clever speech-maker. . . . Castlereagh . . . was the most unpopular man in the kingdom. . . . Lord Sidmouth, to whom Canning had given the sobriquet of 'The Doctor' (from his father, Dr. Addington) was peculiarly hated, as Home Secretary. . . . The Duke . . . was disliked at that time. . . . The four thus named were the principal members of Lord Liverpool's Cabinet. The Premier himself was a nobody. . . ."

The *London Journal* of November 20, 1847, is also worth quoting : —

"At such a crisis, and against such a Ministry, William Hone had the boldness to enter the lists. He commenced the publication of cheap pamphlets, in which the literature was below par, and the main reliance was upon the telling points of the woodcuts. The first was 'The Political House that Jack Built,' with thirteen cuts, after designs by George Cruikshank. . . . This was a parody upon the old nursery rhyme. It took amazingly. Upwards of 100,000 copies were sold. . . . Every one laughed at what Hone had issued, and though it did the Ministry a thousand times the actual damage which even Cobbett's *Register* could have done, they could not prosecute it. The Attorney-General would have been laughed out of Court had he attempted anything of the kind. The light weapons of ridicule went through the armour which a heavier weapon could

not enter.   All the world laughed ; Canning, Castlereagh and Company enjoying the joke, no doubt, as
well as the rest of the people."

The warm and intimate friendship between Hone and
Cruikshank, which had begun about 1815, lasted without
interruption till 1827 ; and the unfortunate estrangement which then sprang up between them cannot be
attributed to the fault of either of the principals, but
to the evil machinations of one who—in the words of
a private letter—so wormed himself into the confidence
of his employer, William Hone, that he even dared, by
his insinuating plausibility, to produce a rupture within
the family circle.   This man, whose name was Percy,
as confidential business adviser, had assumed the entire
control of Hone's money affairs, keeping his employer
in the dark as to the actual state of his obligations,
and for a long time successfully postponing the day
of reckoning by the usual expedient of accommodation
bills.   It was in one of these wretched transactions
that Cruikshank became involved, and the matter
terminated, not only in the ruin of Hone's credit, but
in the destruction of the twelve years' friendship
between him and the artist.

Hone was always lacking in common prudence in
financial matters, and in this matter appears to have
been very much imposed upon by this manager, who
ran up such extravagant bills for advertising, that whatever profit accrued from the work was more than
swallowed up by the expenses.

" That man," writes Mrs. Burn, " sat daily at our
table for years, took his six pounds every Saturday,
and when he had cleared out all the ready cash, left
my father starving at his work on the ' Every-Day
Book ' within the Rules of the King's Bench Prison,
inextricably involved in debt."

The breach with Cruikshank was a source of the
deepest regret to Hone, and had the two parties been

brought together the briefest of explanations would have sufficed to heal it. But they never met again till the close of Hone's life, when Cruikshank came in response to his old friend's wish, and was so affected by the interview he declared to the mutual friend who accompanied him that never again would he have a lifelong difference with any man.

In a subsequently published work called "Aspersions Answered," Hone appends a note in which he makes this allusion to the publishing period during which Cruikshank was associated with him :—

"The pieces I brought out, with which the public are best acquainted, were the products of my own pen. Be their merits or demerits what they may, one real service has resulted from them. By showing what engraving on wood could effect in a popular way, and exciting a taste for art in the more humble ranks of life, they created a new era in the history of publication. They are the parents of the present cheap literature, which extends to a sale of at least four hundred thousand copies every week, and gives large and constant employment to talent in that particular branch of engraving which I selected as the best adapted to enforce, and give circulation to, my own thoughts.

"Besides this, I have the high satisfaction of knowing that my little pieces acquainted every rank of society, in the most remote corner of the British dominions, with the powers of Mr. George Cruikshank, whose genius had been wasted on mere caricature till it embodied my ideas and feelings. . . . Robert Burns had not more kindly feelings when he wrote ' Auld lang syne,' than I have towards my friend George Cruikshank. ' We twa hae paidl't,' and though as regards me, his occupation's gone, our mutual esteem is undiminished.

"The Parodies formerly published by me, I may, perhaps, be allowed to repeat, I always considered as mere political squibs, and nothing else. It is now two years and a half since I commenced to publish, in the course of which time I have issued upwards of one hundred and thirty pieces, chiefly of my own production. Not a week has elapsed during that period, without my having compiled or written something ; but whether it were prose or verse,

> " ' Grave to gay, or lively to severe,'

I console myself with the reflection that, amidst all I have put on paper, there is

> " ' Not one immoral, one indecent thought,
> One line which, dying, I would wish to blot ! ' "

XIII

A BANK RESTRICTION NOTE

ANOTHER publication of Hone's in 1819 had made a considerable stir, and that on account of its piquancy, its appositeness, and direct bearing upon a burning question of the day. Its inception was a sudden inspiration, as in the case of " The Political House that Jack Built."

As a piece of wit and invention the thing was rather poor, and the appeal somewhat shallow ; but it was not inapt, and as an appeal to the popular imagination it went home at once.

Hone had announced the publication of full and accurate reports of the trials of no less than twenty-two innocent persons who, during the last century, had been executed, the victims of circumstantial evidence. But it was just as easy in those days to commit a capital offence as to get hanged undeservedly, one particular form of felony through which many arrived at the gallows being the forging or uttering of the banknotes then so largely in circulation. On December 16, 1818, three men, convicted on September 12th, were hanged at the Old Bailey for this offence.

With such fatal facility could banknotes be imitated, there were presented at the Bank of England in 1816 as many as 17,885 forged pieces of paper money.

Sir Samuel Romilly was at the height of his crusade

against the death penalty for small offences ; and though his Bill to effect this passed the Commons, it was thrown out by the Lords on May 22, 1816. It was then a capital offence to steal privately in a shop to the value of five shillings. In 1785 ninety-seven persons had been executed for the offence in London alone. The capital sentence was often evaded by juries committing a pious fraud, and finding the stolen property, of less value than the statutory five shillings. At the very moment Romilly's Bill was thrown out, there was a child of ten years of age lying in Newgate under sentence of death for this offence against the sacredness of property.

But here we are concerned more directly with the crime of forging banknotes, the problem being—would the number of offences increase if the death penalty were removed? Or would it be wiser to legislate for the removal of the temptation which led to its perpetration upon so large a scale?

The circulation of £1 notes unquestionably led to much forgery and to a melancholy waste of human life. These small-value notes were rough and even rude in their execution, and counterfeits were circulated with as much ease as they were produced. The perpetration of this class of offence had increased out of all proportion to every other class of crime ; and if any man in London was cognisant of this fact, it was William Hone, whose residence was within view of the Old Bailey.

It was this execution, with its peculiar attendant circumstances, which put into Hone's head the idea of devising and issuing his famous Bank Restriction Note. Having made his rough sketch, he sent for George Cruikshank, who immediately made an elaborated copy of the design, and etched the plates.

The " Bank Note " was published January 26, 1819, and the announcement of it advertised in the *Times* ran : —

" *Books published this Day.*
" Bank Restriction Note, printed on Bank-
Post Paper.
" Price 1s.

" An Engraved specimen of a Bank Note, not to be imitated ; submitted to the consideration of the Bank Directors, and the inspection of the Public ; with the Bank Restriction Barometer, or scale of effects on Society of the Bank Note System, and Payments in Gold.

" By Abraham Franklin, Published by William Stone,
" Ludgate Hill."

The typographical error in Hone's name in this advertisement (which ran to February 8th) was corrected the second day. The " Note " and the " Barometer " were sold together, and Hone prosecuted one street-hawker who was found selling the " Notes " without the " Barometer," when an investigation resulted in the discovery that a great number of the " Notes " had been purloined from the printing-office by the errand-boy employed there.

This note, in external appearance, bore some resemblance to the ordinary Bank of England note, being a copper-plate engraving, and printed on what is termed Bank-post paper, but on minute inspection is found to differ very materially. The greater part of the face of the note exhibits the figure of a gallows, from which are suspended several male and female figures, with caps over their faces, the usual appendage to such a situation ; over this gallows appears in letters as a substitute for the number, " No. *ad lib.*" The part where the word expressive of the value of the note is placed exhibits the black wall of a prison, through which are seen several human countenances ; to this is prefixed a rope, the various circumvolutions of which form the letter " L." The promissory part of the note is to the following effect :—

" I Promise to Perform, during the issue of Bank

BANK RESTRICTION NOTE

Specimen of a Bank Note — not to be imitated.

Submitted to the Consideration of the Bank Directors and the inspection of the Public.

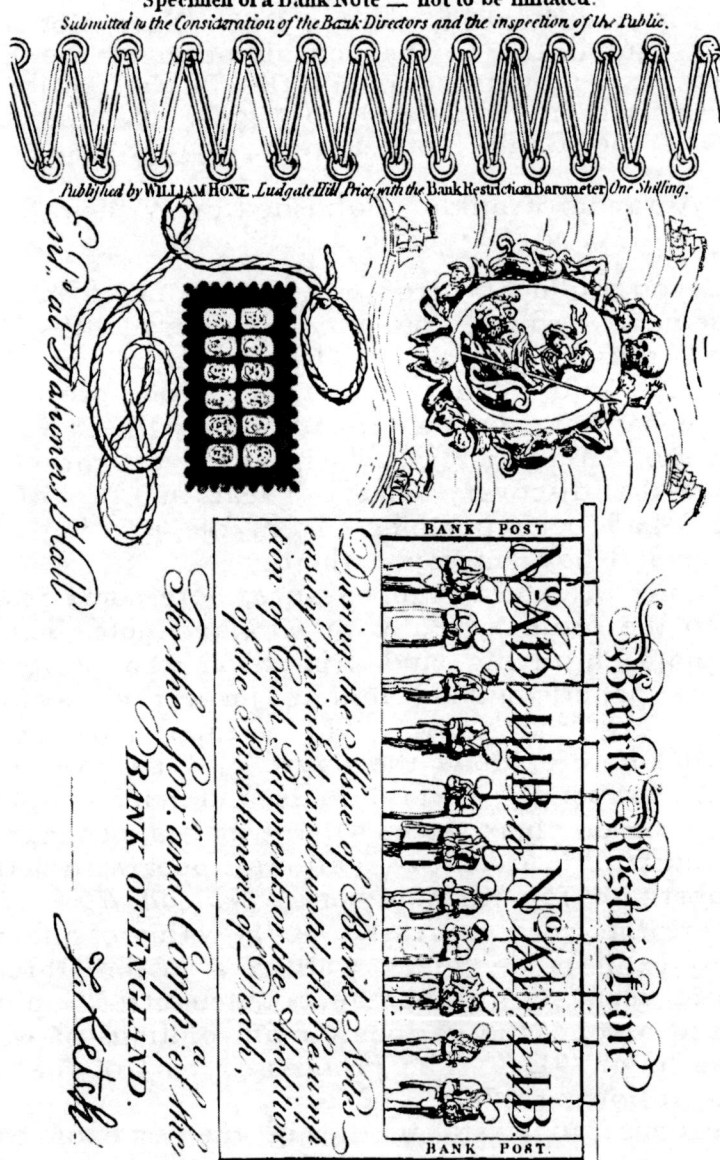

Published by WILLIAM HONE, Ludgate Hill. Price, with the Bank Restriction Barometer, One Shilling.

Notes easily imitated, and until the Resumption of Cash Payments, or the Abolition of the Punishment of Death, for the Govr. and Compa. of the Bank of England, J. Ketch.''

One wag, looking at a specimen in Hone's window, observed that this ingenious note was '' a wonderful execution.''

The Bank of England suspended payments in cash in 1797, and by 1817 the bank paper in circulation amounted to twenty-nine and a half million pounds, while the amount of bullion in the bank at that time represented but a fraction of that amount—in 1819 it had only three and a half millions in gold. Peel's Act (1819) provided for the gradual resumption of cash payments to begin in 1823—as a matter of fact the Bank exchanged its notes for gold, on demand, in 1821—and the withdrawal of all notes under £5.

Immediately on the publication of Hone's satire the *Examiner* had said : '' This banknote is by Mr. Hone, and ought to make the hearts of the Bank Directors ache at the sight.''

In later years arose a dispute between the representatives of William Hone on the one hand and of George Cruikshank on the other, as to whom the credit of designing the caricature note really belongs. James Routledge years ago failed to trace the design to its actual origin, but says that at least one newspaper of the year 1819 (the *Examiner*) attributes the drawing to Hone. The disputants on either side gave very circumstantial accounts of how the idea was conceived.

Let us take the evidence of one of the principals first. The following letter, dated from 263, Hampstead Road, December 12, 1875, and headed '' How I put a stop to Hanging,'' is addressed by George Cruikshank to the editor of *Whitaker's Journal :—*

'' DEAR WHITAKER,—About the year 1817 or 1818 there were one pound Bank of England notes in circulation, and unfortunately, there were forged one pound bank notes in circulation also ; and the punishment for passing these forged notes was in some cases transportation for life, and in others death.

"At that time I resided in Dorset Street, Salisbury Square, Fleet Street, and had occasion to go early one morning to a house near the Bank of England, and in returning home between 8 and 9 o'clock down Ludgate Hill, and seeing a number of persons looking up the Old Bailey, I looked that way myself, and saw several human beings hanging on the gibbet opposite Newgate prison, and to my horror, two of these were women, and, upon enquiring what these women had been hung for, was informed that it was for passing forged one pound notes. The fact that a poor woman could be put to death for such a minor offence had a great effect upon me, and I at that moment determined, if possible, to put a stop to this shocking destruction of life, for merely obtaining a few shillings by fraud ; and well knowing the habits of the low class of society in London, I felt quite sure that in very many cases the rascals who forged the notes induced these poor ignorant women to go into the gin-shops to ' get something to drink,' and thus *pass* the notes and hand them the change.

" My residence was a short distance from Ludgate Hill, and after witnessing this tragic scene I went home, and in ten minutes designed and made a sketch of this ' Bank note not to be imitated.' About half an hour after this was done, William Hone came into my room and saw the sketch lying upon my table ; he was much struck with it, and said, ' What are you going to do with this, George? ' ' To publish it,' I replied. Then he said, ' Will you let me have it? ' To his request I consented, made an etching of it, and it was published. Mr. Hone then resided on Ludgate Hill, not many yards from the spot where I had seen the people hanging on the gibbet, and when it appeared in his shop windows it created a great sensation, and the people gathered round his house in such numbers that the Lord Mayor had to send the City police (of that day) to disperse the crowd. The Bank Directors held

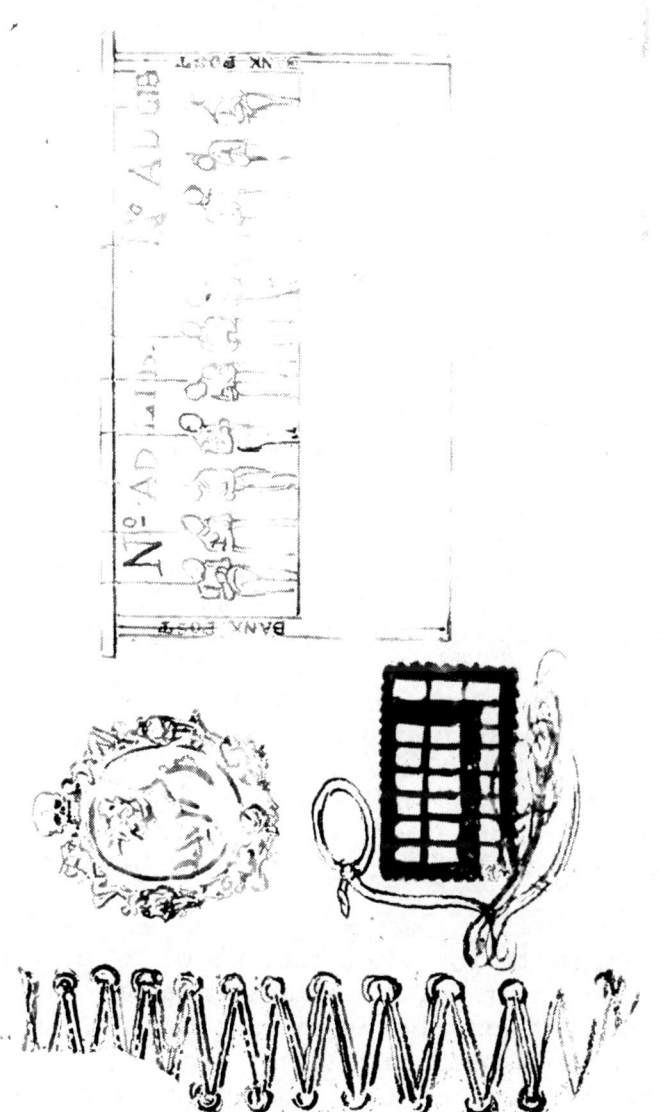

A ROUGH SKETCH, DATED 12 JANUARY, 1846, SUPPOSED TO SHOW BONE'S PENCILLINGS.

a meeting immediately upon the subject, and after that they issued no more one pound notes, and so there was no more hanging for passing forged one pound notes ; not only that, but ultimately no hanging, even for forgery. After this Sir Robert Peel got a Bill passed in Parliament for the ' Resumption of cash payments.' After this he revised the penal code, and after that there was not any more hanging or punishment of death for minor offences."

In a letter Mrs. Burn writes : —

" I remember George Cruikshank did engrave a second plate for the note. Of the night work I know not, nor of the £700 cleared. How could George Cruikshank know, what I believe our father knew not?—the copies sold were many, but who knows how many? Do any of the family? Who worked the plate? I recollect the street being cleared, but as several popular squibs were out at the time, each may share the notability, and I rather think the Matrimonial Ladder was the other chief attraction at that time. But the blockade of people in front of the house was usual on the appearance of every new pamphlet."

Mrs. Burn in one of her family epistles writes on the subject of this controverted origin :—

" I was much surprised to hear that George had claimed it. I remember distinctly the heads within the bars, as sketched by our father, and also the £ rope."

With regard to the circumstance of a second plate having to be engraved, a circumstance on which some stress is laid, it may be explained that at that period the only material used for etching was copper, a metal so soft that after 2,000 or 3,000 impressions had been taken from it, the plate was quite worn out. Hence, when the demand for the engravings was large enough to exhaust the first impressions, a second plate was necessary for the production of a second edition.

Alfred Hone wrote a letter, dated March 18, 1878, to the *Athenæum*, claiming the credit of the design for his father, and giving a number of interesting details concerning the production of the work.

In the *Daily Telegraph* of May 2, 1878, appeared the following advertisement: —

"MRS. CRUIKSHANK will feel obliged if the printer in whose hands the undermentioned steel plates are lodged will forward them to her address, 263 Hampstead Road, 'The Fairy Library' (Cinderella, Jack and Bean-stalk, and Puss in Boots), 'The One-Pound Note'; 'The Children's Lottery Picture.'"

Immediately upon seeing the advertisement Alfred Hone addressed this letter to Mrs. Cruikshank :—

"MADAM,—Early intimacy with Mr. Cruikshank, and the associations arising out of it, have caused us always to entertain great respect for him, and it is with much regret I feel it incumbent on me to write you on a subject which has from time to time given us much pain.

"An Advertisement in the *Daily Telegraph*, to which my attention has been directed, requests that certain Steel plates may be furnished to you, among them that of the One-Pound Note, from which we infer it is your intention to re-produce what we know to have been an error of Mr. Cruikshank's memory concerning the note, in the forthcoming memoir of him.

"Our mother was especially hurt by the claim Mr. Cruikshank made in 1862 to the Design as his own ; whereas the Design originated with, and was made by, my father, who, having been long grieved by the frequent executions for forgery and the uttering of forged bank notes consequent on the circulation of cheap paper currency, had resolved to attack the law authorising it, when opportunity served for him to do so with any prospect of success."

An echo of this controversy appeared in the *Cape Argus* during 1892, a member of the Hone family then residing in that colony.

XIV

INDUSTRY WITHOUT BUSINESS METHODS

FROM this time forward the career of our subject is more or less affected by the state of his health, which remained precarious to the end of his days. But notwithstanding enfeebled health, he toils on from year to year, always finding an incentive to unremitting labour in the growing requirements of his large family. His activities at this period are chiefly in the direction of political pamphleteering.

Energetic and full of activity as he was, Hone never enjoyed robust health, as may be gathered from the MS. memoranda of Mrs. Burn.

Besides the severe nervous debility that often unfitted him for mental exertion, he used to have frequent attacks of illness, and in his early years was subject to quinsy. About 1809 he had rheumatic fever, which settled in his right hand, and for a long time he wrote with the left. Quinsy again troubled him several times, in 1814 occurring the most severe attack. Then Dr. Cribb (who was the last medical man to wear a pig-tail in London) told him he must avoid another, or it would prove fatal. The doctor gave him many hours of personal attendance, and told him to gargle his throat every morning with the rinsings of the bottoms of old port-wine bottles, saying with a quizzical air, " Don't drink the stuff, Hone, and you will have no more quinsy." This advice was followed for years, and there was no return of the malady.

In 1815 came the first apoplectic fit ; another occurred in 1819. Mrs. Burn writes :—

" About 1821, tense with nervous excitement, my father fancied he saw one day the upper part of himself on the opposite side of Fleet Street ; another day his legs only were there ; another time after being from home he could not approach the house (45 Ludgate Hill) from any part, because he fancied it was surrounded by a wall of fire. This he told me very seriously as we sat one day by his office in Bolt Court. Then he immediately remarked on the goodness of God who relieved him of such terrible weariness of body and mental suffering.

" Father and I used to talk on the subject of dreams and hallucinations ; and we concluded they were the effects, the former generally of vivid impressions from peculiar circumstances ; the latter, the results of indigestion or in extreme cases were caused by an over-wrought state of the brain. To such causes he ascribed those strange sensations when he fancied he saw the upper part of himself passing along on the opposite side of Fleet Street ; and the dread which possessed him when he approached home, night after night, always to find the house blockaded from his approach by a dense wall of fire. (I believe Matilda at length had to bring him home.) He confided to me that his mind was as nearly wrecked as it could be, and his frame as well, solely from the effects of over-work, and ever-present monetary embarrassments."

His medical attendant at this time, Mr. Anderson, directed that he should never be allowed to go outside the house alone.

This evidence shows that Hone had a neurotic tendency which manifested itself chiefly when he was fatigued with overwork, a not uncommon condition with highly strung people. The tendency was probably hereditary, as his father had been subject to hallucinations, and particularly to abnormally vivid and disordered dreams. It is very generally recognised that in some neurotic subjects visual hallucinations are produced in fatigued states ; but the seeing of half things, sometimes the top, sometimes the lower half, cannot be readily explained, and may not improbably be attributable to defective eyesight rather than to a disordered brain. The other symptom appears akin to obsession, such as fear of open spaces, of which there are several phases known to exist.

To those who believe in the " duality of the mind," and seek to explain the impressions of some imagined scene in a pre-existence, an anecdote he relates of his own experience serves as a useful illustration.

Being called, in the course of business, to a house in a certain street in a part of London quite new to him, he had noticed to himself, as he walked along, that he had never been there before.

" I was shown," he said, " into a room to wait. On looking round, to my astonishment everything appeared perfectly familiar to me : I seemed to *recognise* every object. I said to myself, ' What is this? I was never here before, and yet I have seen all this : and, if so, there is a very peculiar knot in the shutter.' "

He opened the shutter, and found the knot ! Now, then, thought he, " Here is something I cannot explain on my principles ; there must be some power beyond matter."

And he proceeds to indulge himself in psychological speculations.

As to his untiring industry and business ineptitude, a memorandum of his activities and misfortunes in the year 1818 has been left by Mrs. Burn :—

" Preparing Trials for publication.
" Determining on advices by friends for business—Bookseller & Auctioneer.
" Taking House, 45 Ludgate Hill. Invaded by

Authors to publish—sometimes as many as twenty MSS. per day on numerous Subjects—from Politics to Poetry —which at length necessitated a ' Reader,' and the return of all save the very few worth printing.

" Receiving numerous visitors from all parts of the country.

" Replying to some of the hosts of letters involved a large amount of correspondence.

" Collecting Books for Stock—arranging Catalogue of same—and others for Auction Sales.

" Settling the Boys at school—Mr. Dawson."

A further note by the same daughter reveals the private family affairs of the next few years, and incidentally how the money raised by public subscription was frittered away.

" Message from the *Times*—Mr. Walter advised his informing ' The Committee ' that their continued advertising Subscriptions in most of the papers had absorbed one-third of the amount subscribed.

" A Collector appointed—who levanted with another third.

" The business was loosely conducted, rather allowed to drift ; for a working Committee was never inaugurated, and eventually, out of over £3,000 subscribed and promised, he was benefited only to the extent of one thousand.

" The writing ' Aspersions '—seeing through the press—and also Curran's Speeches—Hazlitt's Essays— and other works.

" Formed extensive and valuable collection for ' History of Parody ' and ' Trials.' Embarrassments obliged the deposit for a sum to relieve pressure— could not redeem the collection, therefore sold and dispersed, which cost him a bitter heart pang—It was a terrible wrench.

" Health gave way several times—had fits of apoplexy—weakness obliged change of air and scene— journey to Bath—can remember no particulars—could it have been on that occasion he visited Dr. Parr? and

14

Rev. Henry White of Lichfield?—I believe he travelled some long distances.

"I do not remember when Percy first took his seat in the counting-house at a salary of three guineas per week, which he scrupulously possessed himself of every Saturday evening during his location—also dining and sitting over his glass, and frequently two glasses of Rum and water, at his own convenient time. Spirits and wine were introduced at table for no one but him. Unhappily, by a certain plausibility, he acquired an influence fatal to the credit and peace of his employer, keeping him ignorant of his financial position—he led him into a system of accommodation bills, and practised petty manœuvrings of his own, under guise of our father's short-comings, who to the last was unaware of his own insolvency. Percy's conduct was a course of treachery. He founded the difference between W. Hone and G. Cruikshank by an action of double treachery. He betrayed an accommodation affair to J.H.B., who revealed his knowledge to my father."

This is a rough note, made long after the events recorded, by an aggrieved person, who has evidently not allowed her grievances to fade from her mind.

A letter from Hone to his friend Childs shows that he is deriving good returns from the sale of the "Banknote," and occupying himself with the projected "History of Parody" to accompany his "Trials."

"LONDON,
"29th. Jan. 1819.

"MY DEAR SIR,—Sincerely do I thank you for your honest and friendly advice respecting the Book, and I shall be glad of your opinion further, after reading the enclosed prospectus, which will appear in the *Quarterly, Gentleman's Magazine, Monthly Repository, Monthly Magazine and Eclectic*.

"The affair of the Note (which is going like wild-fire) hurries me just now, so that I can write you but little, nor would you have that, but for my being unable to send you one without a line.

" Your invitation is most kind, but (curse these
' buts ') I cannot, *must* not stir. The Trials shall
have my full attention—they shall. But before this, I
must get my Note throughout the kingdom. I have
set my heart on its going into every nook and cranny
where a Bank-note goes. Do write me by return, and
tell me your opinion of the thing, and what to do ;
but mind, no post paid.

" To return to the Trials. Your letter on the
necessity of my doing them with all my might, and
to a plan, is weighty and has weight with me—mind
that—with *me*. I will do them uninterruptedly, and
you may rely on it with a good deal of inspiriting from
your epistle, which I shall take up and look at every
now and then, when I find myself likely to flag. My
wife desires me to tell you that she has read your
letter, and that she thinks it the best letter I have
ever received—she made me promise this—and I not
only keep my promise, but agree with her opinion.

" We join in hearty thanks for your remembrance
and enquiries, and beg our respects to Mrs. Childs,
who we may some time or other have the pleasure
of seeing perhaps in this world.

> " I am, My dear Sir,
> " Most sincerely yours,
> " W. HONE.

" MR. JOHN CHILDS,
    " Bungay."

In another letter, a few weeks later, he makes
allusion to the perplexities with which he is assailed
in mind and estate.

> " LUDGATE HILL,
> " 3rd. Feb. 1819.

" MY DEAR SIR,—Yesterday I could not get off
the Notes on account of a spurt which ran us out before
I was aware of it—to-day you have £2 worth enclosed.

" Your kind offer of prospectus-using I most thank-
fully embrace ; indeed, such have been my troubles
of the brain that if I fail in my undertaking, it would
not be wonderful to myself.

" Could I be persuaded of realising something like
certainty for my wife, and be assured that my children
would be so placed in the world as to give her no
uneasiness for their fate, I could pass with cheerfulness to ' where the weary are at rest and where the
wicked cease from troubling.' Perhaps water drinking
and sunshine and good digestion, and a conscience
void of offence towards God and man, may dispel some
of the perilous stuff about my heart, and yet it has
increased on me of late till sense has nearly suffocated—
I feel that my mind is not as it ought to be, I am
very miserable and for want of a friend to sympathise
with, carry about my burden unseen and in silence.

" Old De Foe is a man after my own heart, respecting whom and his works I know more, perhaps, than
any other living admirer of him—his ' Jure Divino '
is indeed a famous old book, and yet I fear would not
(I wish it would) bear re-printing.

" I dined at John Hunt's on Sunday with Mr.
Hazlitt, for whose work on the prospectus I have just
concluded a bargain, and given Mr. Creery this morning copy to begin with—Hazlitt is a De Foeite.

" The affair of the Bible prosecutions instituted by
Strahan & Spottiswoode, King's printers, might be made
of great service to the booksellers. I am morally
certain that by firm co-operation and stout attack, the
patent might be thrown open.—The Booksellers' Committee meet and enquire, and enquire and meet, and
will make a Report which will end in smoke.

" My wife presents her respects to Mrs. Childs. I
am rather late for the mail.

" I am, My dear Sir,
" Yours most truly,
" W. HONE.

" MR. JOHN CHILDS."

Whether conversing with customers and callers at his
shop or slaving with his pen at the desk, there was
always at the back of Hone's mind at this period of
his life his projected work " A History of Parody,"
which was to be his *chef d'œuvre*. As it was to be

a complete vindication of his character, and a final
answer to all his critics, there was no labour or expense
to which he was not prepared to go.

The title-page of the projected work was drawn up
in his own handwriting thus (the date appended
appears to indicate that the work was expected to
occupy him about ten years) : —

" WILLIAM HONE'S
Enlarged
REPORTS
of his
THREE STATE TRIALS
In Guildhall, London,
On the 18th, 19th, and 20th December, 1817,
On Ex-officio Informations
for publishing
THREE PARODIES.
With
A HISTORY of PARODY from
the invention of printing :
Including
Parodies by Royal, Noble, Ecclesiastical
and Learned Personages of England
and Specimens of the Literature
of the Multitude.
ILLUSTRATED BY ENGRAVINGS.
ISLINGTON.
Printed for William Hone, Lower Street,
1829."

Hone's account-books show that he had collected
845 books for this work, at a cost of £443 19s., and
this private memorandum is appended :—

" I have been nearly 2 years engaged in the Inquiry.
Have made long journeys.
Viewed Public Edifices.
Examined Collections.
Turned over many thousands of prints.
Collected under my own inspection.

Most other subjects were indifferent to me, but this is a Work nearest my heart."

He had formed an extensive and valuable collection of prints and books for his "History of Parody" when pressing embarrassments crowded upon him. The whole collection was deposited as security for an advance of cash by a few friends, with the hope of its affording permanent relief. Still the cloud hovered, and gradually increased until the storm of ruin broke over him. The loan could not be returned, and the collection which had cost him so much labour, time, and money was sold under the hammer.

The dispersion cost him a wrench of feeling which few persons can realise, and a sensible depression of energy ensued from which he never fully recovered.

A Note by Alfred Hone.

" The collection was deposited with Alexander Galloway for security, and when it was determined to recover the advance by the sale of the books and prints, I accompanied father daily for about a week to Mr. Galloway's business house on Snow Hill, where, in a room over the shop, the chests or boxes, with their contents, were kept among machine models and lumber, and covered with dust. Here father worked with difficulty, seated on one box, and using two for a table.

" Mr. Galloway did not look in during the time, the shopman having been told to give Mr. Hone access to the room during the time the shop was open. Thus my father prepared the catalogue for the sale of his treasured collection."

The catalogue was most carefully compiled, every volume with the date of its issue, ranging from 1611 to 1817.

That this ill-starred undertaking of Hone was against the advice of his best friends is disclosed in his correspondence, of which the following is only a fragment of that bearing on the subject.

" BLACK SWAN INN,
" WARWICK
" 31st. *March* 1819.

" SIR,—Believing it to be my duty to assist to the utmost in defending Russell, the Birmingham printer, I arrived here on Monday to be present at his trial, and put into Mr. Denman's hands the most efficient of the materials I used in defending myself on each of my Trials in London.

" Russell's affair having terminated by the Prosecutors withdrawing the Record this morning, my business here is ended, but I cannot be in the neighbourhood of Hatton without recollecting your public kindness to me, nor can I leave it without soliciting the honour of paying my respects to you personally, after my return to-day.

" I have the honour to be, Sir,
" Most respectfully and obediently your faithful servant,
" W. HONE."

Received from Dr. Parr by William Hone.

" HATTON,
" *April* 13th, 1819.

" DEAR SIR,—I was much disappointed at not seeing you on the Wednesday. I hope that you returned safe to London, and found your family there in good health.

" I have reflected very seriously indeed upon your situation, and I shall not insult you by making an apology for suggesting to you some precautions. Are you quite sure that a publication of your Trials may not subject you to a second prosecution? For it was some time ago declared from the Bench, that there were circumstances under which the occurrences of a Court of Justice could not be published without a penalty. You are well aware of the peculiarities which distinguish your Trials. Again : I cannot reconcile my mind to the introduction of any other parodies than those to which you adverted before Lord Ellenborough.

The authors and the printers may have escaped notice, but you, by publishing them, may become responsible for the contents. . . . Nobody will confine that declaration to parodies written by yourself, and as to those which were written by other men, it may be said well that the number to which you appealed upon your Trials was sufficient for your vindication. I think that you will alienate many of your well-wishers and provoke your enemies by the introduction of new matter. More particularly I entreat you from the best motives, and upon the best grounds, to spare all ludicrous representations of the Trinity. I say this plainly for your own sake, and I also say it because I am seriously and decidedly an enemy to levity upon subjects which are sacred in the judgment of all believers, whether heterodox or orthodox. I am sure that your genius and your heroism will stand high in public estimation, if you will confine yourself strictly to that which passed when you were in Guildhall.

*   *   *   *   *

" I am, dear Sir, unfeignedly your well-wisher,
" SAMUEL PARR."

From the MS. of Mrs. Burn we learn that that literary celebrity Dr. Samuel Parr was wont to call upon Hone at his Ludgate Hill residence, while the latter sometimes visited the doctor at Hatton.

Calling one day at Ludgate Hill, in 1820, the Doctor made particular inquiries about Hone's family of five daughters and four sons. " And now you have another son, sir ; what name do you intend to give him? " " We think of calling him Samuel, after my youngest brother," replied Hone. " Then add my name," rejoined the Doctor, " and let him be christened Samuel Parr." And this was the name conferred, the baptism being performed at Islington Church by the Rev. Daniel Wilson, afterwards Bishop of Calcutta.

Dr. Parr was a great scholar, a voluminous writer,

a prominent man in his day, and was regarded as the " Whig Johnson."

We find Hone undertaking coach journeys and even journeys by water to various parts of the country, sometimes on business of a quasi-political character, the real purport of which is not always obvious. His journey to Warwick appears to have been to show sympathy with, if not to assist, Russell, who was prosecuted for publishing atheistic literature. But wherever he goes he never fails to be keenly observant, always accumulating in his mind those stores of information of which he made good use in his later and more popular works.

The rural descriptions which are to be found in his " Every-Day Book " and " Table Book " necessitated many trips to the localities mentioned, which he made in company with White, Samuel Williams, and other artists, and which cost him both time and money.

XV

POLITICAL PAMPHLETEERING

FROM 1818 to 1825 he was increasingly occupied, at first with auctioneering and then with publishing. How busy he was with the latter the long lists of his publications advertisements will testify. He wrote, besides the " Political House that Jack Built " and " The Bank Restriction Barometer," " The Apocryphal New Testament," " Ancient Mysteries Described," and many others, besides letters innumerable, all the time collecting much material for a History of Parody. And yet, with all this pen work, his time was incessantly called upon for political business and ward affairs, and in another direction for the investigation and relief of those private cases of distress, in which an appeal to him was never made in vain.

Ministers had not crushed Hone. They had conferred on him immense popularity ; they had made him formidable ; and he went on as vigorously as ever attacking them, and the Prince Regent, in a succession of stinging squibs—" The Political House that Jack Built," 1819 ; " The Queen's Matrimonial Ladder," in allusion to Queen Caroline's unhappy union (1820) ; " The Political Showman " (1821), in which Lord Sidmouth figured as the " Doctor " (his father having been one), and Nicholas Vansittart, the Chancellor of the Exchequer, as " Old Bags."

The political celebrity which accrued to William Hone may, be attributed to the folly of the mistaken policy of the Government in his case. Had his Parody squibs been allowed to run their day, in a short time after publication but a few would have been in existence, and those mostly hidden away in the libraries of collectors.

His sense of the ludicrous was shown by the titles and positions into which he worked the public personages of his political " Facetiæ " and the vein of humour which often runs through the descriptive sketches of more serious writing.

The activity of his mind often led him into the error of framing projects far beyond his power of performance ; hence the delays which depreciated the monetary value of some of his works, and totally precluded the production of others.

Hone's political publications in woodcuts and verse, being something between the newspaper and the pamphlet, hold a unique position. They were always topical and full of invention, and by a happy combination of caricature and satire, oftener than not accomplished the particular purpose they aimed at more effectively than any ordinary newspaper could have done. They moved the heart of the reader in the cause of liberty, roused the spirit of the patriot, and poured scorn and contempt on the hypocrite, the slave, and the tyrant. In word and picture they constituted an entertaining and instructive admixture of notorious matter-of-fact with emblematic allusion. " To Mr. Hone " (said the *Examiner* of December 24, 1820) " is England indebted for originating this important branch of publication." And their success being immediate and very considerable, Hone found imitators in a Mr. Dolby and Mr. Fairburn.

Hone has an anecdote to relate as to the way the first of the satires occurred to him : —

" I was acquitted but," said he, putting both his hands to his forehead, " my brain has never recovered ;

it was overwrought ; I have never been since, what I was before that day. After my trials, the newspapers were continually at me, calling me an acquitted felon. The worm will turn when trodden on. One day, when I had been exasperated beyond bearing, one of my children, a little girl of four years old, was sitting on my knee, very busy, looking at the pictures of a child's book ; ' What have you got there? ' said I—' " The House that Jack Built " '—an idea flashed across my mind ; I saw at once the use that might be made of it ; I took it from her. I said, ' Mother, take the child, send me up my tea and two candles, and let nobody come near me till I ring.' I sat up all night and wrote ' The House that Jack Built.'

" In the morning I sent for Cruikshank, read it to him, and put myself into the attitudes of the figures I wanted drawn. Some of the characters Cruikshank had never seen, but I gave him the likeness as well as the attitude."

And so well did he mimic the character to be introduced, the original of which Cruikshank had never seen, that the drawing which resulted had a most whimsical resemblance to the original intended. He went on to say: " I was told that, at the Privy Council, soon after it was published, the Prince laid it on the table without saying a word, and that after he was gone, some one present said, ' We have had enough of William Hone ' —and no notice was taken of it."

A letter to his friend John Childs hints at the same possibility of another prosecution being provoked.

The " Political House that Jack Built," with drawings by George Cruikshank, was not only the first, but was the best of the series, every line in the design on the title-page being pregnant with meaning. It represents a great military commander-in-chief throwing a sword into the scale, in which lie Bank Restrictions, Bills of Indemnity, *ex-officio* documents, the whole of them outweighed by the opposite scale in which lies

"THE WEALTH THAT LAY IN THE HOUSE THAT JACK BUILT."

To face p. 221.

a pen. The label underneath is " The Pen and the Sword," and the meaning is obvious. On page three is drawn a chest containing Magna Charta, the Habeas Corpus, the Bill of Rights, and about it lie bags of wealth and loose coin ; beneath which is inscribed, " This is the wealth that lay in the House that Jack Built." To this picture is applied an aptly selected motto from Cowper : —

" Not to understand a treasure's worth
Till time has stolen away the slighted good,
Is cause of half the poverty we feel,
And makes the world the wilderness it is."

There follow in succession representations of the military, the magisterial, the legal, the clerical, and the ministerial oppressors : —

" The Vermin that plunder the Wealth
That lay in the House that Jack built."

Then comes a printing-press : —

" THE THING, that in spite of new Acts
And attempts to restrain it, by Soldiers or Tax,
Will POISON the Vermin that plunder," &c., &c.

The clerical magistrate is a striking picture—a double-bodied and disgustingly inconsistent monster, looking and discoursing two ways ; holding up the cross and preaching peace and love among all Christian people, and at the same time dealing out anathemas against presumed political offenders.

Castlereagh, depicted with a cat-o'-nine-tails, is called " Derry-Down-Triangle " ; the last term having reference to that instrument of torture used in Dublin Yard, and Derry-Down connecting him with the nation for whose education the cat was used. Sidmouth, drawn with an infant's feeding-bottle, had had the nickname " Doctor " conferred upon him long before, by Canning when they were political opponents. Canning was a " Spouter of Froth."

Into the real merits of these statesmen it is not necessary here to inquire ; Hone's rhymed description of them runs : —

" This is the DOCTOR of Circular fame,
  A Driv'ller, a Bigot, a Knave without shame ;
  And that's DERRY-DOWN-TRIANGLE by name
  From the Land of Misrule and half-hanging and
    flame ;
  And that is the SPOUTER OF FROTH BY THE
    HOUR,
  The worthless colleague of their infamous power."

There is nothing mincing in these denunciations, and the squib took the popular fancy at once. " Of Circular fame " refers to the infamous circular issued to the Lords-Lieutenant of counties, already dealt with.

Not the least cutting bit of pictorial satire is the corkscrew suspended from the watch of the " Dandy, of Sixty " (otherwise the bibulous Prince Regent), while real pathos appears in the print of John Bull's starving, weeping, ragged family, with the massacre of the people in the background.

" Portentous, unexampled, unexplained,
        What man, seeing this,
  And having human feelings, does not blush
  And hang his head to think himself a man ?
        I cannot rest
  A silent witness of the headlong rage
  Or heedless folly by which thousands die,
  Bleed gold for Ministers to sport away."

A publication so popular, and commanding such large sales as " The Political House that Jack Built," naturally produced imitations in several quarters. One piracy perpetrated, of which some of the woodcuts are

Give not thy strength unto women, nor thy ways to that which destroyeth kings.

Solomon.

QUALIFICATION.

In love, and in drink, and o'ertoppled by debt;
With women, with wine, and with duns on the fret.

THE FIRST ILLUSTRATION IN "THE QUEEN'S MATRIMONIAL
LADDER."

To face p. 253.

still in existence, was "printed for L. Carvelho, London "; another, printed by "J. Dawson, Norwich," was embellished with a mediocre woodcut of "The Clerical Magistrate, Law & Gospel." There can be little doubt that much of the success of Hone's satires was due to the excellence of the cartoons.

The imitations essayed by the "courtly" booksellers were weak and washy as compared with Hone's, and he therefore never felt any serious rivalry.; lacking point and inventiveness, those of the opposite party failed to hit the popular taste, or to promote the cause they advocated. Rarely did he publish political satires from other pens than his own ; one of the very few was "The Man in the Moon." About the same time he issued "A Political Christmas Carol."

It was in connection with this work of William Hone that George Cruikshank suddenly rose to supreme popularity. . . . The work which Cruikshank did for Hone, as "The Political House that Jack Built," the "Political Showman," and lastly, *A Slap at Slop*, produced at the time of Queen Caroline's trial, enjoyed an extraordinary popularity and commanded an immense circulation, the first running into over fifty editions. "The Queen's Matrimonial Ladder" was another great success. The caricaturist's pencil gave the necessary finish to the work of the satirist's pen.

The drawings of the last-named, "all by Mr. George Cruikshank," as Mr. Hone advertised, were severely satirical throughout, from the first, where the royal husband drunk, with a broken wineglass in his hand, the garter falling from his leg, cards and dice and bottles scattered at his feet, and the candles guttering in the sockets ; to where the fat Adonis is being borne away in a barrow to the English cry of "Cat's meat." "Non mi ricordo" was another squib of this year ; it was founded on the convenient memory of Theodore Majocci, one of the principal witnesses against the Queen, who, when cross-examined touching some actions of the King which bore very much against his Majesty, pleaded that he " did not remember." This tract contains satire of the bitterest and keenest ; George IV.'s towering false hair, whiskers, padded garments, and enormous bulk were rendered ridiculously real by the cuts. The affectation of youth by the " dandy of sixty who bows with a grace," was ludicrously obvious to the most clownish capacity.

It was in 1822 that Hone brought out *A Slap at Slop and the Bridge Street Gang*, a very cleverly written broadsheet, newspaper size, with fictitious advertisements and intelligence, every line of which has a direct political or personal aim. This, too, had the advantage of being illustrated by Cruikshank, who was responsible for the idea. Hone, at this time the gossip and companion of Sir Francis Burdett and other reformers, was dining with the artist one day at the Spotted Dog chop-house in Holywell Street, when Cruikshank proposed to Hone to publish a sort of comic newspaper interspersed with caricatures, and consisting of all sorts of curious and eccentric paragraphs. The idea was a happy one, and was acted upon at once, though Hone transformed the original suggestion into a burlesque of the *New Times*, the organ of his mortal enemy, Stoddart.

The object of the satire, which ran through several editions, was Dr. John Stoddart, who had been a leader-writer on the *Times*, but having had a difference with the proprietors, had parted from them, and in 1817 had started a rival daily paper, which he called the *New Times*. In this sheet he constituted himself the champion of " the Bridge Street Gang "—Hone's name for the " Constitutional Society."

Though Hone stigmatises Stoddart's work as " sloppy," he was a capable journalist, a good lawyer, and a sound scholar. His lick-spittle sycophancy won him a knighthood from George IV. in 1826 ; two years later the *New Times* ceased to exist.

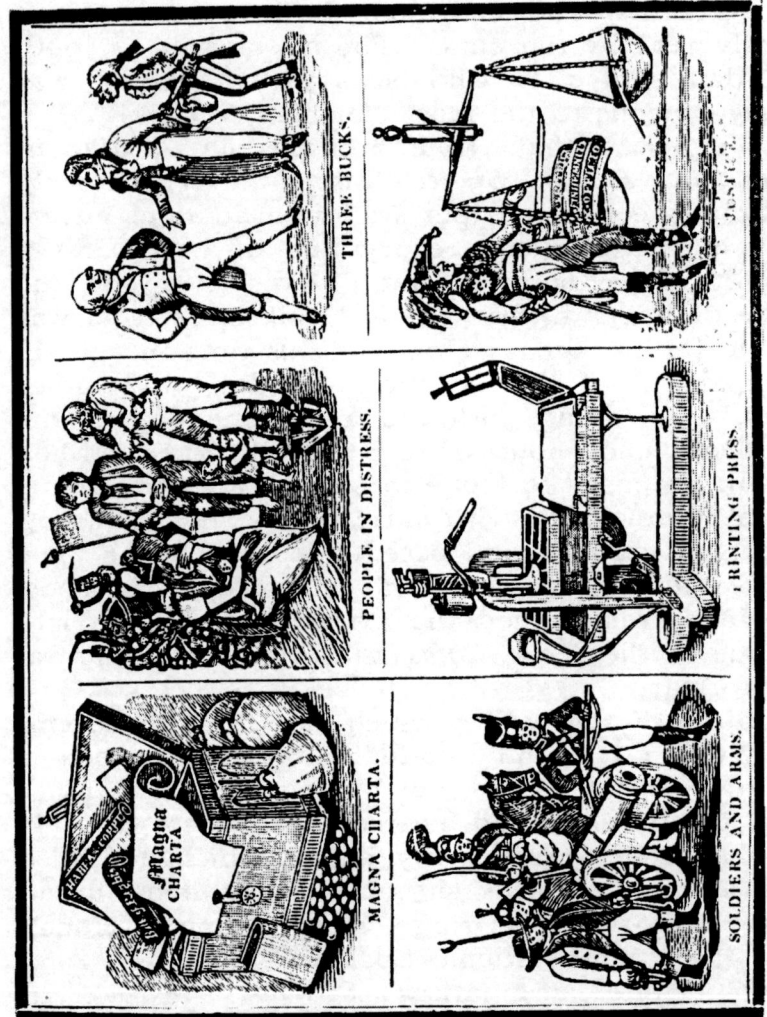

THREE BUCKS.   PEOPLE IN DISTRESS.   MAGNA CHARTA.

JUSTICE.   PRINTING PRESS.   SOLDIERS AND ARMS.

London: Printed by S. Carvalho.

SPECIMEN OF PIRATED ILLUSTRATIONS TO UNAUTHORISED ISSUES OF HONE'S WORKS.

On the day of his third trial Hone had encountered Dr. Stoddart in the precincts of the Court, and there found cause to complain bitterly of his conduct. Stoddart's journal was always ready to perform any dirty work which would be deemed acceptable to those in power ; and he had maliciously circulated a report that a man had been tried and convicted by a jury, and summarily sent to punishment for publishing the very parodies for which Hone, the arch-offender, had been twice acquitted. The defendant's wrath and indignation were intense ; he would proclaim Dr. Slop (a name given to Stoddart before he was dismissed from the *Times* on account of the profane curses lavished by him on Napoleon Buonaparte) a villain to his face, whenever and wherever he should meet him. Thenceforward Hone's hatred of Stoddart will be found to run through all his political publications. As for " the Bridge Street Gang," he regarded that party as the embodiment of all political evil.

The *Slap at Slop*, in the form of an amusing burlesque newspaper, had three pages of parody, and the fourth occupied by a history of the life of the individual aimed at—the venal ministerial time-server " Dr. Slop," who was not only stripped naked, but flayed, dissected, and exposed to the core by this unsparing censor. As Stoddart had been virulent in his abuse of Hone, so now in turn Hone paid him back in his own coin. Even the mock advertisements in this make-believe newspaper were so many minor hits at all sorts of sore places in Church and State, many of them illustrated by woodcuts, grotesque, ludicrous, and stinging, all from the practised hand of George Cruikshank.

The " Man in the Moon," which appeared in January, 1820, and to superintend the publishing of which he excused himself from attendance at the " Fox " dinner, at Norwich, was the second of these facetious pamphlets, and, like its predecessor, distinguished by

15

fancy and satiric wit. The frontispiece represented the back view of a lusty, pot-bellied, elderly gentleman, with very curious skirts to his dandy coat (George IV.), holding up a blanket on a long sword, with which he endeavours to hide the light of an allegorical solar representation of the Press ; he is at the same time addressing a speech to a most fantastical group of twingling little stars, upon spider legs, who are assembled in the lunar senate-house. As one critic said of Cruikshank's drawing, it " was the very poetry of the pencil." There was surely a spice of malice in Hone's dedication of the work " to the Right Hon. George Canning, Author of the parodies on Scripture (to ridicule his political Opponents), and colleague with the Prosecutors of Political Parody: Who, after lampooning Lord Sidmouth, and holding him up to the scorn and contempt of all England, as a Charlatan and *prime Doctor to the Country*, now takes a subordinate part under him as a *Prime Minister*," &c. &c. This " Speech from the Throne to the Senate of Lunataria "—such was the sub-title of the " Man in the Moon "—ran quickly through a number of editions, the twelfth being advertised concurrently with the forty-first edition of the " Political House that Jack Built."

The " Christmas Carol," which followed, had for a frontispiece a handpress, encircled with a serpent, emblem of eternity—this was an expression of Hone's faith in the enduring nature of that institution.

" The Political Showman," with twenty woodcuts by Cruikshank, purports to be an exhibition of such rare and curious " creatures " as Court sycophants and subservient Ministers ; and though the portraits are striking and even stinging likenesses of the public men portrayed, at this distance of time it would be of little use to recall the details for any purposes of identification. The " creatures " and their ways have all been long forgotten. On one fine plate are seen :—

THE
MAN IN THE MOON,
&c. &c. &c.

" If Cæsar can hide the Sun with a blanket, or put the Moon in his pocket, we will pay him tribute for light."—Cymbeline.

WITH FIFTEEN CUTS.

𝔗𝔴𝔢𝔫𝔱𝔶-𝔰𝔢𝔳𝔢𝔫𝔱𝔥 𝔈𝔡𝔦𝔱𝔦𝔬𝔫.

LONDON:
PRINTED BY AND FOR WILLIAM HONE,
45, LUDGATE-HILL.
1821.

ONE SHILLING.

" COURT VERMIN that buzz around
And fly-blow the King's ear ; make him suspect
His wisest, faithfullest, best counsellors—
Who, for themselves and their dependents, seize
All places and all profits ; and who wrest
To their own ends, the statutes of the land
Or safely break them."

This quotation is from Southey's " Joan of Arc "—
Hone dedicates this brochure to the Poet Laureate—and
an equally apt and pungent quotation accompanies each
" curiosity " exhibited by the Showman. Though
Hone's favourite, it did not have so large a sale as
the others. The illustrations should have won it a
wider favour.

The *Statesman*, in reviewing the work, calls it one
of the most humorous publications issued from the
Press. The *Champion* of May 6, 1821, calls it " an
ingenious and laughter-moving satyric squib." Though
it is Cruikshank's drawing which arrests and holds
much of the attention, the literary side of the work is
not without merit, for Hone lays under contribution
Southey and Cowper, Montaigne and Bacon, Fletcher
and Shakespeare, Swift and Goldsmith, and even the
Right Hon. George Canning himself, in the cause of
political waggery ; and the appositeness of the
descriptive text is as marked as that of the pictured
caricature. If evidence of this fidelity of the portraiture
were wanting, it is to be found in the fact that some
political leader-writers of the time referred their readers
to the study of particular pages of " The Political
Showman " for the elucidation of the problems or
mysteries which formed the subject of them.

This series of political pamphlets, which did much
injury to the Government, was beyond the pale of
prosecution. They drew admiring crowds to the
windows of Hone's shop on Ludgate Hill. The series
numbered five, with the titles of " The Political House
that Jack Built," " The Matrimonial Ladder," " The

Man in the Moon," " The Political Showman at Home,"
and " Non mi ricordo." These were published during
the years 1819-22. Cruikshank received half a guinea
each for the thirteen cuts which embellished " The
House that Jack Built " ; and if above 100,000 copies
of the work were sold, as stated, it is to be presumed
that the publisher pocketed by the transaction nearly
one thousand pounds.

The popularity of the squibs equalled their merit ;
altogether more than a quarter of a million copies were
sold, while some went into a thirtieth edition. The
tailpiece of " Non mi ricordo " gives a true picture of
the feelings of the subject of these satires. The King
is represented as on a gridiron, literally grilled by the
fire of cross-examination ; his contortions are a mixture
of the painful and ridiculous ; the print is called
" The Fat in the Fire." After the publication of
A Slap at Slop Cruikshank retired almost wholly from
political caricaturing, and no more—

" To party gave up what was meant for mankind."

Publications so trenchant, so biting, could not escape
criticism. The Quarterly Review, in a notice on
Hazlitt's " Table Talk," compared Hone, Hunt, and
Hazlitt to three asses. The Examiner of January 6,
1822, retorts thus (so far as Hone is concerned) to
what it describes as " Mr. Gifford's gloomy endeavour
at pleasantry " : —

" He assuredly must be allowed to be a very singular
specimen of the race, partaking little of the dull, sub-
missive, bearing-burthen character of the long-eared
tribe, or he never could have caused by his movements
such a hubbub and alarm among all the reverend and
irreverend orthodox animals in Church and State. He
most certainly cannot be of the patient and half-starved
breed of English asses, but must rather be able to
boast of his sprightly and vigorous Spanish blood ;

or perhaps, which is still more likely, he may be one of the Zebra or ' Queen's ass ' tribe—a wild and hitherto untameable race, as we all know.   If these suppositions will not satisfy the inquiring naturalist, he may consult some of the hundred thousand purchasers of the ' House that Jack Built,' the ' Matrimonial Ladder,' and the *Slap at Slop*, who may possibly be better able to decide upon the breed and merits of this frolicsome, high-mettled, independent, and not-to-be-ridden beast."

All the same, Gifford of the *Quarterly Review* was a man of vigorous intellect, and accounted the first critic of his day.

Pamphlets with a political aim, now regarded as mere curiosities of literature, had then a real importance.   Their justification was found in the peculiarities of the times, when men were tried on false pleas.; when men, women, and children in lawful assembly were liable to be trampled under foot by the military ; when innumerable social and political injustices were rampant in this country.   One of Hone's fierce pleasantries is to call attention in an advertisement to the receipt of a prize by Dr. Malthus " for his essay on the moral restraint of war and the blessings of famine, the advantages of pestilence, the comforts of disease, and the piety of decease."   Another shows how the pyramid of the Constitution may be inverted and upheld by bayonets.

Hone never repented of his satirical efforts, and, in fact, reprinted some of them years after their first issue. He strove, by their means, to keep in touch with popular feeling, using business channels for the promulgation of the political opinions he held with real earnestness.

The " Facetiæ and Miscellanies, by William Hone, with one hundred and twenty engravings drawn by George Cruikshank," constituted a volume issued a few years later (republished for William Hone, by Hunt and Clarke, Tavistock Street, 1827) in which these pamphlets, revised, with others of his works, were all bound together. On the title-page was a vignette showing a table, at one end of which was seated the author, in the attitude of writing, and at the other end the illustrator, with pencil in hand—both excellent portraits, and, of course, the work of Cruikshank. The motto is ".We twa hae paidl't." One biographer of Cruikshank (W. Bates, 1879) says of this volume, that he regards it as " perhaps the most interesting and permanently valuable in the whole cycle of Cruik-shankiana." There is an Introduction, of which the scene is the interior of Hone's shop, 45, Ludgate Hill ; the time A.D. 1822, the date of the first collection ; and it takes the form of a dialogue between the pro-prietor and a lady customer, who in buying the satires particularly desires to know the name of the author of them. According to the self-satisfied author she is annoyed to learn the truth. He distinctly claims the whole collection, except " The Man in the Moon," as the product of his own pen.

The pamphlets, by the introduction of good draw-ing and good wood engravings, made a new era in political caricature. In word and picture they were so true, nearly everybody admitted the truth and apposite-ness of them.

Hone lit these squibs and flung them among the mob ; and people, even those who disagreed with them, bought them, read them, laughed, and said, " D—— the fellow ! "—and waited for the next.

"We twa hae paid't."—BURNS.

HONE AND CRUIKSHANK.

To face p. 266.

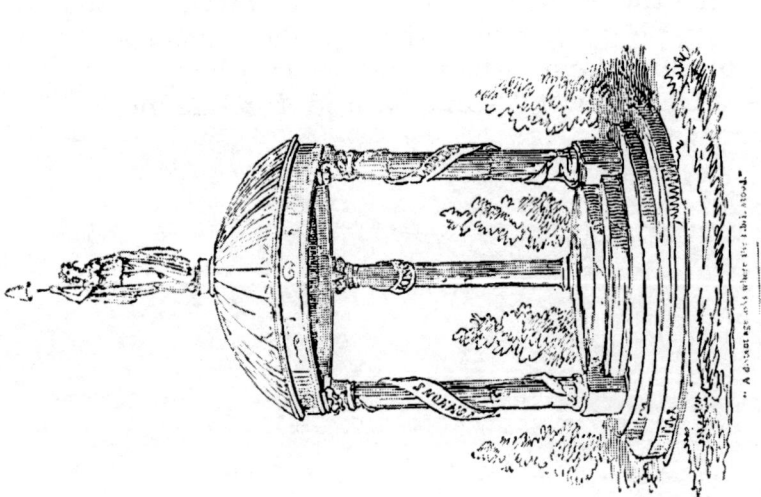

"A drawing-room where the fashi..aliead."

"THE HOUSE THAT JACK BUILT."

XVI

THE QUEEN CAROLINE AFFAIR

IMMEDIATELY after the accession of George IV. the public mind was agitated more profoundly than ever over the affair of Queen Caroline. How far the unfortunate woman herself was to blame for all the trouble which gathered round her need not be inquired into here. There can be no doubt she had for years been deeply calumniated—in 1813 a series of charges formulated against her was published in "A Delicate Investigation into the Conduct of H.R.H. the Princess of Wales, before Lord Erskine ; containing the depositions of all the evidences, copies of Letters, Narratives, Reports, &c., superintended by the Rt. Hon. Spencer Perceval, and then suppressed ; with the Defence."

William Hone, as one of the most prominent publicists in the metropolis, was well to the fore in the agitation—of course, ranging himself on the side of the weaker party, whom he regarded, as did many thousands of others, as the victim of a vile Court conspiracy.

Is it possible for the present-day reader to realise the political conditions under which the people of this country were compelled to live a century ago? Let us quote a graphic table which was printed in 1813 in the *Independent Whig*, at a time when the resources of the country were being drained by the exhausting Napoleonic wars, and ask what terrific and devastating storms would break over the land now if the people were called upon to breathe such an electrically sur-charged political atmosphere as that generated by the extravagances of a licentious ruler. From the 1812 Budget of Mr. Perceval, it appears that the Civil List provided a sum of little less than one and three-quarter millions of money for the upkeep of the Prince Regent's household. The appalling magnitude of this sum, required to support a profligate prince and his concu-bines, was thus set forth in the newspaper named:—

" £1,700,000. Weight (in gold) Fifteen tons, twelve cwt. three quarters, seventeen pounds, six ounces and two dwts.
" The daily pay to His Royal Highness is—
£4,657 : 10 : 8
" Each hour, drunk or sober
£194 : 8 : 0
" Each minute, asleep or awake
£3 : 4 : 8½ "

Is it difficult, with this exposure before us, to trace to its source the nation's cry for peace, retrenchment, and reform?

To understand the episode of Queen Caroline's troubles into which Hone now plunged, it will be neces-sary to recall as briefly as may be the main events in the matrimonial career of that unfortunate princess.

Brought to England for the royal espousal in 1795, Greenwich was the place of debarkation of the Princess Caroline of Brunswick, who landed here in order to become the much injured and unhappy wife of George, Prince of Wales (afterwards George IV.). From this place she passed on to London, in the midst of universal shouts of popular joy, her progress being almost a triumphal procession. Alas! (exclaims Walter Thorn-bury) in how short a time she was destined to rue the day!

Says Thackeray, in " The Four Georges," that

scathing exposure of the founders of the royal line of Brunswick: —

" Malmesbury gives us the beginning of the marriage story—how the Prince reeled into Chapel to be married ; how he hiccuped out his vows of fidelity— you know how he kept them ; how he pursued the woman whom he had married ; to what a state he brought her ; with what blows he struck her ; with what malignity he pursued her ; what his treatment of his daughter was ; and what his own life. *He* the first gentleman of Europe ! "

The Princess of .Wales, as is too well known, had anything but happiness in her married life with this royal libertine and drunkard. If the Prince ever really cared for any woman, it was for Mrs. Fitzherbert. The Princess of Wales always spoke highly of Mrs. Fitzherbert ; she would say: —

" That is the Prince's true wife, she is an excellent woman ; it is a great pity for him he ever broke vid her. Do you know, I know de man who was present at his marriage, the late Lord Bradford. He declared to a friend of mine that when he went to inform Mrs. Fitzherbert that the Prince had married me, she would not believe it, for she knew she was herself married to him."

Mrs. Fitzherbert, with whom the Prince of Wales had gone through a form of marriage in 1782, was a Roman Catholic, and by a legitimate alliance with her he would have forfeited the throne.

Within a few months of the marriage between the Prince of Wales and the Princess Caroline, domestic differences arose, and these unhappy differences, from whatever cause they sprang, terminated in a separation of the royal couple, three months after the birth of their only child, the Princess Charlotte, in 1796.

The Princess Caroline lived by herself at Shooter's Hill and Blackheath, the object of much public sympathy. Then reports to her discredit were carried to the old King, who determined on an investigation.

In May, 1806, was instituted a Royal Commission, consisting of Lords Erskine, Grenville, Spencer, and Ellenborough, all then members of the Cabinet, to inquire into the charges brought against her. She was found to have been imprudent, but guilty of nothing criminal. In 1814 she obtained leave to visit Brunswick, and eventually, she got to Italy, where the life she led was at least eccentric, if not very indiscreet.

On her return to England in 1820, her husband having succeeded to the throne, the Government pressed proceedings against her for adultery. The trial having lasted from August 19th to September 7th, the case against the Queen closed, and an adjournment took place, to allow time for her counsel to prepare her defence. On October 3rd Mr. Brougham delivered his speech for her defence, at great length, and with astonishing eloquence and effect. The case, in the apprehension of what was perhaps the majority of the nation, was left in that state which Scotch lawyers call " not proven." The Government then abandoned their Divorce Bill, November 8th.

Thus ended, in defeat and disgrace to the new King, an indecent and scandalous contest, which had filled right-minded men with unutterable disgust, and which had made every Englishman hold down his head and blush for his sovereign and his country.

At the close of these unpopular proceedings London was illuminated for three nights, and on the 29th the Queen went to St. Paul's Cathedral to return thanks.

In honour of the Queen's visit to the cathedral Hone exhibited from his upper windows in Ludgate Hill a blue silk flag, on which was inscribed in letters of

THE TRANSPARENCY Exhibited by WILLIAM HONE during the ILLUMINATION commencing on the 11th, and ending on the 15th of November, 1820, in celebration of the VICTORY obtained by PUBLIC OPINION *for the Liberties of The People,* which had been assailed in the Person of *The Queen.* The words " TRIUMPH OF THE PRESS," composed of 187 lighted lamps covered the whole House above the Transparency; and on the Evening of the 29th, when *The Queen* went to St. Paul's, it was again exhibited, and the House illuminated in like manner, with Lord Brew's immortal words, " KNOWLEDGE IS POWER."—The Transparency is 13 feet wide, by seven feet six inches high, and was painted by Messrs. George, and James Cruikshank.

TRANSPARENCY WITH WHICH HONE ILLUMINATED HIS SHOP.

To face p. 273.

gold "The People," and from an early hour in the evening he illuminated his house with a brilliant transparency, and a design in blue lamps of the royal monogram, C.R., within a wreath of laurel, typical of victory. The streets were crowded to a late hour, and many of the tradesmen in Fleet Street and the Strand who had failed to follow Hone's example in the matter of illuminating had their shop windows smashed in. The bells of several of the City churches rang merrily throughout the day. Mr. and Mrs. Hone gave a party that night, at which one of the dances and some of the items of music were specially arranged for the occasion—one being a new anthem entitled "God Save the Queen," the *motif* of which was borrowed from the National Anthem, "God Save Great George our King." In Hone's advertisements of that date there appears "A Form of Prayer, with Thanksgiving" for her Majesty, which was also of his composition. The *Birmingham Mercury* (December 11, 1820), in referring to it in commendatory terms, effectively defended the author from the false and calumniating charges of blasphemy which "Ministerialists were fond of bringing against him."

The pathetic ending of it all remains to be told. The unfortunate Queen, Caroline of Brunswick, presenting herself for admission to the Abbey in order to be crowned with her husband, George IV., as his Queen Consort, was rudely repulsed from the doors, both at Poets' Corner and at the western entrance. This was on July 19, 1821. Little more than a fortnight afterwards, on August 7th, she died at Brandenburg House, the victim of a broken heart, or, as Hone puts it in *A Slap at Slop*, she "died of the dagger of Persecution."

On the 14th, when her remains were removed for interment at Brunswick, a shameful riot took place in the streets of London. For some reason or other, which was never explained, the Queen's corpse was ordered to be carried into Essex, *en route* for Hardwick, not through the heart of the city but by the circuitous route of the New Road. The people, who had made common cause with the injured lady, regarded this as an indignity, and in opposition to the King's Ministers and in defiance of the authority of the Horse Guards, they succeeded in forcing the funeral cortège to pass through the Strand and St. Paul's.

The "Matrimonial Ladder" very happily illustrated popular feeling, and excited the public laughter at the expense of the exalted personages whose conduct had merited the nation's derision. It described, in well-marked steps, the whole progress of the question at issue between the King and the Queen ; it was issued in the usual pamphlet form, containing pregnant verse and spirited etchings, and the pamphlet was accompanied by a toy in the shape of a strip of cardboard with more etchings in black and white, doubled to stand of itself like a step-ladder—the two sold at a shilling.

Not the least amusing illustration represented the Regent in a fainting fit and Sidmouth, as the doctor, attempting to restore him. Another clever picture was "The Joss and his Folly," accompanying a racy description of the Pavilion at Brighton.

It was at the Southampton Coffee House in Chancery Lane that Hone, Hazlitt, and Cruikshank were wont to meet to discuss the squibs on the Queen's trial, when the artist "would sometimes dip his finger in the ale and sketch his suggestion on the table." Hone's own account of the origin of this Squib is given in Miss Rolleston's pamphlet.

"I was very sore about my Trials ; I thought it hard that Canning's Parodies had led to place and power, and mine were prosecuted. I wanted to write a 'History of Parody.' I was reading in the British Museum for that purpose—that was the time of the Queen's business, and some of her chief partisans

THE PICTURES ON THE TWO LEGS OF THE CARDBOARD TOY LADDER.

To face p. 276.

came to me. They urged me to write something for her. I refused for some time, till at last they said, ' The Queen expects it of you ' ; and I felt I could no longer refuse, but it troubled me very much. I had gone there to be quiet, and out of the way of politics, about which my mind had begun to misgive me—that is, as to my interference with them. Observe, though God has changed my opinions about religion, I have not changed my politics.

" I did not like my task ; I could not see how to do it, nor yet how to avoid it ; so, a good deal out of sorts, I left the Museum.

" Instead of going straight home, I wandered off towards Pentonville, and stopped and looked absently into the window of a little fancy shop. There was a toy, ' The Matrimonial Ladder.' I saw at once what I could do with it, and went home and wrote ' The Queen's Matrimonial Ladder.' Soon after, a person whom I shall not name, came and offered me £50 to suppress it. I refused and was offered up to £500. I said, ' Could you not make it £5,000? Even if you did, I should refuse it.' "

This origin, like that given for " The House that Jack Built," has sometimes been discredited as " legendary," as the product of Hone's post-conversion days.

As a partisan there was nothing half-hearted about William Hone. He records with evident relish the fact that the Prince Regent was frequently hissed in public, and that when he accompanied the Allied Sovereigns on their visit to the City of London he was careful to take the Duke of Wellington with him in his carriage, sheltering himself under the hearty cheers accorded to the popular hero.

When it was proposed that Queen Caroline's name should be omitted from the liturgy of the Church, Hone's mockery was put into the bitter sentence, " I'll not have her prayed for ! "

Hone had been mentioned by name in the parliamentary proceedings on the Divorce Bill. The Solicitor-

General in his reply, Monday, October 30, 1820, is reported by Hansard to have said:—

" But, my lords, what makes it still more extra-ordinary, my learned friend has not even the merit of invention and novelty in this—the parallel is not his own ; for I find in a newspaper which I hold in my hand, published some days before the speech delivered by my learned friend, an advertisement in these terms, ' Nero Vindicated '—published by whom, my lords? by a name well known, an individual of whom I know nothing, except through the publications he has ushered into the world—' printed by William Hone, Ludgate Hill.' And my learned friend con-descends to make himself the instrument of such a person as that whom I have described—to prefer such charges as these in this high and august assembly against the monarch of this country."

Hone was the publisher of " The Printers' Address to The Queen, and Her Majesty's tribute to the Press, in answer."

The Address was presented to the Queen at Branden-burg House on Wednesday, October 11, 1820, by a deputation of 138 compositors and pressmen, who were most graciously received, and had the honour to kiss Her Majesty's hand. It concluded with the follow-ing paragraph :—

" In future times, should the page of history record the present era as one in which overwhelming power combined with senatorial venality to crush an unpro-tected female, we trust it will also preserve the grati-fying remembrance that the base conspiracy was defeated by the irresistible force of Public Opinion, directed and displayed through the powerful medium of a Free, Uncorrupted, and Uncorruptible British Press."

Her Majesty's reply included the following—

" The press is at present the only stronghold that

Liberty has left. If we lose this we lose all. We have no other rampart against an implacable foe."

Here is a letter which shows that Hone had been busying himself in the Queen's affairs from the commencement of the year. The old King had died on January 29th.

To Rev. R. Aspland.
"*Feb.* 1820.
"My dear Sir,—You witnessed, I presume, Dr. Lindsey's appalling death. It is a loss to the nation, and I fear, a very great one at this time.
"The Queen's affairs will miss his directing mind, when its real wisdom was most essential to her interests.
"The Whigs are sad dogs—they engaged to get her £50,000 per ann. by private contributions ; brought down a message in her name, refusing that annuity from Parliament ; and now cannot agree among themselves to give her a shilling.
"I am, My dear Sir,
"Yours truly,
"W. Hone."

The Rev. Robert Aspland, of Hackney, was a prominent Unitarian divine, and editor of the *Christian Reformer* and several other religious periodicals of the time. It was he who had stood by Hone's side at his trials in the Guildhall to manage the voluminous books of reference used in his defence ; on each of the three days Mr. Aspland had found the authorities to be quoted, furnished hints in the use of them, and prompted Hone time after time in his memorable speeches. Many of the books had been borrowed by the reverend advocate from Dr. William's Library— he was a man attracted by, and indefatigably active in, political and religious efforts of this kind.

Further correspondence throws light on Hone's activities in this matter.

To Mr. Hone.

" SLIGO,
" *July 30th,* 1820.

" MY DEAR SIR,—I write to you in a hurry from a circuit town, but the subject admits of no delay. I am writing a few pages on the present crisis, which I hope soon to have ready, and after our intercourse, you are the man in England who I would soonest have for my publisher. I will leave the terms entirely to yourself. You will give me whatever sum you choose on each edition, and I am only sorry that a poor man's claims prevent his presenting it to you altogether. If you are satisfied with this, do not lose a moment in inserting the following advertisement.

" ' THE QUEEN.
" ' In the press, and immediately will be published,
THE QUEEN'S CASE STATED.
By
Charles Phillips, Esq., Barrister-at-Law.

" ' You shall surely answer it when the poorest rag upon the poorest beggar in this island shall have the splendour of your Coronation garment.' *Vide* statement.

" Write to me the moment you receive this, and direct to me at ' Galway.' I shall, by return of post, enclose to you, if not the whole, at least the greatest part of the Manuscript. Excuse haste and believe me, Dear Sir, relying on your immediate answer,
" Yours most sincerely,
" C. PHILLIPS.

" Tell me all the news and give my best regards to Mr. Aspland. I need not say I am the Queen's friend."

To Charles Phillips, Esq.

" LONDON,
" 23rd. Oct. 1820.

" MY DEAR SIR,—I do indeed, as you suppose, think the Queen triumphant ; hers is, in my honest, sincere opinion, the triumph of honour and innocence, over sensuality and subornation to perjury. I am glad to hear that she has noticed the pamphlet. She is a frank, open-hearted, unsuspicious woman. I have seen and conversed with her. She is shrewd, witty, sarcastic and gay, and so disloyal as to speak what she thinks. . . .

" If you come here, you will have to live down some very strong dislikes, and that will take time, unless you prefer the other course, viz.—to declare that certain good and valuable considerations have assured you of the error of your ways, and afforded you the means of parting from your conscience, till you meet it in the other world.

" You see what a rascal Donoughmore has become. He was ever a most violent declaimer against the King personally—he is bought—but the price is not known exactly. Lord Hutchinson has been always a private friend of the King, and the unhappy man has not had the courage to resist the blandishments of royalty.

" The Editions of your pamphlet are 500 each, and it is now in the 19th. edition, which it has arrived at from the means I have adopted, peculiar to myself. Nothing operates more effectually upon a man than interest, and as mine is co-equal with yours in this affair, and my experience of a better kind, in a matter of this sort, than any other man's in London, you have, perhaps, the best security an author can have for everything effectual being accomplished to promote his object.

" I am, my dear Sir,
" Yours faithfully,
" W. HONE."

The Lord Hutchinson here mentioned by the writer was the close personal friend of George IV. who was commissioned to meet Queen Caroline at St. Omer and make her an offer of £50,000 a year on condition that she relinquished all English titles of royalty, and never visited England. The Queen indignantly spurned the

16

suggestion, and started next morning (June 5th) for England. Lord Donoughmore was Hutchinson's elder brother, who had been on the Liberal side but now supported the Government against Queen Caroline ; hence Hone's just wrath against his time-serving " rascality."

XVII

ANTIQUARY AND CONTROVERSIALIST

MENTION has been made (p. 218) of works other than political and topical which were also engaging Hone's attention during this period—perhaps the period of his greatest activity. At no time did he ever willingly relinquish his researches in the records of antiquity, and he was always too ready to flourish his pen in religious controversy.

As an antiquary, part of his time was taken up in writing his " Ancient Mysteries " and the " Apocryphal New Testament " ; as a controversialist he was answering the " Aspersions " of the *Quarterly Review*.

The researches which he made to support his plea at the trials familiarised him with an obscure section of literature, which, in 1821, resulted in the publication of a curious and interesting volume, " The Apocryphal New Testament, being all the Gospels, Epistles, &c. attributed in the first four centuries to Jesus Christ, His Apostles, and their Companions."

No sooner was the work published than it was fiercely attacked all round, the most savage onslaught being made by the *Quarterly Review*, the sting of which was the reviewer's pretended assumption that Hone was only the " editor," being " a poor, illiterate creature, far too ignorant " to have written it himself. Hone was furious. He addressed a letter and a challenge to the *Quarterly*, and in 1824 published " Aspersions Answered : An Explanatory Statement

243

addressed to the Public at large, and every Reader of the *Quarterly Review* in particular."

The same malignant spirit in the *Quarterly* which had assailed poor Keats was now manifesting itself against William Hone. He replied to a second article in it by publishing a pamphlet, "Another Article for the *Quarterly Review*." In the same spirited manner he engaged in a controversial correspondence with Dr. Samuel Butler, Archdeacon and Headmaster of Shrewsbury School, who, in 1836, became Bishop of Lichfield and Coventry." Dr. Butler, whose grandson of the same name, it is interesting to recall, is the author of "Erewhon," retracted his aspersions and afterwards became friendly with Hone.

The second of these twin antiquarian publications, being less polemical, may be dismissed more briefly.

"The Ancient Mysteries Described, especially the English Miracle Plays, founded on the Apocryphal New Testament Story," appeared in May, 1823. Hone printed eight of these Mysteries or Ancient Miracle Plays, the precursors of the English drama, which he had found in MS. at the British Museum and now gave to the world. To these he added, as variations and illustrations, other ancient ecclesiastical shows, such as "The Feast of Fools," "The Feast of the Ass," "The Boy Bishop," "The Descent into Hell," and even "The Giants in the Guildhall"—not all exactly ancient, though all of them curious and diverting. It was in this way Hone supplied interesting and amusing matter to the uninitiated, and won for his antiquarian publications a wide and well-deserved popularity. The illustrations to this book, thirteen in number, were more than usually quaint. Underneath the frontispiece, representing the Fool with his Bauble, were the lines:—

" When Friars, Monks, and Priests of former days,
  Apocrypha and Scripture turned to Plays,

The Festivals of Fools and Asses kept
Obey'd Boy Bishops, and to crosses crept,
They made the Mumming Church the people's rod,
And held the grinning Bauble for a God."

An interesting correspondence passed between Hone
and Walter Wilson, the biographer of De Foe, the latter
desiring assistance in the collection of his material.
Hone had to refuse his request, being so fully occupied
in bringing out his " Ancient Mysteries " ; but the
tone of the letters shows the closeness of their intimacy.

A number of other books, none of which made any
particular stir in the world, were being issued by Hone
at this time. His best publishing period lasted from
1818 to 1826, during which his output, having regard
to the class of literature in which he trafficked and
the methods of publication then employed, was really
considerable.

But, though Hone had " found himself," though
he took an intense pleasure in the work with which
he busied himself unremittingly day by day, he was
never getting one penny the richer, no matter what
quantity of stuff he was selling. How seldom it is
that the bookish man is equipped to encounter the
actualities of business bargaining ! In William Hone,
indeed, it would seem that the competitive spirit was
all but absent.

The Hone period of publishing, be it remembered,
was *par excellence* the age of parody and piracy, and
the market was flooded with hundreds of cheap and
trashy reprints which are now either extinct or represented by the few rare copies treasured in the libraries
of the chap-book collectors. They were mostly produced by unscrupulous and impecunious printers, men
who defied the law because, being little better than
literary scavengers, they were not worth prosecuting.
Hone did very little in this line ; for though he printed
a lot of trash, it was trash honourably paid for, as far
as his means allowed.

XVIII

THE "EVERY-DAY BOOK"

HAVING abandoned his career as a satirist, Hone devoted his later years to antiquarian research for the purpose of publishing antiquarian information in a popular form, and presenting it in such a manner as not only to be understanded of the people, but accessible to those of average means. To this congenial work he brought to bear his well-tried powers of research, and displayed all that indefatigable perseverance which always characterised his labours, whatever they were. The result of all this was the publication of the "Every-Day Book" in 1825 and 1826, the "Table Book" in 1827, and the "Year Book" in 1832.

Had the public realised the true value of Hone's work at the outset, he might, perhaps, have been saved the ignominy of a debtor's prison. At that stage in the history of periodical literature publishing was by no means a lucrative trade, and the publisher who meddled in political affairs usually found himself labouring under an additional disadvantage.

The first number of "The Every-Day Book" was published January 1, 1825, and as projected the issue of the work was to occupy twelve months. A "number," consisting of a sheet of thirty-two columns, with engravings from original designs by "superior artists," or from rare old prints and drawings, was published every Saturday, at the price of threepence. The "Monthly Parts," comprising four of these weekly numbers, were "sold by all vendors of periodical works in town and country " at one shilling each.

Such was the success of the work, a second volume was announced in January, 1826, which duly appeared, and ran a similar course in popular favour. By the close of the year the "Every-Day Book" had been completed in 104 numbers, or 27 parts, and was being offered in two octavo volumes of 1,700 pages, at 14s. each volume.

A letter, dated February 15, 1825, addressed to S. J. Button, Esq., Pilgrim Street, shows the pecuniary straits to which he was constantly reduced while bringing out these works.

"MY DEAR SIR,—Can you favour me with a loan of £25 till the 27th? I am sadly tied by the leg here and the booksellers will do nothing by *sending* to ; so that by their indifference to messages and my indispensable attention to ' Every Day,' I am really in a vexatious plight. I have artists to pay, and they, poor fellows, cannot be put off. The work is doing better every week, and yet it keeps me poor by its very success in the country where it is increasing fast. Withal I am very unwell for want of a run out, and I dare not venture on it till Saturday. If you can do this for me it will serve and inspirit."

There are other letters of a similar nature which disclose an almost chronic state of impecuniosity ; this must suffice here—it well illustrates the struggles common to literary men whose love of letters dulls their acquaintance with figures.

Hone's accounts of the expenses incurred by him in getting up the "Every-Day Book," in respect of drawings and cuts, are so admirably kept, item by item, each under its respective date, from January 1, 1825, when No. 1 was first put into preparation, to the last entry for No. 66, April 1, 1826, that one wonders why such a show of business habits and such exactitude in accountancy never resulted in the man's commercial success. The name of the draughtsman and of the engraver in each case is given with the cost set against it, as :—

						£	s.	d
Feb.	8.	No. 2.	Twelfth Night.	Drawing.	G. Cruikshank	2	2	0
Feb.	8.	No. 2.	Twelfth Night.	Cutting.	H. White	2	0	0
Sept.	3.	No. 36.	Candler's Fantoccini.	Drawing.	G. Cruikshank	2	2	0
Sept.	3.	No. 36.	Candler's Fantoccini.	Cutting.	White	2	15	0
Dec.	24.	No. 52.	Bungay Watchman.	Drawn by self			—	
Dec.	24.	Bungay Watchman.		Cutting.	White	0	12	0
Jan.	21.	No. 56. { Skating on the	Drawing.	G. Cruikshank	3	3	0
Jan.	21.	No. 56. (Serpentine.	Cutting.	White	3	3	0

The total charges for designing and engraving the whole of the illustrations amounted to £660 12s. 6d. This includes a lump sum of £150 for " out-of-pocket expenses," set forth as under:—

" Charges on the above Engravings and Numbers of the ' Every-Day Book ' for fees to Parish Clerks, Sextons, and Porters ; Gifts to Showmen ; Civility money to persons exhibited ; Gratuities for information and permission to sketch, and for Stage hire and other travelling expenses every week, to Islington, Canonbury, Hagbush Lane, Hornsey, Highgate, Tottenham, West Wickham, and Greenwich, and to Bullock's Museum, Cross's Menagerie, Bartholomew Fair, Charlton, and other Fairs, and different places in town and country ; frequently accompanied by Artists, and always bearing their charges ; besides sums paid for the loan of books, prints, and drawings, &c., &c., at least, £150."

The illustrations, not only those of Cruikshank but many of the others—those of S. Williams, for instance —compare favourably with the best woodcuts of the present day.

Hone sometimes made sketches himself. In

Volume II. he gives a long account (p. 321) of the elephant which was shot dead in Mr. Cross's Menagerie, Exeter Change, in consequence of the dangerous symptoms which it had developed. The initials to the drawing of the unfortunate elephant as he lay dead show that William Hone and George Cruikshank visited the scene together.

During the summer of 1825 Hone took some quiet lodgings near Pentonville, in order that he might get on with his work without the interruptions incidental to shopkeeping in the city.

In the "Every-Day Book," under date May 8th, is a description of a walk out of London towards Canonbury, in which the following passage occurs :—

" Having crossed the back Islington Road, we found ourselves in the rear of the Pied Bull. Ah, I know this spot well ; this stagnant pool was a ' famous ' carp pond among boys. How dreary the place seems ; the yard and pens were formerly filled with sheep and cattle for Smithfield market ; graziers and drovers were busied about them ; a high barred-gate was constantly closed ; now all is thrown open and neglected, and not a living thing to be seen. We went round to the front, the house was shut up, and nobody answered to the knocking. It had been the residence of the gallant Sir Walter Raleigh, who threw down his court mantle for Queen Elizabeth to walk on, that she might not damp her feet ; he, whose achievements in Virginia secured immense revenue to his country ; whose individual enterprise in South America carried terror to the recreant heart of Spain ; whose lost years of his life within the walls of the Tower, where he wrote the ' History of the World,' and better than all, its inimitable preface ; and who finally lost his life on a scaffold for his courage and services.

" By a door in the rear we got into ' the best parlour,' this was on the ground floor ; it had been Raleigh's dining-room. Here the arms of Sir John Miller are painted on glass in the end window, and we

found Mr. John Cleghorn sketching them. This gentleman, who lives in the neighbourhood, and whose talents
as a draughtsman and engraver are well known, was
obligingly communicative, and we condoled on the
decaying memorials of past greatness.

"On the ceiling of this room are stuccoed the five
senses ; Feeling in an oval centre, and the other four
in the scroll-work around. The chimney-piece of
carved oak, painted white, represents Charity, supported
by Faith on her right, and Hope on her left. Taking
leave of Mr. Cleghorn, we hastily passed through the
other apartments, and gave a last farewell look at Sir
Walter's house ; yet we made not adieu to it till my
accompanying friend expressed a wish, that as Sir
Walter, according to tradition, had there smoked the
first pipe of tobacco drawn in Islington, so *he* might
have been able to smoke the last whiff within the walls
that would in a few weeks be levelled to the ground."

Now, evidently this description was written from actual
experience, though the walk was not taken precisely
on the day of the month already named. Preserved
among the family papers is the following memorandum
in Hone's neat and legible handwriting, and having at
the top of it a humorously drawn figure of a pied bull
smoking a pipe—the drawing apparently executed by
the same hand :—

" PIED BULL, ISLINGTON,
" 21*st*. *May* 1825.

"Memorandum made on the spot, by us the undersigned, now assembled for the purpose of looking at
this house, previous to its being pulled down. That
we have done so, and each of us smoked a pipe, that
is to say, each of us one or more pipes, or less than
one pipe, and the undersigned George Cruikshank
having smoked pipes innumerable or more or less—and
that each of us did cause to be brought, or did bring,
to wit, by and through the undersigned David Sage,
whose father, David Sage the elder, is about to pull
down the house, many to wit, several pots of porter, in
aid of the said smoking, and that the same being so

drunk, he, the said David Sage, at the suggestion, and
by desire of the not so undersigned, brought wine,
to wit, port wine at 3/6 per bottle (duty knocked off
lately) wherewith, and with other ingredients, bowls
of negus were made by the undersigned William Hone
and partaken of by each of us—the first toast being
given 'To the Immortal Memory of Sir Walter
Raleigh.'   Intervening sentiments and toasts being
expressed and drunk, the next of importance was the
Country of Sir Walter and ourselves—' Old England '
—We, the first three undersigned, came here for the
high veneration we feel for the memory and character
of Sir Walter, and that we might have the gratification
of saying hereafter that we had smoked a pipe in the
same room that the man who first introduced tobacco
smoked in himself.   The room in which we do this,
is that described in the Every-Day Book of this day
by W. H.   In short, we have done what we have said,
and there is nothing more we can say, than this, that
as Englishmen we glory in the memory and renown of
our revered countryman.

> " WILLIAM HONE, *Chairman.*
> " GEORGE CRUIKSHANK.
> " JOSEPH GOODYEAR.
> " DAVID SAGE."

The signatures are autographs, and they were doubtless a very merry party who honoured the memory of
Raleigh that fine May day.   This is one of the few
glimpses we get of Hone away from the cares of
business, and in the merry mood of pleasure-making.
Joseph Goodyear was an engraver on wood, born in
Birmingham, where he was apprenticed to Tye.

Legend says that William Hone took up his residence
in Canonbury Tower for a short time during the writing
of Volume I.   It is precisely the kind of thing he would
do, on account of the literary associations which cluster
so thickly round that ancient structure.   Oliver
Goldsmith is supposed to have produced some of his
works here about the year 1767 ; Samuel Humphreys,

author of "Ulysses," died here in 1737, and Christopher Smart, the "mad poet," once rented rooms in the building. A number of other eminent names in literature have added lustre to the history of Canonbury Tower, all of which would be known to William Hone, and perhaps suggest the atmosphere of the place to him as the source of literary inspiration. And it was perhaps a safe retreat from duns.

"Oh for a year without quarter-days!" Thus sighed the man whose whole time, thoughts, and energies were occupied upon a glorified calendar. William Hone was living at 45, Ludgate Hill—on the site now occupied by the railway-bridge—and the time of stress and tribulation which wrung this exclamation from his lips was the "inevitable" quarter-day which arrived in March, 1826. The final blow in the long-impending disaster fell on April 4th, when he was arrested for debt, and carried off to the Lock-up House. Upon his surrender to the "Rules of King's Bench," he was lodged for a time at Mr. Poole's, tobacconist, 2, Suffolk Street ; whilst his wife and family, being thrust out of the Ludgate Hill premises, found a temporary refuge with his father, until a small house at 22, Belvedere Place, Southwark, was secured for them, it being the custom then for a debtor to "reside within the Rules."

The King's Bench Prison, Southwark, was one pile of buildings occupying an extensive tract of land, and having within its high walls 224 rooms, a coffee-house, and two public-houses ; also shops and stalls for the sale of meat, vegetables, and the other necessaries of life ; while the people walking about, or enjoying themselves in various forms of amusement, was little calculated to impress a stranger with the ideas of insolvency and distress or even of confinement.

The Prison buildings had been burnt down by the Lord George Gordon rioters in 1780, the year of Hone's birth ; but they had been very speedily rebuilt. Imprisonment for debt, it may be noted (except when fraudulently contracted) was abolished in 1861.

Referring to this break-up of the home, a rather pathetic note, considered from a literary man's point of view, made by the son Alfred in later years, is found among the family papers:—

" A perfect set of father's publications was kept in a chest in the little lumber-room at the top of the house, at Ludgate Hill. When the break-up came, this chest was forgotten and left behind ; mother had a perfect recollection of this."

Settled down, Hone occupied himself with literary, work " within the Rules," almost as unconcernedly as if he were entirely free. Others before his time, and since, have similarly employed their talents under the shadow of this prison. Here, for instance, Dr. Syntax, otherwise the eccentric William Coombe, wrote his " Tour in Search of the Picturesque " in 1822 ; and not literature alone has been wooed " within the Rules " —a few years later poor Haydon painted his " Mock Election," which was purchased by George IV. for £500. Art is a kinder mistress than letters—at least, for writers of the solid type of William Hone.

From January 1, 1825, the impecunious author had been engaged upon his " Every-Day Book," getting it out regularly in threepenny numbers. He continued his writing in the prison, getting out the current weekly number in the lock-up, the publishing being taken over by Hunt and Clarke, who issued for him the shilling monthly part that April.

Here is a business letter from Mr. Hunt, addressed to " Mr. Hone at Mr. Poole's, tobacconist, 2, Suffolk Street, near the King's Bench Prison ":—

" *April 22nd*. 1826.

" MY DEAR SIR,—We will at all costs advance the £60 to save the furniture. It seems difficult (though

I don't know why it should be so) to persuade you that nothing could cause the hesitation on our part but the actual difficulty of finding the money. To do it next Wednesday will occasion great inconvenience—for it cannot be done without putting off payments that ought not to be postponed.

" I mention this simply in order to convince you (taking for granted that you give me credit for sincerity) that since Mr. Evans first explained the receipts, there was only one question with us, namely, *could* we advance the money?

" I forgot to remind you to-day of the general advertisement for our catalogue, which the printer waits for. It must not be long.

" Can you let Cox have some part of the proof of Index to-morrow morning to correct?

" Very truly yours,
" H. L. Hunt."

The plight he was in, and the course he proposed to pursue, are best set forth in his own words, as we find them in a letter to his old friend John Childs.

" In the Rules of King's Bench Prison,
" 24 *April*, 1826.

" ' *Every-Day Book.*'

" Dear Childs,—My family is thrust out from Ludgate Hill, and I am in the Rules of King's Bench Prison. From the moment I found my affairs irretrievable, which was within two hours after I was arrested (it being made plain to me by my Solicitor, and I had not dreamed of it before) I worked like a horse to put the ' Every-Day Book ' beyond the reach of destruction, by transferring it to Messrs. Hunt & Clarke, in trust for my Creditors, and every sheet of every thing out of my own power, or the power of any one man to touch in preference to another. All was removed into their Warehouse in a few hours, and my papers secured with the books necessary to the conduct of the work ; and I was transferred hither, after writing a number in the Lock-up House. Since then, I have got out last week's, arranged the Index, so as to make the first volume an immediately productive asset, and have just got the proofs from the printer's, which, when read, will go to press.

"My wife and family are in great distress. They ran for shelter to my Father's, and I went to prison with 3/6 in my pocket—and this a week before one of my daughters was to have been married.

"It is not possible, I think, that my creditors will refuse the proposition that will be submitted to them generally, and to which those who have been already seen have assented, for the continuation of the 'Every-Day Book,' and employing me, under Trustees, at such a rate as shall maintain my family on the smallest weekly allowance, until I have satisfied them in full. It is my wish, and will be my endeavour to do it, and nothing short of being allowed to make that endeavour, and pay them 20/- in the £, will satisfy me.

"To remove all suspicion that I might desire the benefit, as it is called, of the Insolvent Court, I have forborne entering the Prison walls, which is a requisite enjoined by the law, before a debtor can petition for relief. Bankruptcy seems altogether out of the question. It would be the best thing for *me*, and the worst for my creditors, and as I am willing to work for them, at the price of bare existence, they will scarcely reject the offer.

"My direction is 'Mr. Hone, at Mr. Poole's, Tobacconist, 2 Great Suffolk Street, opposite the old Windsor Castle, Borough, London.'

"Though I have lacked necessaries, I mean meals, since I have been here, I have not made known that I had not the wherewithal to obtain them, for I am not a beggar. Had I been dishonest to my creditors, I should not have been in want.

"I am, dear Childs,
"Yours sincerely,
"W. HONE."

With what mixed feelings the bankrupt received, a month or so later, the following letter from his publisher, addressed to him at Belvedere Place, may be best imagined by those who have most endured life's bitter ironies. The newspaper cutting is carefully pasted at the top of the note-paper, thus: —

" 'According to the *Colonial Times* (a Hobart's Town paper), Mr. HONE, the brother of the political squib writer of that name, is receiving from his various appointments in that colony, the following salaries :—

	£	s.	d.
As Master	480	15	4
For House Rent	115	7	4½
As Commissioner of the Court of Requests	298	13	4
As Chairman of the Quarter Sessions ...	177	17	6
Total ...	£1072	13	6½

" If to this sum is added his present salary, as Acting Attorney-General, Mr. HONE'S income will not be far short of 2,000*l* per annum ! ! ! When the gentlemen of Westminster-Hall read this statement, they will be of opinion that Mr. HONE has been, at least, tolerably successful.'

" MY DEAR SIR,—I send you the above from this day's *Herald*, that you may rejoice at the fact, and laugh at poor Thwaite's spite.
" Will you oblige me with an answer, by bearer, to my queries of yesterday? I must know, in order to make the requisite arrangements for publishing.
" Very truly yours,
" HENRY L. HUNT.
" *Wednesday, 23rd. August.*"

An extract from a letter at the close of that fateful year shows William Hone, though nominally a prisoner in confinement, still busily and industriously engaged

on the work which ever had a fascination for him, and
by means of which he hoped to extricate himself
and his family from difficulties.

> " 22 BELVEDERE PLACE,
> " SOUTHWARK,
> *Dec.* 18*th.* 1826.
>
> ". . . I think I begin to see daylight through the
> gloom of my late distresses, and if I can turn my per-
> verted faculties a little more to the right, I may struggle
> through at no distant period. Be this as it may, I
> shall wait patiently, and endeavour silently.
>
> " I end the ' Every-Day Book ' with the next number,
> and hope is resolving into certainty that the work,
> when completed, will yield something, which those who
> have expected nothing will be glad to divide, though a
> trifle, amongst themselves, and the rest who have taken
> vengeance in their own hands, and obtained nothing
> unhappily, but a good bill from their own legal
> advisers, will have the option of the same dividend.
>
> " As to ' being in the world again,' I am scarcely
> more out of it than I was at Ludgate Hill. It's true
> I have not so many friends fluttering about me, but
> in other respects I am altogether as I was, ' except
> these bonds.' I thank God, however, that in this small
> house we are more comfortable than I could imagine
> possible."

The dedication of the first volume ran : —

> " TO CHARLES LAMB, Esq.
>
> " DEAR ——, Your letter to me, within the first
> two months from the commencement of the present
> work, approving my notice of St. Chad's Well, and
> your afterwards daring to publish me your ' friend,'
> with your proper name annexed, I shall never forget.
> Nor can I forget your and Miss Lamb's sympathy and
> kindness, when glooms overmastered me ; and that
> your pen spontaneously sparkled in the book, when my
> mind was in clouds and darkness. These ' trifles '

17

as each of you would call them, are benefits scored upon my heart, and
   " I dedicate this volume
    " To you and Miss Lamb,
     " With affectionate respect,
       " W. HONE.
" *May 5th.* 1826."

On the completion of the work Lamb paid that graceful rhymed compliment to " friend Hone " which is so often quoted. In the middle of the volume there was also an interchange of rhymed compliments between the two, the well-known Quatrains to " ingenuous Hone," and his laboured Quatorzians in reply.

The second volume of the " Every-Day Book " was " respectfully dedicated by William Hone, to the Right Honourable the Earl of Darlington—' as an encouragement of the old Country Sports and Usages chiefly treated of in my Book '; 27th. February 1827."

Of the " Every-Day Book " he said he could have continued it for six volumes full of interesting matter. He told a friend that he remembered Brand, the antiquary, and described him as—

" a tall, robust, Johnsonian sort of man, without Johnson stoop. He loved his bottle of port and dessert, to loll over his wine with some noble friend, turn over his illustrated Pennant, and recall interesting anecdotes of the characters of past times. Sunday was his working day—and he used to say on Saturday, ' Oh ! I have to preach to-morrow.' "

Brand's " Popular Antiquities " was doubtless a source of inspiration to the later antiquary.

XIX

THE "TABLE BOOK"

MONTH after month, for another year, the work of completing the first, and writing the second of his famous Miscellanies, went steadily forward. But under what bodily strain and mental suffering these well-known works were produced, few who are familiar with them seem to know.

On Christmas Day, 1827, the indomitable scribe makes the note :—

"The next number of the 'Table Book' is the last—so wills the public. . . . W. H."

The man of letters being "no man of business," his affairs were now taken in hand by a friend, who interviewed Messrs. Hunt and Clarke, and found that the "Every-Day Book," representing the unremitting toil of many weary months, would result in no pecuniary benefit whatever to its author. It was found, further, that a sum of £400 was still required to settle with Hone's creditors before his liberation could be effected.

But the year 1827 was fraught with other, and deeper, distresses than unproductive labour. Writing to a friend, William Hone makes this allusion to his sons William and John :—

"I have the satisfaction to say that my eldest son has remitted half his pay, since he has been at sea, in liquidation of debts he had contracted previously, and he has written so as to persuade me that the good seed is outgrowing the tares.

" Little Jack, whom I shipped off to France, has returned, after a six months' voyage, and I have put him to a good school (I have found one) where the little chap is fagging with all his might and delight at navigation, that he may get off to sea as quickly as possible, and, in spite of all my teaching, and though he saw above thirty sail wrecked off Yarmouth, and not a soul saved, he is eager to go aboard again, and actually desires to have ' a brush,' as he calls it, at fighting ! This is a son of mine ! "

The elder boy had been appointed to H.M.S. *Procris*, commanded by Captain Waldegrave. Let a letter disclose the beginning of a series of domestic afflictions which added to the imprisoned debtor's other distresses :—

" 22, BELVEDERE PLACE, SOUTHWARK,
" 13th. *December* 1827.

" DEAR CHILDS,—Since you were here in the Summer, distress has poured upon us in floods. One fact, from the interest you took in our son William's welfare, you ought not to be ignorant of—he is dead ! You may have learned, perhaps, by the papers, that our second son, Alfred, was run over in the Strand a week ago. His skull was fractured, and at that time there was every appearance of mortal termination. From the time he was brought home, he vomited blood for fifteen hours, and was insensible. He is now gradually recovering, though not out of danger, and I wished to write William, from whom we had not heard of late, though we wrote him letters. My wife went yesterday to receive his pay, but chiefly for the purpose of inquiring where his ship was stationed ; she was answered that his pay was stopped, and this mode was feelingly adopted to prepare her for the intelligence of his death. She dragged herself home scarcely alive, with a paper indorsed that he died 18th. October. Her grief was too absorbing to leave thought or anxiety for particulars. If I do not mistake that date was the day of the battle of Navarino. This is all that I know or conjecture.

"You will do me a favor if you communicate this to Mr. Filby, whose kindness, as well as yours, I will remember. I am too full of sorrow to say more than God bless you and yours.

" W. HONE."

An extract from another letter will supply a few details of the bereavement :—

"First, however, I must thank you for the consolatory sentiments you express towards us in our affliction, for the loss of our poor boy, William, respecting whom we have since heard that he was found dead in his hammock, in Leith Roads, and that he appeared to have expired three hours before, having gone to rest in apparent health."

It was little comfort to the bereaved family to receive the captain's testimony to the deceased's intelligence, ability, and officer-like conduct.

Then the son John—" little Jack," as his father fondly calls him—gets his appointment to H.M.S. *Gannet* in the following year, and goes to sea again. Strangely enough, he soon afterwards meets with his death by a fall from the yard-arm.

But this is anticipatory. To return to the close of 1827, we learn from a letter that Hone himself was in bodily suffering :—

"MY DEAR SIR,—If you can let me have the Legend of the Bridge, with some notice of the painter of the picture, which is in the hands of the engraver, it will oblige me—particularly so, should it be convenient to drop it to me on Monday—the wood block will be ready, and they might appear next Saturday.

"To say truth, I am o'er wearied with my troubles, and my spirit is too severely wounded to get up when I want it, and at this moment the Article would help me, for I have only one engraving for my sheet next week, save yours, and for the life of me cannot devise another.

" Let me not, however, press you inconveniently— merely do me the favor of a line by bearer—a word— aye or nay—and I shall arrange accordingly.

" Since I wrote you last, I have been under the hands of the surgeon—for a complaint I had unwittingly neglected—and the operation, and the altogetherness of my difficulties in this place, have prevented me from writing T.Q.M.[1] as I purposed—I have literally been unable.—You, I am sure, must be aware that ' the heart alone knoweth its own sorrows,' and that there are times when it can neither make them known, nor bear the weight of ordinary business in addition. I pray you let this be (as it truly is) excuse and apology for seeming neglect. Will and power I have been little able of late to connect.

" I am, My dear Sir,
" Yours sincerely,
" W. HONE.

" 22 Belvedere Place,
    " 1st. Dec. 1827.
      " To C. C. Wilson, Esq."

The advertisement which offered for sale " The Every-Day Book Complete " also announced a new work to commence on January 1, 1827, which, like its predecessor, was to be issued in weekly and monthly sections. This was the " Table Book," the first number of which appeared with the New Year, 1827. To this work Hone invited the communications of correspondents on topics of interest, and current gossip on events of the day, which, with his own writings and the embellishments of his artists, he hoped to make into a literary kaleidoscope, which would blend information with amusement, utility with diversion, or, as he put it in rhyme :—

---

[1] A frequent contributor to the " Table Book."

" Cuttings with cuts, facts, fancies, recollections,
Heads, autographs, views, prose, and verse selections,
Notes of my musings in a lonely walk,
My friends' communications, table-talk,
Notions of books, and things I read and see,
Events that are, or were, or are to be,
Fall in my TABLE BOOK—and thence arise
To please the young, and help divert the wise."

Hone laid many of his literary friends under contribution, as may be noted by the observant reader of this compilation.

How one contributor was obtained is disclosed in the autobiography of Mrs. Charles Cowden-Clarke ; it is the story of a first literary effort which led to many very notable achievements by the same pen. Miss Mary Novello, as she then was, had just become engaged at the age of seventeen to her future husband. It was of the year 1826 she thus writes in " My Long Life " (T. Fisher Unwin, 1896) : —

" I made my first attempt in literary production. My only confidant was my sister Cecilia. I wrote one short paper, entitled ' My Arm Chair,' signed merely ' M.H.' These initials I meant to represent ' Mary Howard,' because my father had in his juvenile days, enacted the part of Sir John Falstaff as ' Mr. Howard ' at some private theatricals. I sent my paper to the office where Hone's ' Table Book ' was published, and to my great joy, and to that of my sister-confidant, my paper was promptly accepted, making its appearance in an early subsequent number of that interesting periodical. To figure in the same volume where dear and honoured Charles Lamb was contributing his selections from the ' Garrick Plays ' was in itself a greatly-to-be-prized distinction, but my happiest triumph was when I showed the paper to my Charles, telling him it was written by a girl of seventeen, and watched his look of pleased surprise when I told him who that girl was.

" I may here mention that this contribution of mine to Hone's TABLE BOOK was followed by five others, respectively entitled ' My Desk,' ' My Home, ' My Pocket-Book,' ' Inn Yards,' and a paper on the ' Assignats ' in currency at the time of the French Republic of 1792. The paper was headed by a printed facsimile of an ' Assignat di dix sous,' from one that had been given to me by my kind old tutor, Monsieur Bonnefoy."

Life in the King's Bench must have appeared but a dull grey thing to a bright young girl in the first bloom of womanhood. Mrs. Cowden-Clarke, in her charming reminiscences, tells us of her intimate acquaintance in early life with Leigh Hunt, John Keats, and other literary lights with whom her family were on visiting terms. Here is an episode of the kind which occurred soon after she—still Miss Mary Victoria Novello—had become engaged to Charles Cowden-Clarke : —

" Another visit, but of a very different kind, that year, was paid by my Charles and me together. He took me to see William Hone, who was then detained, by temporary money difficulties, ' within the rules ' of the King's Bench Prison ; so dingy and smoky were the regions through which we had to pass ere we arrived there, that a morsel of smut found its way to my face and stuck thereon during the first portion of our interview with Mr. Hone. When Charles perceived the black intruder, he quickly puffed it off and went on with his conversation.

" A day or two afterwards, when Hone again saw Charles, he said to him, ' You are engaged to Miss Novello, are you not? ' ' What makes you think so? ' was the reply. ' I saw you familiarly blow a smut off the young lady's face, to which familiarity she made no objection ; therefore, I naturally guessed you were engaged to each other.' "

The " Table Book," like its predecessor, soon became popular ; the reception it met with may be gauged by

the high commendation passed upon it by Christopher
North : —

"Reader, did you ever see Hone's Every-day Book?
You cannot do better than buy it directly. . . . You
will meet with spirit-stirring descriptions of old
customs, delightful woodcuts of old buildings, as well
as many a fine secret learned among the woods and
fields, and whispered by the seasons' difference. . . .
He has deserved well of the Naturalist, the Antiquary,
and the Poet by his Every-day Book, and also by
his Table Book."

Hone's edition of Strutt appeared about this time.
Probably there was no other man then living more
capable of editing Joseph Strutt's "Sports and Pastimes
of the People of England," which had been first
published in 1801, the year before the author's death.

Part I. of Hone's edition of "Strutt's Sports," to
be issued in ten monthly parts, with 140 engravings,
was announced for February 1, 1828. The price was
to be one shilling each part, or on superior paper, two
shillings, and if coloured, three shillings. The
publishers were Hunt and Clarke. In 1834 a new
edition, "with copious index," was published by Thomas
Tegg & Son.

XX

WILLIAM HONE AND CHARLES LAMB

WE have now reached a period in Hone's life when something requires to be said of an acquaintance with one who holds a more distinguished place in our literature than any who have hitherto been mentioned ; one, too, who arouses in his admirers the most intense and ardent affection. There is a sheer pleasure in even writing his name—Charles Lamb. Sir Walter Scott or Oliver Goldsmith may be the *most* beloved of writers, but Charles Lamb " has not left his peer " ; he, far beyond all others, is the *best* beloved, and it is impossible to imagine that any other author will ever appeal to us so compellingly as he does.

When the two met cannot, in the present state of our knowledge, be definitely stated. In his " Life of Charles Lamb " Mr. E. V. Lucas remarks that " to the best of his knowledge " the acquaintance began after Hone had sent to Lamb a copy of his " Ancient Mysteries." This book was published probably some time in May, 1823, as Lamb acknowledged its receipt in a letter dated the 19th of that month and it was announced in the June number of the *London Magazine* as having been " lately published." Mr. Lucas, however, is in error as the above-named letter was not the first one that passed between the two, for, some eighteen months earlier, Lamb had written to Hone in reply to a communication in which the latter had, evidently, sent some details concerning " Graces," perhaps after having read in the November number of the *London*

Magazine the Elian essay, " Grace Before Meat." So, at least, one judges from the letter referred to, which was first printed in 1870 in " The Complete Correspondence and Works of Charles Lamb." The letter runs thus :—

" 9 *Nov.*, '21.

" DEAR SIR,—I was not very well nor in spirits when your pleasant note reached me, or should have noticed it sooner. Our Hebrew brethren seem to appreciate the good things of this life in more liberal latitude than we, to judge from their frequent graces. One, I think, you must have omitted : ' After concluding a bargain.' Their distinction of ' Fruits growing upon trees,' and ' upon the ground ' I can understand. A sow makes quite a different grunt (*her grace*) over chestnuts and pignuts. The last is a little above Elia.

" With thanks and wishing grace be with you.

" Yours,

" C. LAMB."

One is inclined to · surmise that some sort of an acquaintance may have taken place even earlier than the preceding date, although we have no evidence of such, for in his journeyings to and fro between his rooms in Great Russell Street, Covent Garden, and the East India House in Leadenhall Street, Charles Lamb must have passed Hone's shop in Ludgate Hill (where the latter had set up as a bookseller since 1818) at least twice daily and, quite conceivably, may have entered it in search of some literary treasure or other, and by some humorous or witty remark have engaged Hone's interest. Another possible source of introduction may have been Lamb's friend, Hazlitt, who in 1819 employed Hone as the publisher of his " Political Essays." Either of these assumptions seems more probable than that the intimacy should have originated as the result of Hone's having first written to Lamb after the appearance of the essay in November, 1821. For it should be borne in mind that the contributions to the *London*

Magazine were signed with a pseudonym, and all that Hone would have known would be that their author was a certain " Elia " whose identity with Charles Lamb was known to a few friends only. And even supposing that Hone had written to Elia under care of the editor of the magazine and the letter had been forwarded by the latter, it is hardly likely that he would " give himself away " by signing his proper name as Lamb did in his reply. And, of course, if Hone communicated directly with Lamb by letter addressed either to the India House or elsewhere he must have been less of a stranger than has hitherto been assumed. If it be objected that, had the two been known to each other at the date in question, Lamb could quite easily have popped into the shop in passing and so thanked Hone personally and would doubtless have done so, we reply that Lamb was then temporarily living in Dalston and his route lay some distance away from Ludgate Hill.

The third letter to Hone is one of thanks for an " excellent pamphlet " which is apparently that published by him early in the year 1824, entitled " Aspersions answered: an Explanatory Statement to the Public at large and every reader of the *Quarterly Review*." Two other letters follow, undated, but conjecturally belonging to the same year.

It is not until the year 1825, shortly after Hone had begun the publication of his " Every-Day Book," that the friendship appears to have become established. From that time onwards up to 1834, the year of Lamb's death, the intimacy continued and the various editions of Lamb's Letters contain some twenty-six letters written to Hone, most of them bearing on Lamb's contributions to the " Every-Day Book " and " Table Book," in the latter of which appeared the " Garrick Extracts " from the old dramatists which were published in 1835 along with the third edition of the " Dramatic Specimens."

In the *London Magazine* for May, 1825, were printed Lamb's pleasant and kindly verses " Quatrains to the

Editor of the ' Every-Day Book ' "—which opened with the line, " I like your book, ingenuous Hone," and of which the conclusion ran as follows :—

" Dan Phœbus loves your book—trust me, friend
        Hone—
    The title only errs, he bids me say :
For while such art, wit, reading, there are shown
    He swears, 'tis not a work of *every day*."

The phrase " friend Hone " seems to have called forth all his rapturous gratitude, for in his Dedication of the first volume of the periodical to Charles Lamb in May, 1826, he refers to it, as he had done previously in a letter now published for the first time :—

> " GATE HOUSE, HIGHGATE,
>   " *Sunday*, *May*, 1825.

" DEAR SIR,—' My dear Sir,' at the head of a letter to you, is too formal—I think it much better to say, then—

" DEAR LAMB,

" Because, to be plain, I must call you so. ' Friend Hone ' in print is so kind, and then there's such courage, in *public*, to say you dare to encourage my friendship, in *private* I cannot resist a glow of affection for such an assistance towards a poor mortal like me, who only is, (*sic*) and never can be more than, a creeper, where others are runners.

" Now for my ' say '—There being some sun this May morning, I purpose to shock Miss Lamb and you about 2 o'clock, with a call and an appetite, such as it is, and to eat out my thanks, and excite all your risibility, suavity, compassion and gravity—for melancholy, mirth, and I are one.

> " I'm more than
>   " Yours sincerely,
>   " W. HONE."

The Quatrains were copied by Hone into No. 30 of the " Every-Day Book " which appeared on July 23rd and were followed by his own quatorzians (irregular sonnets), two of which are here given :—

" In feeling, like a stricken deer, I've been
    Self-put out from the herd, friend Lamb ; for I
Imagined all the sympathies between
    Mankind and me had ceased, till your full cry
Of kindness reach'd and roused me, as I lay
    ' Musing—on divers things unknown ' : it bid
Me know, in you, a friend ; with a fine gay
    Sincerity, before all men it chid,
Or rather, by not chiding, seem'd to chide
    Me, for long absence from you ; re-invited
Me, with a herald's trump, and so defied
    Me to remain immured ; and it requited
Me, for others' harsh misdeeming—which I trust is
    Now, or will be, known by them, to be injustice.
            *   *   *   *   *
" As to the message from your friend above :—
    Do me the favour to present my best
Respects to old ' Dan Phœbus ' for the ' love '
    He bears the *Every-Day Book :* for the rest,
That is, the handsome mode he has selected
    Of making me fine compliments by you, 'tis
So flatt'ring to me, and so much respected
    By me, that, if you please, and it should suit his
Highness, I must rely upon you, for
    Obtaining his commands, to introduce me
To him yourself, when quite convenient ; or
    I trust at any rate, you'll not refuse me
A line, to signify, that I'm the person known
    To him, through your friend Lamb as
                    " *Your Friend,*
                            " WILLIAM HONE."

It is quite evident that Hone was no poet, and we have not quoted his very prosaic verses for the purpose of poking fun at him or of depreciating his poetic efforts, but merely to show the effect on him of Lamb's kindly sympathy and " friending," and how sincere was his gratitude. The concluding quatorzian is also necessary to understand Lamb's reference to " this last interlineation," in his letter to Hone of July 25, 1825, printed on page 273.

In the summer of 1825, Lamb's health having broken down, it was found necessary for him for a while to leave Colebrook Cottage, Islington, where he had been living since the autumn of 1823. He sought health and quiet farther afield in the village of Enfield, and while there his cottage was occupied by Hone, who, on a broiling day in July, penned the following amusing epistle which he used as " copy " for the " Every-Day Book "—in which it was printed in the number for July 23rd, the same number in which Lamb's verses and his own appeared. It is headed " A Hot Letter " and is addressed to " Captain Lamb, Brighton."

"MY DEAR SIR,—I anticipated a sojournment in your ' neat little country cottage ' during your absence, with more pleasure than I expressed, when you made me the offer of it. I imagined how much more comfortable I should be there, than in my own out-of-town single-room. I was mistaken. I have been comfortable nowhere. The malignity of an evil star is against me ; I mean the dog star. You recollect the heat I fell into during our Hornsey walk. I have been hot ever since, ' hissing hot,—think of that Master Brook ' ; I would that thou wert really a brook, I would cleave thy bosom, and, unless thou wert cool to me, I would not acknowledge thee for a true friend.

" After returning from the coach wherein you and your lady-cousin [1] departed, I ' larded the lean earth ' to my own house in town. That evening I got into a hackney-coach, to enjoy your ' cool ' residence ; but it was hot ; and there was no ' cool of the evening ' ; I went to bed hot, and I slept hot all night, and got up hot to a hot tea breakfast, looking all the while on the hot print opposite, Hogarth's ' Evening,' with the fat hot citizen's wife sweltering between her husband and the New River, the hot little dog looking wistfully into the reachless warm water, her crying hot boy on her husband's stick, the scolding hot sister, and all the other heats of that ever-to-be warmly-admired engraving.

---

[1] " Bridget Elia," of course.

" The coldest picture in the room, to my heated eye, was the fruit-piece worked in worsted—worsted in the dog-days !

" How I got through that hot day I cannot remember. At night, when, according to Addison, ' evening shades prevail ' the heat prevailed ; there were no ' cool ' shades, and I got no rest ; and therefore I got up restless, and walked out and saw the Morning Star, which I suppose was the dog star, for I sought coolness and found it not ; but the sun arose, and methought there was no atmosphere but burning beams ; and the metropolis poured out its heated thousands towards the New River, at Newington ; and it was filled with men, and boys, and dogs ; and all looked as ' comfortable ' as live eels in a stew pan.

" I am too hot to proceed. What a summer ! The very pumps refuse ' spring ' water ; and I suppose, we shall have no more until next spring.

" My heart melts within me, and I am not so unhuman as to request the servant to broil with this letter to the post office, but I have ordered her to give it to the newsman, and ask him to slip it into the first letter-box he passes, and to tell him, if he forgets, it is of no consequence, and in no hurry ; he may take it on to Ludgate Hill, and Mr. Hone, if he please, may print it in his ' Every-Day Book.' I dare say he is too hot to write, and this may help to fill up ; so you'll get it, at any rate. I don't care if all the world reads it, for the hot weather is no secret. As Mr. Freeling [1] cannot say that printing a letter is privately conveying it, I shall not get into hot water at the post-office.

" I am, my dear Sir,
" Your warmest friend, till winter,
" I. FRY.

" COLEMAN COTTAGE,
" *Sun Day*.

" P.S. I am told the sight of the postmen in their scarlet coats is not bearable in London ; they look red-hot."

---

[1] Francis Freeling, Secretary to the G.P.O.

To this letter, over which he must have chuckled when he read it in the " Every-Day Book," Lamb replied :—

" ENFIELD,
[25 *July*, 1825.]

" DEAR H——,—The Quotidian came in as pleasantly as it was looked for at breakfast time yesterday. You have repaid my poor stanzas with interest. This last interlineation is one of those instances of affectation rightly applied. Read the sentence without it, how bald it is ! Your idea of ' worsted in the dog-days ' was capital.

" We are here so comfortably that I am confident we shall stay one month, from this date, most probably longer ; so, if you please, you can cut your out-of-town room for that time. I have sent up my petit farce altered ; and Harley is at the theatre now. It cannot come out for some weeks. When it does, we think not of leaving here, but to borrow a bed of you for the night.

" I write principally to say that the 4th of August is coming,—Dogget's Coat and Badge Day on the water. You will find a good deal about him in *Cibber's Apology*, octavo, facing the window ; and something haply in a thin blackish quarto among the plays, facing the fireside.

" You have done with mad dogs ; else there is a print of Rowlandson's, or somebody's, of people in pursuit of [one] in a village, which might have come in : also Goldsmith's verses.

" Mary's kind remembrance,
" C. LAMB.

" MR. HONE,
" Colebrook Cottage,
" Islington."

It was, probably, while Hone was living at Highgate that the following incident, related by the author of " Some Account of the Conversion from Atheism to Christianity of the late William Hone," took place: " Next to Peckham Rye, or rather before it, he [Hone] loved Hampstead Heath ; there he used to see much of

Charles Lamb, of whom he always spoke with true affection. He told me, ' One summer's evening I was walking with Charles Lamb, and we had talked ourselves into a philosophic contempt of our slavery to the habit of snuff-taking ; with the firm resolution of never again taking a single pinch, we threw our snuff-boxes away from the hill on which we stood, far among the furze and brambles below, and went home in triumph ; I began to be very miserable, was wretched all night ; in the morning I was walking on the same hill ; I saw Charles Lamb below, searching among the bushes ; he looked up laughing, and saying, " What ! you are come to look for your snuff-box too ? " " Oh, no," said I, taking a pinch out of a paper in my waistcoat pocket. " I went for a halfpenny-worth to the first shop that was open." ' "

During the two years (1825 and 1826) that the " Every-Day Book " ran, Lamb contributed several articles, all more or less characteristic of his delightful style. It was not, however, until Hone brought out his " Table Book " in the year following the cessation of the former publication that Lamb became a constant contributor. His extracts from the Garrick plays appeared, with few exceptions, every week during 1827. He found during the latter part of the preceding year much pleasant occupation at the British Museum, which greatly relieved the tedium of having so much spare time on his hands following his retirement from the India House. In September, 1826, he told his Quaker friend, Bernard Barton, that he was going through a course of reading at the Museum and that he had two thousand of the Garrick plays to go through, a tithe of which he had " despatch'd " in a few weeks. It was, he said, " a sort of office to me ; hours, ten to four, the same. It does me good. Man must have regular occupation, that has been used to it." The first extract appeared in the fourth number, and the concluding one in No. 53.

He introduces the series in an interesting letter to
the editor : —

" DEAR SIR,—It is not unknown to you, that about
sixteen years [1] since I published ' Specimens of English
Dramatic Poets, who lived about the Time of Shakespeare.' For the scarcer Plays I had recourse to the
Collection bequeathed to the British Museum by Mr.
Garrick. But my time was but short, and my subsequent leisure has discovered in it a treasure rich
and exhaustless beyond what I then imagined. In it
is to be found almost every production in the shape of
a Play that has appeared in print, from the time of
the old Mysteries and Moralities to the days of Crown
and D'Urfey. Imagine the luxury to one like me, who,
above every other form of Poetry, have ever preferred
the Dramatic, of sitting in the princely apartments, for
such they are, of poor condemned Montagu House,
which I predict will not speedily be followed by a hand-
somer, and culling at will the flower of some thousand
Dramas. It is like having the range of a Nobleman's
Library, with the Librarian to your friend. Nothing
can exceed the courteousness and attentions of the
Gentleman who has the chief direction of the Reading
Rooms here ; and you have scarce to ask for a volume
before it is laid before you. If the occasional Extracts,
which I have been tempted to bring away, may find
an appropriate place in your ' Table Book,' some of
them are weekly at your service. By those who
remember the ' Specimens ' these may be considered
as mere after-gleanings, supplementary to that work,
only comprising a longer period. You must be content
with sometimes a scene, sometimes a song ; a speech,
or passage, or a poetical image, as they happen to
strike me. I read without order of time ; I am a poor
hand at dates ; and for any biography of the

---

[1] It was really nineteen years since the first edition
appeared (1808), but, as he confessed, he was " a
poor hand at dates."

Dramatists, I must refer to writers who are more skilful in such matters. My business is with their poetry only.

"Your well-wisher,
"C. LAMB.
" *January* 27, 1827."

Most of Lamb's letters to Hone during this period— over a dozen—relate more or less to these extracts.

In pursuing our narrative of the course of this notable friendship it will be necessary to anticipate in some slight degree the events of the next few chapters.

The " Table Book " was short-lived ; it ran only for twelve months. During the next two years, 1828 and 1829, very few letters passed between the two friends, so far as the published letters of Charles Lamb enable us to judge. Friendly intercourse, however, was not at an end, as we find Lamb, in a letter usually dated May 2, 1828 but almost certainly written on the 21st of the month of that year, inviting Hone to Enfield for the following day to meet their common friend, Walter Wilson, whose " Life of De Foe," in which both Lamb and Hone were much interested, was to appear a year or so later.

In 1830, Hone's worldly affairs were at a low ebb and his friends were endeavouring to set him up as a coffee-house keeper in Gracechurch Street. Lamb, ever ready to help a friend in time of need, was very active in his behalf. To Southey he wrote the following charming letter : —

"*May* 10, 1830.
" DEAR SOUTHEY,—My friend Hone, whom you would like *for a friend*, I found deeply impressed by your generous notice of him in your beautiful ' Life of Bunyan ' which I am just now full of. He has written to you for leave to publish a certain good-natured letter. I write this not to enforce his request, for we are fully aware that the refusal of such publication would be quite consistent with all that is good in your

character. Neither he nor I expect it from you, nor exact it ; but if you would consent to it you would oblige me by it, as well as him. He is just now in a critical situation ; kind friends have opened a coffee-house for him in the City, but their means have not extended to the purchase of coffee-pots, credit for Reviews, newspapers and other paraphernalia. So I am sitting in the skeleton of a possible divan. . . . Our object is to open a subscription which my friends of the *Times* are most willing to forward for him, but think that a leave from you to publish from you would aid it.

"But not an atom of respect or kindness will or shall it abate in either of us if you decline it. Have this strongly in your mind.

"Those 'Every-Day' and 'Table Books' will be a treasure a hundred years hence, but they have failed to make Hone's fortune.

"Here his wife and all his children are about me, gaping for coffee customers ; but how should they come in, seeing no pot boiling. . . .

"C. LAMB.

"P.S. . . . I write from Hone's ; therefore Mary cannot send her love to Mrs. Southey, but I do.

"Yours ever,
"C. L."

The "certain good-natured letter" had been written to Hone by Southey and contained kindly and appreciatory references (see pp. 297-8).

In the issue of the *Times* containing these letters was printed a subscription list headed by the name of "Charles Lamb, Esq." who contributed the sum of £10. Other subscribers were "Five old Friends of Mr. Hone—each £10 " ; " Mr. Tegg, Cheapside, £20 "; "His Grace the Duke of Bedford £20," and several more. In all, in this first list, a total of £165 was contributed.

To help further in the good cause Lamb also wrote to his friend Basil Montagu, who was told that he was a good soul of himself and needed no spurring, " but if you can help a worthy man," added Lamb, " you will have *two worthy men* obliged to you."

In a short time enough money was obtained, and Hone opened the coffee-house on June 19th, as may be seen from the following letter written by Hone to Effingham Wilson of the Royal Exchange. Wilson was a bookseller, who published among other works the poems of Alfred Tennyson, a review of which by A. H. Hallam appeared in Moxon's *Englishman's Magazine* for August, 1831.

> " 13 GRACECHURCH ST.
> " 18 *June* 1830.
> " MY DEAR SIR,—We have finally resolved on opening this house to-morrow—Saturday—and there are announcements in the window to that effect. You may inform any of your friends therefore, and all you can mention it to in the course of the day, that the ' Grasshopper ' will be opened at 6 in the morning.
> " Yours sincerely,
> " W. HONE.
> " ' Good Beds and early Breakfasts.' "

Hone's occupancy of the " Grasshopper " lasted for about three years, and he still found time for literary or journalistic pursuits, for in the following year he edited his " Year Book," a periodical meant " to supply omissions upon subjects that the ' Every-Day Book ' and the ' Table Book ' were designed to include." Lamb did not contribute any articles, but two of his poems appeared there for the first time, viz., " To C. Aders, Esq. on his Collection of Paintings by the Old German Masters," and in the last number but one, " The Change," lines written on his old friend Louisa Martin. John Clare, the Northamptonshire peasant poet, whose friendship with Lamb dated from the time when the latter was contributing his Elia essays to the

London Magazine, sent Hone a sonnet in praise of
" Friend Lamb."

After 1830, so far as we know, Lamb wrote only
two letters ; one in 1833, the other in 1834, early in
the year in which he died.   The first one is in acknowledgment of " a note from me to C.L. (Hone endorses
the letter) written in January preceding and sent by
young Will Hazlitt.   Received in my paralysis."

" *March* 1, 1833.

" DEAR FRIEND,—Thee hast sent a Christian epistle
to me, and I should not feel clear if I neglected to
reply to it, which would have been sooner if that vain
young man, to whom thou didst intrust it, had not
kept it back.   We should rejoice to see thy outward
man here, especially on a day which should not be a
first day, being liable to worldly callers in on that
day. . . .

" Our little [1] book is delayed by a heathenish injunc-
tion, threatened by the man Taylor.   Canst thou
copy and send, or bring with thee, a vanity in verse
which in my younger days I wrote on friend Aders'
pictures?   Thou wilt find in it a book called the Table
Book.[2]   Tryphena and Tryphosa, whom the world call
Mary and Emma,[3] greet thee with me.

" CH. LAMB.

" 6th of 3d month 4th day."

It is not clear why Lamb used Quaker phraseology
in this letter to Hone, whose recent conversion was
certainly not to Quakerism.

The last letter, with which we close this chapter on
the intimacy between Lamb and Hone, was written
in response to an appeal from the latter for Lamb's
support in his application to the Literary Fund Society.

---

[1] " The Last Essays of Elia," published in 1833.

[2] Here Lamb's memory was at fault ; the poem was
printed in the " Year Book."

[3] Emma Isola, the Lambs' adopted daughter.

Writing to John Scott on February 1, 1834, Hone informs him that he had written to his " friend Mr. Charles Lamb " who was, he stated, the only man who knew him intimately, " but," he goes on, " I fear from Miss Lamb's illness, which is of a very peculiar nature, he may be ill himself, and though I have written to Enfield it is just possible I may not hear from him in answer." Hone's references to Lamb's being at Enfield show that he could not have heard from him for some considerable time, for the Lambs had left that village almost a year previously. He was distinctly in error in supposing that Lamb, whatever sorrow might be overshadowing him at the time, would be neglectful of an old friend who was in distress and needed help, or fail to come to his assistance with monetary or other aid if such assistance were necessary and possible. The reply was written from Edmonton the day after the date of Hone's letter and runs thus : —

" CHURCH STREET, EDMONTON.
" 7*th* *Feb.* 1834.

" MY DEAR SIR,[1]—I compassionate very much your failure and your infirmities. I am in affliction. I am come to Edmonton to live altogether with Mary, at the house where she is nursed, and where we see nobody while she is ill, which is alas ! the greater part of the year now. I cannot but think your application, with a full statement to the Literary Fund, must succeed. Your little political heats are many years past. You are now remember'd but as the Editor of the ' Every-Day ' and ' Table Books.' To *them* appeal. You have Southey's testimony to their meritoriousness. He must be blind indeed who sees aught in them but what is good hearted, void of offence to God and Man. I know not a single Member of the Fund but to whomsoever you may refer to me I am

---

[1] This formality was due to the fact that the letter was to be seen by other eyes than Hone's.

CHARLES LAMB.

To face p. 322.

MARY LAMB.

ready to affirm that your speech and action since I have known you—ten or eleven years I think—have been the most opposite to anything profane or irreligious, and that in your domestic relations a kinder husband or father, as it seemed to me, could not be. Suppose you transmitted your case, or petition, to Mr. Dilke, Editor of the *Athenæum*, with this note of mine—he knows me—and he may know some of the Literary Society. I am totally unacquainted with them.

" With best wishes to you and Mrs. Hone,
" Yours faithfully,
" C. LAMB."

XXI

GETTING OUT OF KING'S BENCH PRISON

WE find Hone at last rousing himself and making an effort to get away from confinement ; and when the full tale of his troubles has been told it will be acknowledged that he was not easily spurred to action. In the following appeal to his trusty legal friend Parkes we seem to recognise in the piteous writer a sort of modern Job, upon whose unfortunate head calamity had succeeded calamity, till the poor wretch was overwhelmed with the burden of his miseries :—

" BELVEDERE PLACE,
" SOUTHWARK.

" DEAR PARKES,—During the last few weeks I have often wished you were in Town, for I should have had your advice and the benefit of your co-operation with an unexpected friend in an unhappy crisis of my affairs. Possibly, however, you may essentially advantage me even at a distance.

" Since I saw you, one of my young sons who had taken a liking to the sea was confirmed in it by a trip to Charente, on board a vessel in the wine trade, and in my endeavours to bind him apprentice, which the difficulties of my constraint rendered nugatory, I accidentally stumbled upon a gentleman who in a day or two bound John to a respectable shipowner and fitted him out on board an East India Trader.

" In the course of the summer, he has actively turned his attention to me, and insisted on my accepting his services to get me out of this place. I laid open to him the whole of my affairs in every particular, and

instead of being disheartened by the thorough view
I gave him of them and of myself, he said everything
was just as he expected from what he had heard and
observed of me, and that mine was precisely the case
he knew how to deal with. He accordingly had interviews with Messrs. Hunt & Clarke in order to determine what proposition the state of accounts might
enable him to make the creditors. From the day I
came hither, I had been doing all in my power to
increase assets, and had proceeded with hope, and
latterly with cheerfulness from Messrs. Hunt & Clarke's
repeatedly assuring me that things were going on
very well. The accounts took a considerable time
making out, and when they were completed to the
30th. of September, to the surprise of Mr. —— and
scarcely less of Messrs. Hunt & Clarke themselves,
they presented this miserable result—that my unremitted
exertions for more than a year and a half in the
purlieus of a prison, have involved me so much deeper,
as to leave me without the least power of drawing subsistence for my family beyond a few weeks further, or
of even extricating my person from restraint.

" This turn in my affairs is to me appalling, but
Mr. ——, who is a thorough man of business, and
who has a warm heart and a cool head, is undismayed.
He has seen some of the parties interested, and well
considered all the circumstances, and determined to
persevere, under the conviction that with a sum of
£400, he can finally settle with every creditor, and
obtain my liberation ; at the same time this mode will
ultimately ensure some permanent advantages to my
family, which any other proceedings would inevitably
destroy. Under a firm persuasion that this sum may
be privately obtained, among a few individuals, he
urges me to disclose my situation where I can with
propriety. He knows not whom to point out, but
leaving that to me to discover, he desires me to reckon
on his personal exertions till he has got me out ; and
on the sum of £50 from himself as part of the £400,
adding as a reason for not doing more, that though
his business is prosperous, his family is large, and he
is far from opulent.

" It is better known to you, perhaps, than any one else, that my stay-at-home habits and literary indulgences were ill calculated to the formation of friendships, and that, in fact, while I have been known to all the world, I am without any personal friends, except yourself and one or two who have no means wherewith to assist me. You may also have derived, from your knowledge of mankind, that this place of retirement is as little inviting as the centre of an Irish bog, and I assure you I have had the benefit of entire seclusion, for from those who knew me before I came hither, I have not had a single solicitation to be allowed an opportunity of disclosing their earnest desire to serve me. In short, I know not whither to look for aid, yet, through the exertions of an excellent man I can be extricated from all my difficulties, and by his long-sightedness, and judicious arrangement, be assured of final benefit to my family.

" From the opportunities you have had of seeing and knowing me, I think you would almost vouch that dishonour could not be coupled with my name, yet as you have known very little of my concerns since you left London, I think it necessary to affirm that were even an enemy to write the history of my frightful distresses and embarrassments, he would be unable to point out a single transaction that would lessen my integrity in the estimation of those who at any time have been pleased to think well of me. Notwithstanding this, and chiefly on account of my solitary habits, I scarcely know to whom, except yourself, I can represent the circumstances.

" Although I have not been within the walls of a prison, I and my family have had a large share of suffering. With the coming in of the summer, disease came in upon us, generated by our sleeping amid the malaria of this place, which I can well remember to have been a marsh. For the last four months sickness has not been out of the house, and during that time, till within the last three weeks my daughter Matilda has been in most imminent danger with inflammation of the lungs, which almost wore out my wife and myself through our night watchings.

" In the midst of all my wife fell dangerously ill of a fever, and while she was lying helpless in one bed, my daughter was almost a corpse in another—and at the same time the scarlet fever was among five of the young ones. At last I became ill myself, from a complaint I had neglected, in my earnest anxiety for those about me, and through the necessity I was under of almost hourly trying my invention for the weekly sheet which gave us bread. At last, about ten days ago, I became so bad as to require immediate surgical advice and I made it known to Mr. Lawrence, who came over, examined me, and determined on an operation immediately, which I underwent on Friday last. In short, out of this place I must get, or I shall pass out of life. Had not Mr. —— unexpectedly arisen to my relief, my spirit must have broken under the conflict. If happily I can be got out, he has a plan for obtaining me something of a public nature in the City, which his influence and connections can secure. In that event, I shall have the prospect of passing a few years with my excellent wife in comparative happiness, and the end will be better than the beginning of my life, for I have hitherto had nothing but vicissitudes, and if I had not considered my children the burthen of my evening prayers would have been that I might not awake to the miseries of another day.

" I commit myself, my dear friend, to your consideration, with a sure hope that in my extremity you will effect whatever may be in your power. Since I began to write Mr. —— has been here. In addition to his own he has obtained another £50, and by to-night's post I shall address myself in another quarter. Do not think I design to press too heavily upon you on this occasion.

" And believe me, dear Parkes,
" faithfully yours,
" W. HONE."

A letter to another friend makes allusion to this illness, and gives an interesting résumé of the events of the past two years or more :—

" Since my Trials, I have struggled amidst mental

infirmities and pecuniary embarrassments for the support of a large family. I had been out-reasoned by sincere friends, desirous of my welfare, into the notion that I could become a man of business, and they persuaded and assisted me, till my unfitness for the position became apparent to them as well as to myself, and I could go on no longer.

" Under the hope of retrieving my affairs, I commenced the ' Every-Day Book ' in January, 1825, whereon I persevered with unassisted labour until the month of April in that year, when the state of my mind and faculties rendered me unable to proceed without bodily exercise in the fresh air. I therefore left my home, with my books and papers, for a room at the back of Pentonville, and being unfit for society, spent the summer in a solitary manner, overwhelmed with hypochondria, working out my book, sheet by sheet, and taking fitful and lonely walks in a state of miserable distraction till the weather drove me back to Ludgate Hill. I there found the November term was approaching, by an influx of writs and Sheriffs' Officers.

" How I struggled through that fearful winter, at what expense of money in fees and costs, and with what wear and tear of mind and loss of spirits, I have no remembrance ; my recollection of it is as a long and terrible dream. At last, on the 4th. April, 1826, I was carried to a Lock-up House, and there, on the next day, I was made sensible of what I had before no idea, that my affairs were irretrievable, and by the advice of Messrs. Hunt & Clarke of Tavistock Street, who were my creditors as well as friends, I surrendered to the King's Bench, and abode within the Rules, while they undertook the management of my publication. Proposals were made to my creditors which they rejected, and in the opinion of Mr. H. L. Hunt, nothing remained for me but to finish the ' Every-Day Book,' and do anything else in my power to produce assets, and hitherto I have laboured on in this place to that object. In the spring of the present year Mr. —— insisted on my accepting his endeavours to settle my unhappy affairs and set me free, and to whom I thoroughly disclosed them, and referred him for other requisite particulars to Messrs. Hunt & Clarke, who furnished him their accounts as soon as they could be made out to the 29th. of September last.

" Their accounts are appalling—they almost as much surprised Messrs. Hunt & Clarke as they did Mr. —— and me ; my unremitted exertions during more than a year and a half of alternating hope and despondency, have involved me so much deeper that I am without the power of further maintaining my family, or of extricating my person from duress. I wish I could explain without running in to wearisome details, by what means I have fallen into necessitous circumstances. This being the Term, by obtaining what is called a day-rule, I could and would have waited on you, but on Friday last I was obliged to submit to an operation at the hands of Mr. Lawrence, which has placed me in a condition not to move about. I scarcely need to add that I shall await, with no small anxiety, in expectation of a line.

" I am, dear Sir,
" Your most respectful,
" W. HONE."

The " thorough man of business " who had taken upon himself the active management of the helpless debtor's affairs was Moxhay, a biscuit baker, who had large contracts with the East India Company. He seems to have been one of those fussy, incompetent busybodies ; and though at first he inspired Hone with immense confidence, all his efforts to extract the debtor from his difficulties, without recourse to the Insolvency Court, proved to be unavailing ; and by the end of September, 1828, William Hone was gazetted a bankrupt, and released from the King's Bench, after a confinement of nearly two and a half years.

Whether the poor author's affairs received the best of attention and fair treatment at the hands of his publishers is rather doubtful ; but the dealings between them were certainly complicated by the failure of Hunt and Clarke. The gossips of the time spoke of this unexpected insolvency as the " most awkward failure " the trade had known ; and although the firm's position must have been known a long time to the managing partner, H. L. Hunt (a nephew of Leigh Hunt), no one seems to have been more surprised at the collapse than the other partner, poor Cowden-Clarke.

From the rough draft of a circular letter evidently intended for his creditors found among his papers it seems that Hone now took, or at least proposed to take, matters into his own hands. The draft, having appended to it a list of nine creditors, to whom there is a total indebtedness of nearly £300, is thus worded :—

　　　" 22 BELVEDERE PLACE, BOROUGH RD.,
　　　　　　" 20th September, 1828.
" SIR,—The issuing of a Commission of Bankruptcy against me, after the unfortunate failure of a measure which you had kindly assented to for my release, emboldens me to urge upon your recollection that I have now been in custody nearly two years and a half. Under these painful circumstances, and as the proceedings at your suit have long since ceased, I venture to entreat your instructions to your Solicitor for my liberation, which can be effected by his addressing a simple note to the Marshal, authorising my discharge. This course will assist my free surrender at the first meeting of the Commissioners on Tuesday next, will enable you to prove your debt, and I scarcely need to add that it will confer on me a lasting obligation.
　　　　　　" I am, Sir,
　　　　　　　　" Yours most respectfully,
　　　　　　　　　　" W. HONE."

Released from the prison " rules," Hone and his family at once removed to Newington Green, Islington, where he had no sooner arrived than he sat down, as usual, to his desk to commence upon a new work, the latest projection of his busy brain. This was " Poor

Humphrey's Calendar," which, according to the advertisements, was to be entirely written and got out within three months, New Year's Day, 1829, being announced as the date of publication. Being without the means of paying for the woodcuts, for the paper and the printing, his good friend John Childs came to his assistance, and the work progressed without further hindrance.

"Poor Humphrey's Calendar" happily appeared to time, bearing the name and address of Matilda Hone as publisher. It was in the usual tabulated calendar form, a folio to each month of the year 1829 ; its contents being a gallimaufry of eventful dates and remarkable characters ; of curious conceits and pithy, sayings, mysterious warnings, and marvellous prognostications ; of odds and ends of antiquarian lore and fragments of great poetical beauty—all brought together in a delightful jumble of exquisite fooling, as only a compiler of such wide research and sound literary judgment could bring together in the space of fifty brief pages. Hone could caricature with his pen the follies and quaintness of antiquity with just the same facility as Cruikshank manifested with his pencil in the treatment of such subjects. Posing as a sort of burlesque Nostradamus, he called himself "Poor Humphrey," "the only seventh son of an only seventh son," "an Unborn Doctor of the High School of Freeknowledgists," "the sole Resolver of all Lawful Questions to Inquiring Students in the College of Learning." The brochure was an amusing satire upon the old astrological almanacs :—

> "All who are over wise
> All who are otherwise
> All who are never wise
> All who are weather wise.
> Over or other, or never or weatherwise
> All should read Humphrey, and be altogether wise.
> *So saith Poor Humphrey*."

Here we have, in fact, poor William Hone masking in the cap and bells of a jester, while there was no fire on his hearth, no bread in his cupboard. The pathos of the situation is but too transparent in certain matter printed on the back page—it is an appeal "to the Reader," soliciting patronage for "Matilda Hone, at 29, Russell Court, Brydges Street," who has on sale (we learn from the family papers the extent of her pitiful little stock-in-trade) "Engravings by ancient and modern Masters, with a moderate price marked on each print." Is it necessary to look to the foot for the signature, when we read that the advertiser, taking the public into his confidence, with a personal familiarity, will " gratefully esteem the kindness of encouragement " which he " entreats " for the little print shop? Who else would wind up an advertisement with anything so characteristic of the signatory as this :—

" Let me add, that I have not the slightest pecuniary interest in the undertaking, but I have a deep anxiety for my daughter's welfare, and endeavour to further it by the present urgent address, and by making her the publisher of this little work.

" W. HONE."

Hone, in issuing this Calendar, was again a vindicator of the freedom of the Press. For a long time the Stationers' Company and the Universities of Oxford and Cambridge had prevented any one else issuing almanacs without their licence, claiming under certain vague letters patent the exclusive right to publish them. Not till the end of the eighteenth century had any one challenged this claim to privilege, and it was 1834 before the heavy stamp duty of 1s. 3d. per copy on almanacs was repealed by Parliament.

For the little print-selling business upon which he had launched his daughter Hone had rummaged his own possessions to the utmost scrap in order to make up her modest stock-in-trade. But there was no demand for prints in Russell Court or Bell Alley. He was living at Newington Green, happy in the thought that he was occupying the house in which old Doctor " Civil Liberty " Price had once received the visits of such men as Hume, Franklin, and Canton.

Having resolved to extricate himself from the toils, Hone anticipated by a week or so his formal release from the Rules of the King's Bench Prison, and is found by the first day of August far away in the north country, enjoying his newly found freedom with all the zest which a long and close confinement would naturally, confer. How he was furnished with the means for this excursion is not known ; but it is not improbable he had received money on account of some literary commission he had undertaken, which necessitated travelling and personal investigation. In an unfinished letter this notable writer, whose career ended almost before the railway era dawned, gives a description from actual experience of the birth of a pioneer railway, and a personal impression—certainly a very faint one—of George Stephenson. He appears to have been present, as an invited guest, at the opening of the Bolton Railway, August 1, 1828.

In the following August we find William Hone again in the North of England. Probably the pressing needs of a wife and ten children had driven him to con- template some great change in life, to make a desperate effort to extricate himself at once and for ever from his harassing monetary difficulties. He pays a visit to Liverpool with a view to raising money for " a certain purpose " of the utmost importance to his family—and undertakes what was perhaps the most momentous expedition of his life. The mission proved a failure ; he failed to inspire confidence owing to the evil reputation still clinging to his name as the author of the " Parodies " ; opulent patrons declined his overtures—whatever they were—and he was unable to obtain an interview with Dr. Raffles, the eminent Independent Minister, to whom he wrote a most urgent letter.

A fortnight later he is still in Liverpool on this " affair of the utmost importance to his family " ; and he even purposes going farther north, apparently on the same errand, the importance of which will not permit of his keeping a promise of very old standing to review the book of his dear friend Wilson, " The Life of De Foe." To which effect he thus writes to another friend, Mr. Thomas Hurst, a member of the well-known publishing firm Longmans & Co. :

" An affair of the utmost importance to my family, and which alters their and my destination in life, so far as I had conceived of it two months ago, brought me to this town about three weeks ago. At the time of my leaving London I expected to return within a week, and to do what I could in a needful and kind way for my old friend Mr. Walter Wilson's Life of De Foe. Circumstances, however, compel me to progress further north, and will keep me from home so long and so alter my pursuits when I return, that I am persuaded I shall not have leisure to write such an Article for the *Westminster Review* as I desired, or perhaps ever put pen to paper for the press on any matter of moment to the public. It is not till I am assured of this that I make the communication, and on every account I do it reluctantly. As respects the work in question I had not intimated my intention to the Editor of the *Westminster*, and therefore I suggest the propriety of your taking such steps as may seem necessary to you for notice of the book in that *Review*. The copy I received from you is locked up at Newington Green, and therefore I have not the means of placing it in your hands till I get back."

" MANCHESTER, 22 *November*.
" I had written thus far when I was called away to the coach without opportunity to conclude, and under

REV. SAMUEL PARR, LL.D

(After a Picture by Opie.)

REV. DR. RAFFLES.

pressure of affairs since I came hither, it escaped me till this (Sunday) morning that I had not posted off my letter. You will do me the justice, I hope, to believe that I much regret my inability to perform what I had volunteered for De Foe, and should have executed with pleasure on behalf of both author and publisher. I certainly never devised anything more satisfactory, or that I should have executed perhaps with better knowledge of a subject wherein I willingly put pen to paper. As it is I can say no more than that I shall be obliged by your intimating to Mr. Wilson in terms accordant with my own expressions of feeling, that I have withdrawn upon compulsion."

A postscript adds :—

" The copy of De Foe which I received, at the same time with my own, for Mr. Hazlitt, I took to him the same day, and left him gratified by receiving it, and in the best disposition to set to work upon it kindly."

The exact nature of Hone's scheme cannot be discovered ; it may have been a project of a semi-social character ; we know, for instance, he was always interested in the savings bank movement ; but whatever it was it never materialised. He returned to London a disappointed, if not a broken-spirited, man. He felt himself abandoned by those to whom he had rendered greatest service. This mission, whatever it was, was apparently the turning-point of Hone's life.

XXII

THE " YEAR BOOK "

To recapitulate—the " Every-Day Book " was published by Hone himself, in weekly numbers and monthly parts, till the April of 1826, when the publishing was taken over by Hunt and Clarke, the two volumes of this work appearing in the course of 1825-6. The " Table Book," published for William Hone by Hunt and Clarke, followed immediately after, and was completed by November, 1827. In the September of 1828 William Hone was declared bankrupt ; six months later, in the April of 1829, Hunt and Clarke became bankrupts.

After the latter failure the two works were printed by W. Clowes, who sold all the printed stock and stereotype plates to T. Tegg. This publisher apparently did not find the work unremunerative, as he paid Hone £400 to write a companion work, the " Year Book," which duly appeared in 1831-2.

Inside the cover of Part II. of the " Year Book," issued in February, 1831, is printed the following " Notice ".:—

" To the Independent Livery of London.

" Gentlemen,—It has been, and is now, more than ever, my anxious desire to be one of your Bridge-masters.

" On the present occasion, however, I will trouble you with no more than that declaration ; but, feeling persuaded of your general kind wishes and friendship, I earnestly entreat you to bear in remembrance, that it is my intention, if I am living, to become a Candidate on the next vacancy.

"I am, Gentlemen,
"Yours most respectfully,
"WILLIAM HONE.

"13 Gracechurch Street,
"*January* 21st. 1831."

It is scarcely necessary to say William Hone did not get the appointment he sought. It is only in the United States of America that the flowery paths of literature lead to honourable employment in the public service.

By 1835 all rights in the four works had passed out of the author's hands. Tegg must have reaped a rich harvest from the publication of Hone's "pleasing compilations" (as the *Times* called them), a harvest in which the author had no participation. By 1838 some eighty thousand copies are said to have been sold; and a family memorandum estimates—on what basis is not stated—that a thousand copies of the "Every-Day Book" yielded a profit of £412, and the same quantity of the "Table Book" £206.

Till recent years this firm was reissuing Hone's famous volumes; indeed, William Tegg & Co. were reprinting the "Trials" and the "Freedom of the Press," two of his minor works, in 1876.

Tegg in 1874 reprinted the "Every-Day Book" and the others from the stereotyped plates, properly repaired. The only additions were to the "Year Book" —namely, "My Father's [Hone] Narrative, written by Himself," and "Decker's Raven's Almanack, foretelling of the Plague, Famine and Civill Warre, that shall happen this present year, 1609; in quarto, black letter."

At that date (1874) none of the contributors to the four volumes were believed to be alive, and Tegg did not feel himself justified in further disturbing the work of his old friend the editor and author.

Reprints of Hone's ever popular works have appeared from time to time, Messrs. Ward, Lock & Co. in 1887 venturing on the original plan of issuing them in monthly parts—twenty-seven at sixpence each.

Had Hone written nothing else than his " Every Day Book," " Year Book," and " Table Book," these works alone would entitle him to the respect and esteem of all book-lovers. It is always a matter of deep and lasting regret that William Hone was ever seduced from the compilation of such entertaining miscellanies of antiquarian lore to the thorny and profitless wilderness of polemics.

Hone's four volumes were the first of their kind. Without under-estimating the value of that useful and excellent work, it may safely be predicated that Chambers's " Book of Days " owed its inception to Hone's " Year Book." But it possesses neither the antiquarian nor the historical value of the latter, which enshrines a mass of curious information, much of which would probably have been lost but for Hone's wide research and love of the good old times. He was a literary Autolycus, a picker up of trifles, not of great value individually, but collectively of inestimable worth.

The home at Newington Green, humble as it was, it was found impossible to maintain for more than fifteen months. At the instigation of Mr. Tegg and with the assistance of other friends a coffee-house, known as the Grasshopper Hotel, Gracechurch Street, was taken for the impecunious writer and his family. The effort was well meant, but how uncongenial such surroundings would be to one of William Hone's habits and temperament only his more intimate friends could realise.

At the instigation of these private friends the Hone family took possession of the coffee-house, which was to be managed by Mrs. Hone and her elder daughters.

DOCTOR SOUTHEY'S NEW VISION.

THE ILLUSTRATION TO HONE'S PARODY, "A VISION OF WANT OF JUDGMENT,
BY SLUMBER'D SOUTHEY."

To face p. 297.

But they immediately found themselves in a painful exigency, which increased daily. The friends then came to the conclusion that a public appeal would have to be made, and the well-wishers of William Hone throughout the kingdom were earnestly solicited to afford the means of completing the fittings in his new establishment, as already mentioned (p. 276). It was pointed out in the advertisement for help that Hone had ceased to have an interest in any of his literary productions, and that from none of them had he ever derived any material advantage. Subscriptions were invited to be sent to three different banks, two booksellers, and to Messrs. Fisher and Moxhay, biscuit-bakers, 55, Threadneedle Street. The appearance of the discarded Moxhay's name is interesting ; Hone may have misjudged the man.

The money was forthcoming, and for the next couple of years or so William Hone and his family are installed in Gracechurch Street. Wherever he was, if William Hone could find a desk and writing materials, he could generally manage to forget most other things, even his troubles.

He was not long in finding more congenial matters than coffee-selling to engage his attention.

Between the parodist and Robert Southey had long existed a deadly enmity—Hone had published a bitter travesty of the poet's " Vision of Judgment." The animosity was reciprocal, but it came to a sudden and surprising termination soon after the publication of the " Table Book," led up to by the generous advances of the poet (see p. 277).

In 1830 the Poet Laureate published his " Life of Bunyan," in which he alluded to William Hone in a very handsome manner, greatly to the latter's delight. A Press notice of the new work called it " a hasty and tumultuous " compilation ; and presently proceeded :—

" But that for which we chiefly notice this work

of Mr. Southey, is the very last sentence in it, wherein is contained his frank and honourable recommendation (though not more than they deserve) of the works of one whom the iron hand of oppression would have levelled with the dust—

" In one of the volumes collected from various quarters, which were sent to me for this purpose, I observe the name of W. Hone, and notice it that I may take the opportunity of recommending his ' Every-Day Book ' and ' Table Book ' to those who are interested in the preservation of our national and local customs. By these very curious publications their compiler has rendered good service in an important department of literature, and he may render yet more, if he obtain the encouragement which he well deserves.

" Not only we, and the person mentioned in this paragraph, but all the friends of pure English literature —all the curious in old English customs—in short, all intelligent men, with the hearts of Englishmen in them— owe Mr. Southey their gratitude for this recommendation : it springs from a just taste and right feeling united."

The *Times* of May 21, 1830, in alluding to Southey's patronising notice, printed the correspondence, which, it said, " displayed in an advantageous light the modesty of Mr. Hone and the amiable and candid disposition of Mr. Southey."

XXIII

HONE'S POLITICAL AND RELIGIOUS VIEWS

POLITICS, like religion, being controversial, exercised a sort of fascination upon William Hone ; and, therefore, it is not surprising to find him taking an active interest in the great Reform movement which was then agitating the country, notwithstanding the shock his faith in political friendship had received and his abandonment of political publishing.

England was ruled by rotten boroughs, and parliamentary elections were a laughing-stock, openly conducted by bribery and intimidation. In Hone's time the English people were undoubtedly ready to make an English revolution, in emulative example of the French—as witness the Spa Fields Affair, the Luddite Riots, and the countless agrarian disturbances accompanied by rick-burning and other acts of incendiarism —but they found no leaders. Hone at his best was only a dreamer, seeing visions of constitutional reform ; even the more fiery Cobbett was no Danton, though he had been a soldier and was always " a man of the people."

The Reform Bill was first introduced into the House of Commons, March 1, 1831, by Lord John Russell. The abandonment of the measure and the strangely, hurried dissolution of Parliament on April 23rd caused immense political excitement throughout the country. Between this date and June 14th, when the newly, elected Parliament assembled, political bodies worked at high pressure, and the country was at fever heat.

Here is an informative letter addressed by our subject to a Manchester weekly newspaper devoted to the interests of democracy.

"To the Editor of the *Voice of the People.*
"13 GRACECHURCH STREET, LONDON,
"11*th. May* 1831.

"SIR,—In the last *Voice of the People,* directed to me from your office and delivered by the post this morning, and which is the first of your Journals I have seen, you propose to call a meeting of six hundred Deputies 'at Mr. Hone's Coffee-house, Gracechurch Street, London.' I desire to state, in your next *Voice of the People,* that this is without previous inquiry or communication with me, directly or indirectly.

"In consequence of this unwarranted association of my name I wish further to represent that, in my opinion, such a meeting of deputies in the Metropolis will be hailed as a powerful body of auxiliaries by the revolutionary and Tory enemies of Lord John Russell's bill, which aims at securing a more beneficent Parliamentary Reform and a greater extension of the elective franchise, than I ever expected would be proffered in my life-time, by any administration, or sanctioned by any sovereign.

"The meeting cannot be held at this house—I hope it will not be held at all.
"I am, Sir,
"Yours sincerely,
"WILLIAM HONE."

An extract from another letter which Hone addressed about this time to the editor of an important newspaper, but to which he did not append his name, gives us a further insight into his views of the bench of bishops as legislators. He says "the office of a bishop is high," and "episcopal incomes are notoriously excessive." He proceeds:—

"Allow me to suggest further, that, as Clergymen are carefully excluded from the House of Commons, it would be as well to consider the propriety of allowing the Episcopal Bench to remain in the House of Lords. A clergyman is exempt by law from all temporal affairs, on account of the necessity for his constant attention to ecclesiastical duties, and this spiritual avocation has been so carefully provided for, that he is not allowed to farm any lands or tenements, under a penalty of ten pounds per month, and avoidance of his lease ; on the same account, he is not either to trade or sell, on pain of forfeiting treble the value of the merchandise."

In all this political excitement Hone is seen as an observer, rather than an advocate, as one recording rather than one taking part in events. The ardour of his political faith had cooled very considerably, and the year after the Reform Bill passed he expressed the opinion that the reform effected had exceeded the wishes of moderate men—including himself—and he " feared the Government had, like Frankenstein, raised a monster they could not tame."

While his political ardour had been cooling down, his religious views had none the less been undergoing a change.

Years before William Hone's formal conversion to Christianity—indeed, from the very moment of his trials—he always evinced a soreness at the charge of atheism implied in being twitted with the publication of the Parodies—that he made money out of free-thought literature.

Nothing would provoke Hone's pen to prolixity so much as a charge of infidelity. There are extant interesting letters to Hume and others that bear out this. His attitude towards Romanism is shown in a letter to the Rev. Joseph Blanco White, the man who taught Pusey the use of the breviary, and in another addressed to Dr. T. I. Forster, of Hartfield, both friends and contributors to his miscellanies.

Such was Hone's love of religious equality, we

find him in 1828 raising his voice, or rather wielding his pen, with as much earnestness as if he had himself been a Protestant Dissenter, in the condemnation of the *Regium Donum*, a kind of State bribe to keep the Dissenters in a condition of subservience and bondage. His eloquent protest had no immediate result, and it was reserved for the Liberation Society to continue to press those objections to what the great body of English Dissenters had long considered inconsistent with their avowed principles.

When a little later he publicly joined a religious community he became a devout Christian. In the vigorous days of his early manhood—in his " wayward youth," as he expressed it—his independence of thought never assumed a more terrible aspect than a mild form of Nature-worship. In consonance with the freedom he claimed for himself, he had a wide tolerance of other men's religions. When the time arrived for his formal adhesion to a Christian denomination he selected Protestantism of the most uncompromising evangelical variety, perhaps because he found the sect most advanced politically. Having embraced it, he lived up to it consistently, leading a life, not only of good works and social service, as he had always done, but breathing an atmosphere from which all forms of worldliness were excluded, and in which the salvation of the individual soul is the supreme and constant concern of each.

He was ever a kindly disposed man, and judged by his life's work, it may be said of him that though he might think wrong, he could not, wilfully, do wrong. In his earlier period his religion was rooted, not in Belief but in Life. So he became a Reformer. Absorbed in other men's affairs, his mind was never in contact with the realities of life, as they affected himself. This was the measure of his failure. In his later years he seems to have adopted the attitude that religion is primarily a life of pure inwardness, which for its due expression demands, as of paramount necessity, an organised Church. So he joined himself to the religious community which approached nearest to his ideals, his broad tolerance not being too nice as to the precise label he should wear.

XXIV

CONVERSION

THE coffee-house venture, like Hone's other commercial enterprises, proved ineffectual to keep his head above water for long. How the end came is best told in his own words, contained in a letter written to his brother in Van Dieman's Land, recapitulating the events of the two past years—eventful years in which occurred family changes of no small import, including their mother's death, the writer's paralysis and broken health, the seizure of his goods by creditors, and, *mirabile dictu!* his "conversion" to Christianity on the New Year's Day of 1832.

> "PECKHAM RYE COMMON,
> "*22nd. April,* 1834.

"MY DEAR BROTHER,—I find among a heap of papers which I may never have health or spirits to sort, a letter I wrote to you near twelve months ago, to acquaint you with our Mother's death. It was then a great effort with me to write, for my faculties were stunned by a paralytic stroke in the January preceding, which deprived me in an instant of the use of my right side, and for many weeks an hour of further life was not with me a probability.

"The blow impaired my memory, and even now I have not recovered the recollection of many occurrences, and I continue to forget things I did an hour ago. In a far worse state, I received the intelligence, on the 20th of April last, that our Mother had died that morning, and unfit as I was to go to Percival

Street, I yet went thither and with all the ability I could muster, arranged for her funeral. I returned home to suffer consequences from such exertion, which I had not anticipated, and my wife went to the funeral.

" Before this event, I found myself in a furnished lodging in Camberwell, to which I had been removed in a helpless state from Gracechurch Street, and while in that state, the property of the family had been taken possession of by creditors of the business, and finally I was stripped of every atom I possessed in the world ; dispossessed of a home to return to, my family dispersed, and I without a friend I could look to, but Almighty God, who had been my merciful support throughout my affliction.

" In my deep sorrows, He and He alone has been my helper. This language from me will be new to you, but you will understand it better than I did at one time.

" For more than two years—before God in His providence laid His hand upon me, I had been led to seek Him, if haply I might find Him, and I was drawn to earnest and anxious prayer, to be enabled to pray aright ; at the same time reading intently in the Scriptures, yet comprehending little of what I read, for I sought the conviction of my natural understanding, and missed ground, at every step, for want of faith, and through ignorance of the way. The Almighty, however, was dealing with me, and ever and anon, I had gleams of light upon His blessed Word, which showed me the darkness in which I groped, and caused me to pray for further illumination.

" I picked up a little book, ' Scougal's Life of God in the Soul of Man,' which was very useful to me, but, above all, ' Cecile's Remains,' which had been presented to me by a Quaker gentleman from the country in 1825, upon the express condition that I would read it, and which I had read. I read it again with other eyes, so that it scarcely seemed the same book.

" I had not been accustomed to attend a place of worship, but shortly after my residence commenced in

Gracechurch Street, I went regularly to the Parish Church of Allhallows, Lombard Street, and in most of the supplications in the Church Liturgy, my heart unfeignedly concurred during the service. The pulpit was not ill filled, but to me it was not *well* filled. I wanted something more than the simple, plain discourse of a well-intentioned clergyman. I wanted food, and came away comparatively hungry.

"At length, on New Year's Day, 1832, the first time I had deviated from Allhallows, I sent the children into the Church, and passed on, not knowing or determining into what place I should go, but thinking of going to Surrey Chapel, I went down Fish Street Hill, until coming to Eastcheap. It struck me that as Mr. Clayton had left the Weigh-House, somebody worth hearing must have succeeded him. I had been there only once, about thirty-five years before, and making my way upstairs, got in just before the text was given out.

"Through the Minister, Mr. Binney, a startling summons was delivered to me in the course of the sermon, and I came away with my mind disturbed, but deeply solemnised. I must be brief. In a very short time it pleased God to break down my self-will, and enable me to surrender my heart to Him. I read His word with prayer for His light upon it, and I seemed to know, though I could not comprehend, to feel, though I could not understand, its truth. To my wonder, everything appeared changed—the world and its pleasures, literature and its choicest works, had lost their charms—in short, I found that I myself was changed, and the mystery of salvation, through the blood of Christ, God made manifest in the flesh, is to me, through the eye of faith, and by the power of grace, a precious truth, by which my rebellious will has been subjugated, and my heart reconciled to God. . . .

"Your affectionate Brother,
"WILLIAM HONE."

On January 27, 1832, Hone was stricken with paralysis whilst attending the service at the Weigh

House, the visitation being so severe that he was long denied the privilege of Mr. Binney's ministry, only once being able to walk so far from his house at Peckham Rye until the June of the following year.

With one class of readers, and a very large one too, the character of William Hone, from this epoch in his career, will probably gain in its attractiveness ; it is not improbable, however, there may be others with whom it will lose.

We have seen William Hone a strong man of independent thought, confident in his own opinions ; we have esteemed him as the father of a family pursuing his daily avocations with an industry that never flagged, and often with an enthusiasm in which his manifold cares and responsibilities were for the time forgotten ; we have admired him for the active part he played in public life, and particularly for his unflinching attitude in a position of peril, as the champion of popular liberties.

Hone was now long turned fifty years of age, and his life so far—as men count such things—had been a failure. Bankrupt in estate and broken in health, with the heavy responsibilities of a family still resting upon his shoulders, what outlook had he on life? What hope did he possess for the future? Would his old friends come to his assistance again? Or, did he not feel that by his incorrigible commercial incompetence he had wearied their patience, that he had completely exhausted their indulgence? Who shall say what his feelings were when he was now casting about for a new anchorage? Was he seeking new friends, or was he realising that there was some other support, some more abiding source of comfort, which hitherto he had always missed? Who shall judge him?

"*Aug.* 15*th.* 1834.

"MY DEAR MR. HONE,—There is amongst us a cordial desire to meet your wish, and to receive you as a Brother in the Lord. The reason for our not immediately and instantly acting, consists not in any want of confidence in your profession and feelings, but first, my wish to associate some of your family with you ; and second, in a feeling of the expediency, in a case like yours, of a little more than ordinary delay, for the sake of outsiders' opinion, seeing that the same act in a Dissenting Church, is looked upon as more important, and as implying more, than in some other institutions that might be named. . . .

"Your Friend,
"T. BINNEY."

In a further letter on the subject Mr. Binney refers by name to the married daughter: —

MY DEAR MR. HONE,—Tell your daughter Emma, from me, that I have no hesitation about the propriety of her wishes being met, and that if any delay may for a little time arise, it will be from the desire that she should be accompanied in her admission to the Church, by those whose presence on such an occasion would add much to the pleasure and impressiveness of the service.

" My wish is to associate some of your family with you—not only Emma—but those others whom I have seen, and who are not so far forward, or so well known to me, as either you or she ; and secondly in the feeling of the expediency in a case like yours (which your own good sense will see exists) of a little more than ordinary delay, for the sake of other people's opinion—for the sake also of the Church, and of Christianity too. We feel that you would be glad that there should be everything that would command respect, and nothing to provoke the remark or observation of those that are without. I shall hope, however, soon to see you, and both resume this subject, and hear how you are proceeding."

Commenting on the foregoing letter, Hone writes thus to his daughter, Mrs. Hemsley: —

" Well, my dear child, this is on Mr. Binney's part praiseworthy circumspection—he owes this caution to his Church, and is bound to pursue it as its Pastor. There is nothing in it to discourage, but much to invite us to hold on, without shrinking or impatience. It is the Christian's duty to wait in patience, and it is my duty to exhort you to perseverance in faith and prayer, and in communion with God—communion with a Church is secondary to this. However we may both desire for ourselves, our desires go forth too, for your dear Mother and sisters, that they too may be united, if it please God, as I pray it may, in the visible fellowship of a Christian community, and sure I am that it will increase the happiness of you and myself, that they should go with us—that neither you nor I should go alone, with the feeling that we have left some behind us in our impatience, to whom our hearts are knit, and whose hearts may feel that we have hastened to attain for ourselves, while disregarding their desire also to attain the object of our common hope, a Christian association.

" Your affectionate Father,

" W.. HONE."

Dr. Binney now begins to put the matter in formal shape, and invites Hone to prepare a " statement."

Monday Evening,
" *Oct.* 22*nd.* 1834.

" MY DEAR SIR,—I believe you know our mode of proceeding at the admission of persons to the Church— the candidates remain in the vestry, while the Church receives some statement satisfying it of the genuine profession, so far as we can judge, of the individuals desiring admission. Your case is peculiar, and will excite no ordinary interest ; and it has been thought by some, that if you would draw up some brief statement of the dealings of God with yourself, and the progress of religion in your family, it would be a satisfaction to many who will wish to hear more in such a case than in ordinary ones, and who know nothing of you but your name. To others it appears more eligible to make use of extracts from the letters I have in my possession, as they would be seen not to be written

for an occasion like that before us. I thought it best
to state both views—I shall feel that I am quite
furnished with the papers I have, but if you should be
disposed to take the trouble of putting down a few
things for next Sunday evening, and allow me the
liberty of using it—in whole or part—with anything I
have, as may appear best, I shall be obliged. If you
should feel that it would be a satisfaction to your own
mind to have the recollection of furnishing as full and
satisfactory a statement to the Church, of your change
of views and feelings as possible—then, prepare it, and
it shall be used.

" Many know you as the ' notorious ' Mr. Hone—
many, I mean, of our people—they would thus know you
as the humble, the believing, and the converted, bearing
his willing testimony to the power of God's grace—Consult your own mind and feelings.

Praying for every spiritual blessing to rest richly
upon you and yours.

" I am, my dear Sir,

" Very truly your Friend,

" T. BINNEY."

Hone was by no means reluctant to comply, and the
" statement " was duly prepared by him. This document,
not unnaturally, was looked upon by the family as one
of considerable importance, and they were much concerned in after-years when it was thought to be lost.
Miss Matilda Hone interviewed Rev. T. Binney, just
before the death of the latter, respecting its where-
abouts, and writes : —

" Mr. Binney said : ' There is a statement that your
father gave me, and which I read at the most impressive
Church meeting I ever experienced. Why, your mother
and sisters were there ; you must have been present.
I shall never forget that evening.' I told him that was
one object of my visit, and wished to know if it might
be printed. " I will have the Church Books searched,
hauled over ; of course if it is there, you had better have

the original, or rather a copy of it from the Church Books to ensure correctness."

Search was made, the original was found, and from it this copy is now made. It is closely written on four sides of foolscap, in Hone's neat hand. Either from a psychological or from a religious aspect, it is a remarkable document ; it is retrospective, it is introspective, and in every way peculiarly characteristic of the man. Accompanying it, also in Hone's handwriting, but on another sheet of blue post-letter paper, is the formal list of candidates for admission to the Church. It has actually gone through the post, addressed : —

" For
    " The Rev. Thomas Binney,
                    " Kennington Common,"

and bears the post-office date—" Ja. 3. 18 (Paid) 35."

" A STATEMENT upon which WILLIAM HONE humbly presumes to claim fellowship with the
             Church of God.

" My life has been crowded with incidents, none of which can be particularised without extending this paper beyond the limits obviously prescribed to it.
" When the promulgation of what was called the ' New Philosophy ' disturbed many a happy home, I was in my boyhood. At sixteen years of age, with feelings alive to every quick-coming event, consequent upon the Revolution in France, and with curiosity awake to every revived opinion denominated new, I quitted my paternal roof to work my way in the world. To my young eyes all seemed fair and beautiful. The New Philosophers prophesied a coming reign of universal philanthropy and happiness, and the downfall of superstition. In common with many other youths I learned from their writings that Religion was a childish dream, the Bible a fable-book, and that all

institutions for religious purposes were mere devices of the crafty to enslave the ignorant.   I became so imbued with this wretched lore, that I should not have believed a sincere believer in Christianity existed, if I had not known, beyond the possibility of mistake, that my own Father was one.   I am reluctant to say how far my desperate unbelief extended, and it is needless to relate by what degrees it lessened in the course of years ; but it may be an instructive fact, a kind of lesson to be remembered by parents, and by young persons who may become parents, that at different periods of my subsequent life, some of the little religious sayings impressed upon my memory in infancy, would suddenly arise to recollection, apparently uncaused, accompanied by unwelcome thoughts, occasioning for a few minutes certain misgivings.   I have sometimes been startled on the recurrence of some short passage of Scripture, which I had not remembered for years and which seemed almost inaudibly uttered in my Father's voice.   At other times I have been surprised upon finding myself humming a tune and stanza of one of Watts's Songs, until that moment forgotten from infancy. Frequently, of later years, have occurred passages which my Father had been accustomed to cite, particularly these—' My son, give me thy heart.'—' Train up a child in the way he should go, and when he is old he will not depart from it.'   The frequent remembrance of these passages forced upon me very serious reflections.

" For the sake of brevity I refrain from specifying any of the circumstances which have marked a life of self-will, waywardness, and disquietude.   After forty years of incessant turmoil, and vain endeavour to derive happiness from objects of sense, and the usual sources of intellectual gratification, I have attained to that peace which the world can neither give nor take away. In my struggles formerly, I struck out into the gulf-stream of Politics, and drifted into its very vortex. There was no happiness for me in that whirlpool, and with exhausting efforts I succeeded in reaching the pleasant region of Literature.

" There I strove to solace myself with books, and renewed an old and fascinating intimacy with works of art. Still I was uneasy. My heart refused to be quieted even in country retreats, among calm and peaceful scenery, and when I sought to pacify it by walking out in the turbulence and uproar of tempests, I did but ' shift the place, and keep the pain.' My pen had been engaged upon political frivolities, and, under feverish excitement of mind, upon something worse, as regards its tendency in a religious light. I resolved to employ it in efforts for general instruction and recreation. My labours in that way were heavy and unceasing, and the fatigue increased my gloom. In that state, I longed for the simplicity of my excellent father's mind. He was living, and he was happy. Had the world been mine, I would have exchanged it for his serenity.

" Long before the recurrence of those events which rendered my name familiar to the world, I had so acquainted myself with the Bible as to have acquired reverence for it, as a book containing facts more extraordinary, and infinitely more wisdom than I could gather from history, or all the writings of all the philosophers. In my estimation their philosophy shrunk to nothing in comparison with the vast moral wisdom of the scriptures. I had read, and understood the controversy between the Church of Rome and the Reformed Churches, and detected and detested the fraud of papal usurpation. This reading led me into much of Theology and Controversy upon other points. I now rushed into Biblical criticism, and with this addition to my former reading ; I fancied I had constructed for myself a satisfactory religion, and, had I been pressed to the declaration, I should have conscientiously affirmed myself a Rational Christian. According to my comprehension of the Saviour's character, I admired it, and I believed as much as I could of his Miracles. There was a glimmer of light in my head, but no warmth in my heart. I conceived I could be quite religious enough at home on Sunday, while reading the New Testament, without going to any

Chapel. It was a maxim with me that ' Conduct is Worship,' and to do what is right is all that God requires. I tried to persuade myself that all this was perfectly true, yet I had secret fears that there was something more in religion than I had found out. My suspicions were speedily verified. Domestic troubles had accumulated upon me, and under the weight of sudden calamity, I needed powerful support ; in the storm of my mind I turned to Rational Religion for help—it blew away from me, like a heap of chips in a hurricane.

" The successive four years of my life were passed in hurryings, and in stillnesses which afforded me much leisure. Retrospective views of my circumstances were painful, and my conceptions of what the future might bring forth dismayed me. I refer now to my temporal concerns. The dangers I would have shunned, I ran upon. I considered, and it struck me forcibly that there must have been more than common causes beyond those that were seen, to operate upon me such a series of misfortunes. From the moment that this view stood out, in its reality, I took courage, and endeavoured to disentangle my affairs, firmly believing that whatever might be the issue, Providence would order all things right. This was the first time I had conceived of Providence interfering in such a way. In the midst of this, the trouble of my soul, in relation to itself, drove me to earnestly seek God in strong and fervent ejaculations—I had desired to pray but could not, and now, every night upon my pillow before I slept, and every morning before I rose, I supplicated God in silence, that He would teach me how to pray, and what to pray for. I persevered until, in time, I went upon my knees. Meanwhile I endeavoured to understand the New Testament, and prayed to God to show me the meaning of what I read. Usually, at these times, I read rapidly, in great agitation and left off confusedly.

" I loved my wife and children as my own life-blood—the sight of them was terrible to me. My dear wife, whom I had married when we were both young,

I had detached from attending upon the worship of God, to which she had been brought up by a pious mother, and my children had neither been instructed by me in any religious duty, nor had I taken them to a place of worship. My reflections upon these defaults were insupportable. Latterly, however, I had led the four younger ones into a church, with the hope that their two elder sisters who were adults, and at home with me, might follow. While doing this my mind became less distressed, but not less anxious. I heard nothing from the minister in the church-pulpit but what I assented to—still, however, it was not satisfying—it served only to increase desires for something more.

" On New Year's Day, 1832, being Sunday, I left my children at the church-door to enter by themselves, while I turned off, not knowing whither to go, yet hoping to hear somewhere an experienced faithful-hearted preacher. Until I got to the corner of Eastcheap, I forgot the Weigh-house ; I then remembered that I had been there about eight-and-thirty years before, and there, by the Providence of Almighty God I was led once more. I heard Mr. Binney—my conscience admitted every reproving sentence in his discourse applicable to my own case, and on going home I retired immediately to my own room and fervently prayed. From that time it pleased God to keep me in private supplication. During about three months in that year I was in temporary lodgings at Kingsland, and when unable to get to the Weigh-house, I attended the faithful ministry of Mr. John Campbell— with that exception throughout the whole of 1832, I was regularly at the Weigh-house.

" Before going to Kingsland in 1832 I perceived in myself a growing indifference to the public occurrences of that eventful year, and books and persons I had formerly liked, became distasteful to me. I could not write with pleasure upon any of my usual subjects, and with difficulty I maintained a brief conversation upon literary topics which I had been accustomed to treat fluently. A change had come over me for which

I could not account. I had plenty of domestic troubles but my heart was at rest, and my mind stayed, and I wondered.

" I was soon led, however, to believe, and I now firmly believe, that at that time Divine grace had said to my tumultuous heart, ' Peace, be still.' I had been accustomed to pray with extreme fervour that God, of His infinite mercy, would accept my confessions of sin, grant me true repentance, subdue me wholly to Himself, and do with me as He pleased. I continued to find relief and happiness in constant prayer. I supplicated mentally while I walked the streets, and this I continued to do after I left Kingsland, praying in my heart all day long, while fully occupied in the perplexing concerns of my daughter's business, which had necessarily devolved upon me, in consequence of her having been seized with a brain fever.

" Briefly—it pleased God to reconcile me to Himself. I had penitently yielded to Him, as I was, a penitent sinner, having nothing to offer to Him but a contrite heart, softened by grace, through faith in the atoning blood of the Saviour. I have a hope beyond hope, even an assured peace in believing, that if it please God to keep me, as He has hitherto kept me, I may be testified as an example of the Power of Divine Truth upon the Heart. At the beginning of the last year, 1833, the Almighty laid His hand upon me while I was engaged in His worship, and suddenly suspended my mental and bodily functions ; and while under that infirmity I was visited with heavy calamities of another kind ; but in these distresses I have been enabled to feel and declare that ' He does all things well.'

" I humbly thank Him that my faith has never wavered. Every infliction from His hand has driven me closer to Him, and been sanctified by His holy spirit to enlarge my views of His abundant mercies, and ne'er-failing Providence. I praise His holy name that He enables me to declare ' It is good for me that I have been afflicted.' What I deemed the desolation of my family has been, by the order of His

Providence, a gracious answer to my prayers and tears
in their behalf. The mother of my children, my dear
wife, now dearer to me in our declining years than
when I first loved her in my youth, recalls with fond
recollections the religious teachings of her infancy.
When we were children we had been accustomed to
go together to the house of God, and now, after an
estrangement of nearly thirty years from attendance
upon His service, we again together turn our feet
thitherward—and the countenance of our Heavenly
Father shines upon us. He has subdued us to Himself,
and each of us seeks union with the Saviour's Church.
With us, too, comes one of our daughters with her
husband, whose attendance upon Mr. Binney's ministry
has issued in the submission of their hearts to their
Saviour and their God. And with us come also three
of our other daughters, in whom, I believe, the dealings of God with their father wrought astonishment
and caused them to enquire, ' How can this thing
be? ' They have successively fallen under God's
messages through the same awakening ministry at the
Weigh-house. It is the belief of each of us that we
come in obedience to the heavenly call, each of us
praying in behalf of all, that the love of God, our
Father, and the grace of our Lord and Saviour Jesus
Christ and the fellowship of the Holy Spirit, may be
with us now, and henceforth. Amen. Even so."

The list of candidates which accompanied this confession of faith, also in Hone's clerkly handwriting,
was as follows:—

" WEIGH-HOUSE,
" *Tuesday, 30th December*, 1834.
ADMITTED MEMBERS.
WILLIAM HONE, of Peckham Rye Common, Parish of
St. Giles, Camberwell, County Surrey. Born
at Bath 3rd. June 1780, and baptized in the
parish church there.
Married at St. Anne's, Soho, by banns, 19th
July 1800, to

SARAH, his present wife, formerly Sarah Johnson : Born in Southwark 30th. Nov. 1781—baptized some years afterwards by the late Rev. Rowland Hill, at Surrey Chapel.

Four daughters of William and Sarah Hone Admitted Members, *viz.*

SARAH, born 20th. July 1801—married 13th. July, 1822 to Jacob Henry Burn, who is now living.

FANNY, born 5th. April, 1803—married 29th. April 1826 to Thomas Hemsley, hereafter mentioned.

MATILDA, born 26th. July 1805—unmarried—She, and her two sisters above mentioned, were baptized in their infancy.

EMMA, born in the Parish of Christ Church, County Surrey, 14th. March, 1814—unmarried, and baptized by Mr. Binney at the Weigh-house, on the above day, previous to her Admission. Also, three other daughters of William and Sarah Hone Baptized by Mr. Binney, viz.—

ROSE, born Parish of St. Bride's, Fleet Street, City of London 27th. August, 1818.

ELLEN, born . . . same parish . . . 31st. March, 1822.

ALICE, born . . . same Parish . . . 8th. December 1825.

Likewise a son-in-law of William and Sarah Hone, Baptized and Admitted Member, viz.—

THOMAS HEMSLEY of King Street, Tower Hill, in the Liberty of the Tower, Parish of St. Botolph, Aldgate, Middlesex, Optician (son of Thomas Hemsley, late of the same place, deceased, by his wife Elizabeth, formerly Elizabeth Seaton), born at Newington Butts, County Surrey, 11th. June 1798—married Fanny Hone, as above. Also the three children of the said Thomas and Fanny Hemsley were baptized by Mr. Binney, viz.—

Thomas, born Thursday 16th. August, 1827.

William, born Wednesday 27th. May, 1829.

Fanny, born Sunday 20th. February, 1831.

All born in the Liberty of the Tower, St. Botolph, Aldgate, Middlesex."

XXV

LIFE AT PECKHAM

LATE in the year 1833 Hone and his family removed to Rose Cottage, Peckham Rye Common, and spent three years in this pleasant spot, remaining there for several months after he had become sub-editor of the *Patriot*, and only leaving it when it was found that the journey to town was too great a tax upon his strength. He then removed to the office of the paper, 5, Bolt Court.

The few years spent at Peckham, being amidst pleasant surroundings, seem to have filled him and his family with happy memories, which they did not fail to record in a number of reminiscent notes left by them.

For a few months in 1833, Mr. and Mrs. Hone, with their younger children, had lodged at Woodland Cottages, Grove Lane, Camberwell, to recruit his health after the stroke of paralysis. It was there he became acquainted with Miss Rolleston, who was his next-door neighbour.

Once more in a permanent home of his own, and particularly in surroundings of a more congenial character than those of a City coffee-house, the patient began to mend, though his progress was slow.

A visit to Grove Lane, Camberwell, in the June of 1833, is described in *Notes and Queries* of the year 1880. The interviewer, an admiring friend, was received in a small back room with glass doors, opening on to a neat garden. Among the *dicta* given forth by Hone on that occasion, was the futility of history as a teacher, that it was a fallacy to imagine that nations would be taught by it. He acknowledged his indebtedness to De Foe's " Time's Telescope " for the idea of his " Every-Day Book." The visit was repeated a fortnight later, when Hone presented his visitor with a rough likeness of himself, drawn in pencil by George Cruikshank.

William Hone's personal appearance in 1833 has been described in *Notes and Queries* by his friend Fuller Russell, who says : —

" He was rather corpulent, and dressed very plainly ; he had a lofty forehead, keen eyes, grey and scanty locks, and a very expressive countenance."

Another description is given of him by Samuel Carter Hall in his " Retrospect of a Long Life," ii. p. 29 : —

" Hone was a small and insignificant-looking man ; mild, kindly, and conciliatory in manner, the very opposite of the traditional demagogue. He must have read a vast deal ; there is evidence of that in his memorable defences as well as in the books he edited and bequeathed as valuable legacies to posterity."

In the summer season it seems that Sunday-school treats on the Common were of frequent occurrence, and it was the delight of the Hones to supply the water for making the tea from their well, though the pump was usually kept fastened to prevent tramps making too free use of it. Miss Rolleston writes of these sunny days, under date 1834 : —

" I found him there, happier than ever, boiling the tea-kettle over his cottage hearth for the rejoicing party of a Sunday School Anniversary on Peckham Rye, running backwards and forwards with it followed by his own little girls, with all the glee of a child."

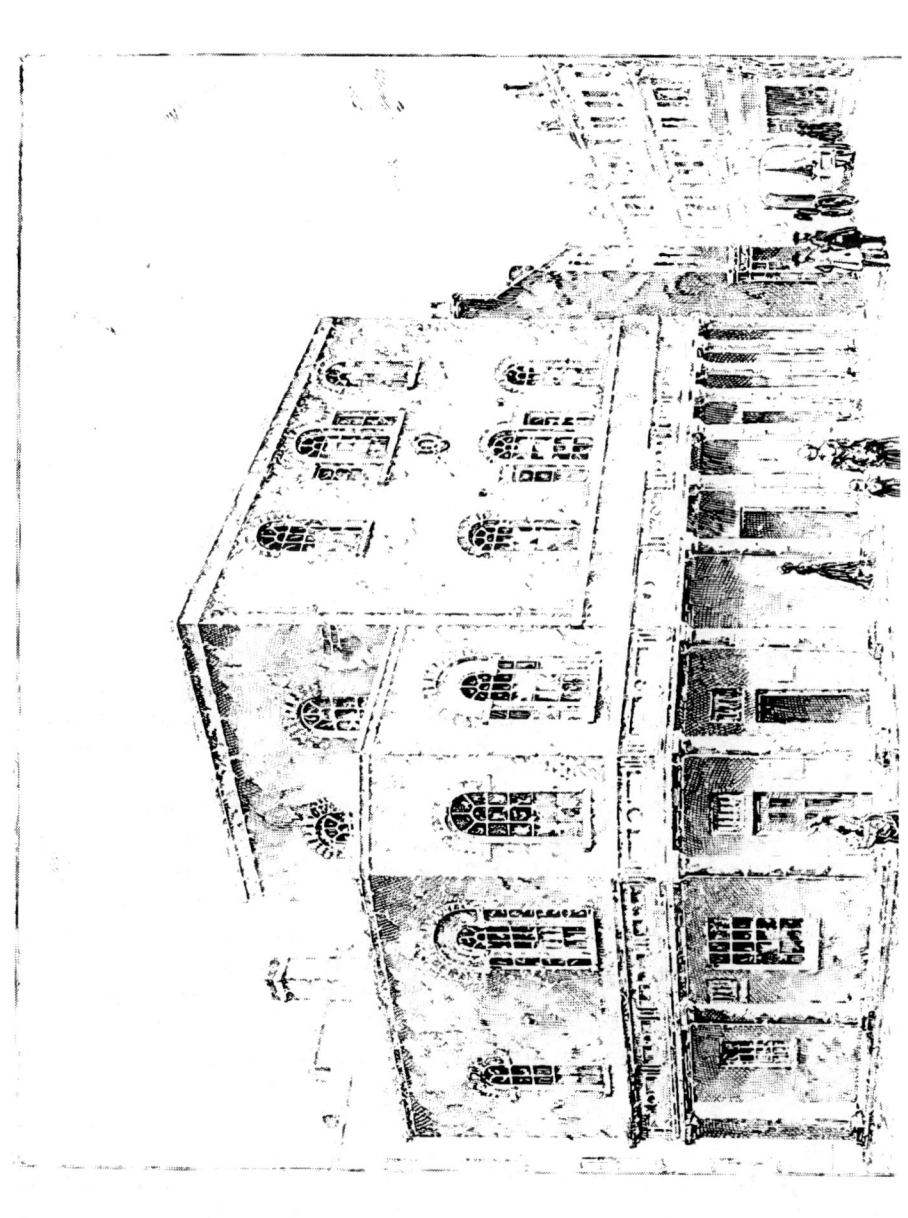

The oft-repeated statement that William Hone became a preacher is without foundation. The only occasion on which he held forth to a congregation was at a camp meeting on Peckham Common in the August of 1835. The incident is fully and circumstantially set forth in a letter, addressed to one of Hone's daughters, very many years after, by the Rev. George Verrall, who was a witness of what took place. He was afraid he might break down, but when once started, had delivered a short and simple address on the existence of a God in forcible style.

Progress in the institution of family devotions is duly reported to his spiritual adviser:—

" *June*, 1834.

" MY DEAR SIR,—' Faith cometh by hearing, and hearing by the Word of God.' I bless God for drawing me to the hearing of your sermon on this text—on the first Sunday in the year 1832.

". . . I left Gracechurch Street, and went to lodge with my wife and two little ones, on Kingsland Green ; while there I heard the Rev. John Campbell, who, in a remarkable discourse, opened to my view the eternal power and Godhead of Christ. That discourse opened my eyes, and raised my mind from its sleep of death in Unitarianism. . . .

" You may remember that it was whilst I was listening to you at the Weigh-House, on Sunday, the 27th of January last year, that I was struck by the hand of God with paralysis, and carried into your vestry as one dead. I have only been able to hear you once since, until yesterday, when I walked from this place (Peckham Rye Common) with my wife and one of our little daughters.

" While in this quiet and remote place, we have attended at Mr. Powell's Baptist Meeting in the Rye Lane. It is a small Church, of poor and despised people.

" Up to that time, much as I desired help from God to commence His worship in my family, I had been restrained through false shame. My wife and

21

children were strangers to my voice in prayer. I came home from hiring the servant, and telling my wife that I feared we were leading the life of heathens in our family, proposed that we should attempt to hold morning and evening worship. My dear wife was affected to tears, and that very evening we commenced. When my sons and daughters have been with us from Town, I have persevered in this course. Mark what has happened—my two daughters, who were indifferent to religious truth, are now under strong conviction. Surely God, who has mercifully subdued me, is carrying on His gracious work in the hearts of my children.

> " I remain, my dear Sir,
> " With great affection,
> " Yours most respectfully and sincerely,
> " W. HONE.

" The REV. THOMAS BINNEY."

Change of thought induces a change of custom, even of Christmas customs:—

> " PECKHAM RYE COMMON,
> " 24*th. Dec.* 1834.

" MY DEAR SIR,—It has hitherto been a custom with me and my wife, to have all our children about us on Christmas Day—that is, as many as were within reach. This year the family meeting is to be at my son-in-law, Thomas Hemsley's, on Tower Hill. With the exception of Samuel (who is in the Blue Coat School), we expect all will be present, and with them the annual turkey, the seventeenth, which of custom, comes from John Childs of Bungay.

" Aforetime, the day has been with us, one of rude merriment—a noisy carnival.

" We meet to-morrow under circumstances which will solemnise our cheerfulness. I feel assured of being able to get into the Stage Coach, and reach the Weigh-House in the morning, when I expect to meet all my family, with the exception of little Samuel, in the House of Prayer—

> ' Lord how delightful 'tis to see
> A whole assembly worship Thee.'

—anon we may have a little chat about the superstitions surrounding the keeping of Christmas. Our good old Puritan forefathers loved plum-porridge, but refused to eat it at Christmas for fear of symbolising with Episcopacy—their successors forget, or neglect, the self-denying obligation, and the receipt for plum-porridge having been lost, they unscrupulously, at this season, eat plum-pudding. Well, let every man be persuaded in his own mind.

"Forgive my smiling on paper. . . .

"I remain, my dear Sir,

"Yours faithfully,

"W. HONE."

A letter written from Peckham Rye, in February, 1834, to his friend John Scott, presents Hone in the character of an applicant for assistance from the Literary Fund:—

"Your intimation of Mr. Gaspey's intention to support my proposed application to the Literary Fund Society is very acceptable, and most kind—for, in truth, moving about is disturbing to my limbs, and the purport of my visits painful to represent—and now, such proceedings on my part are almost out of the question. On my return home Mrs. H., who has been my most solicitous and affectionate nurse under the calamity with which it has pleased God to visit me, I found rather unwell, and in less than half an hour, after putting her feet into warm water I had the utmost difficulty in getting her into bed, where she turned delirious, and whence she has never since removed. This was on Saturday, and you may imagine my situation in a lone place, with no one in the house but my three little girls. I am worn down by fatigue. My poor wife's illness proceeds from over-exertion and anxiety under our exigence. To-day the fever is abating, and my utmost care must be directed to keep her up from exhaustion, and prevent its termination in Typhus. You see how much I have on my hands and heart.

"The Rev. Mr. Lambert, of the old church, Camber-

well, has, unknown to me, interested Mr. Harrison of
the Literary Fund Committee, and will place in that
gentleman's hands my statement for the purpose of
being introduced by him at the Meeting on Wednesday.
I avail myself of your friendship to say, that there is
a way in which you ' can be of use ' in this matter. So
far, and so long, as you have had a personal knowledge
of me, be so good as to certify it in writing, with that
favourable opinion of my character on which I presume
the esteem you have of me is founded. I should have
imagined that one who has so moved in the world as it
has been my lot to do, might fairly be supposed of
good character—that the absence of assault in that particular, from a host of assailants on public grounds,
would be circumstantial evidence that my reputation
presented no point of weakness. I am told, however,
that I should have testimony to my ' respectability,'
in a moral sense—now, if you have ever heard anything
ill of me, it will be proper that you should be silent,
but as I believe you have not, because I think it is not
in the power of a living being to urge with truth anything to my prejudice, so from what you may have
observed and heard of me the other way I venture to
bespeak your good opinion. Such a paper in the hands
of your friend (who I am happy through you to consider in this matter my friend) Mr. Gaspey, to be
produced by him on Wednesday, I shall esteem a
service. I believe I could command a hamper of
such testimonials, but one from you would be evidence
to him, and his knowledge of you would enable him
to hand in such a paper with confidence. My friend
Mr. Charles Lamb is the only man who knows me
intimately—all my other intimacies have been with
books—but I fear from Miss Lamb's illness, which is
of a very peculiar nature, he may be ill himself, and
though I have written to him at Enfield, it is just
possible I may not hear from him in answer. As you
will see Mr. Gaspey, you will perhaps intimate to
him my utter need—I find I owe £40 within a pound
or so—the whole of it presses, for it is to little trades-
people, and for rent and taxes to Christmas last. If

I am enabled to discharge that amount, I think it possible that I may scramble on with my pen, and under the restorative influence of that Power which affected me, be enabled to pick up something for the future support of my family. Already I feel the vivifying effects of the weather, and I think this epistle may warrant my belief that my pen may yet indite a good matter. I have not written such a letter since I have been here. I am sorry to say, that, for a particular reason, I do not pay its postage. With the kindest esteem."

Thomas Gaspey was a well-known author ; among other works he wrote " The Lollards," " The Witch Finder," and " Other Times ; or, the Monks of Leadenhall."

William Hone, having seriously taken on religion, and found immense spiritual strength and consolation in it, was not unnaturally looked upon by the devout of his own faith as a brand plucked from the burning. As such his soul's " experiences " could not but be regarded as peculiarly valuable. It is therefore not surprising that he was frequently urged, almost importuned, to write the narrative of his life and conversion.

Exactly why William Hone never wrote the narrative of his conversion may be left to conjecture. It would seem that on reflection he had no relish for figuring as the subject of a tract. The fact remains that when he died, in 1842, the promised tract was not forthcoming, much to the disappointment of his religious friends. The same reluctance may have been part of the reason why the autobiography of his later years was never accomplished.

The first to rush into the breach was his admiring neighbour, Miss Rolleston, who soon after his departure wrote to Miss E. Hone: " Is there any autobiography left of your dear father? He told me once that he had a quantity of rough sketches by him. Does any one contemplate a memoir of him? " Possibly this officious lady was not overwhelmed with grief to learn the truth, for with evident zest she set about remedying the omission without delay.

To her precipitancy must be attributed the fact that a full and authentic biography of William Hone has not appeared till now. Without further consulting the family or submitting the proofs of her writings to Mrs. Hone she forthwith published a lengthy' pamphlet, entitled " Some Account of the Conversion from Atheism to Christianity of the late William Hone." A second edition, reprinted from the *Loughborough Telegraph* newspaper, with additions, appeared in 1848, and a revised issue, with " further particulars," in 1853.

While the work contained a number of interesting details, there were certain errors of statement in it to which the Hone family took exception and refused their countenance. The same objection applied, to a lesser extent, to a similar pamphlet which was written by J. E. Howard, F.R.S., for the Religious Tract Society. It is Tract No. 1,042, entitled " Recollections of William Hone, Thirty Years an Atheist, afterwards a Happy Christian," and is adorned with a woodcut depicting William Hone inquiring of a studious child with the Bible, " My little girl, what are you reading? "

XXVI

SUB-EDITOR OF THE *PATRIOT*

In December, 1835, William Hone became sub-editor of the *Patriot* at a salary of £2 a week, and a few months afterwards took up his residence at the office of the paper, 5, Bolt Court.

Although convenient to him in one respect, it was by no means a desirable place of residence for an invalid. In October, 1836, he complains that he feels worn out—" the reporters were here in the house all night, and all night the doors were slamming between the goings to and fro of them, and the compositors in the news-office ; and broken rest unnerves me."

The events of his life at this period are best gleaned from the following letter, addressed to a friend, which Hone wrote from Peckham Rye, March 26, 1836 :—

" Soon after I last saw you Mr. Woodthorp, the Town Clerk, proposed to me that I should undertake a business which had been referred to him by the Court of Common Council, namely, a revision of certain evidence taken before the Thames Navigation and Port of London Committee, together with a statement of the Proceedings of the Committee relating to the Navigation of the River Thames, and certain alleged obstructions to the Commerce of the Port—an Inquiry which had been entered on about three years ago in consequence of complaints and communications from Sir John Hall, on behalf of the St. Katharine Dock Company. For this purpose the Town Clerk gave me his room, and

I proceeded to bring into order a mass of documentary papers, and then set in doggedly to the labour of preparing the whole, which, by a vote of the Common Council, was ordered to be printed.

" Soon after Lord Mayor's day, Mr. Thomas Challis and Mr. H. Dunn of the Borough Road School came to see me there, and proposed to me to undertake the Sub-Editorship of the *Patriot* weekly journal. I had been prepared to expect such a proposal from conversations I had had with Mr. Binney, and accepted the offer.

" My first *Patriot* appeared on the 9th. of December, 1835, since when I have attended at the office daily. I had been led to expect that the labour would be trifling, and that my attendance from 10 to 3 daily would afford me, within those hours, some leisure. Such leisure, however, I have not yet found, for the business of the paper has often detained me at Bolt Court until midnight.

" Meanwhile I went to the Town Clerk's at every spare hour, sometimes between 7 and 8 in the morning, and after leaving Bolt Court when I sometimes worked at the Navigation Evidence also until midnight. I was carrying on two businesses, therefore, at the same time.

" In a day or two after the opening of Parliament, Mr. Robert Thompson obtained a committee of the House of Commons to enquire and report on the Navigation of the Port, and this movement on the part of Government rendered nugatory much of my toil. I had gone carefully through the Minute Books of the Thames Navigation Committee for more than three years past, in order to give a history of the proceedings of the City authorities from the earliest period of their enquiry, until its close in October. I had prepared for printing the evidence taken in shorthand, together with an Index for convenient reference. I have been most cautious in avoiding the substitution of any word that would in any degree vary the sense of a speaker's language, but I have suppressed gross vulgarisms and barbarisms, and made Harbourmasters, Lightermen, Pilots, and even Common Councilmen talk something like English.

" During the progress of the whole, I have often risen through the winter at 4 o'clock, and worked, scarcely taking time for breakfast, until I went off by the stage to Town, where I staid late, and returned early the next morning, and so on, day by day.

" After I got into the Index, I had distressing symptoms of having over-laboured. This day week I came home at 3 o'clock, hoping that quiet for the remainder of the day, and the rest of the Sabbath, would restore me. I could not rally at all, and went to bed early. On Sunday I rose about 7, and felt no better. I walked out on the Common, invited by the loveliness of the weather. My youngest daughter and my grandson were with me, and we had walked a few hundred yards when my mind became confused, my sight obscured, and I had general indications of oppression of the brain. Instead of returning home, I managed to get into a stage, and sending the children home, went on to my surgeon's, Mr. Smith, in Gracechurch Street, from whom I got leeches and medicine, and came home under the care of one of my daughters. The next morning I ventured into Town, to the *Patriot* Office, but was compelled to leave—I could do nothing of consequence to the paper. Here I have remained ever since.

" My first effort was to write to Mr. Woodthorpe, apprising him of my situation, and the necessity of my relinquishing the Index, for, paining me as it does to give it up, I feel that to continue it and the *Patriot* would be insanity. For the present, the *Patriot* will give me as much work as I can bear.

" It is important that I should keep that, for although it yields me but £2 a week, yet that comes regularly. The paper ought to afford more, but it does not."

The *Patriot* was established as a weekly newspaper in February, 1832, to represent the religious views and prevailing sentiments of the evangelical Nonconformists, and it at once came to be regarded as the political instructor of the Protestant Dissenters of the

country. It was the champion of "Unfettered Protestantism, Evangelical Truth, and Religious Freedom,"
and did brave work in fighting against Church rates
and the other inequalities and abuses of the times.
Coming into existence in the momentous year of the
Reform Bill, its career was coincident with the era of
parliamentary reform. It took its full share in the
abolition of slavery and in the repeal of the Corn
Laws ; though generally at one with the Whigs, it
was never seduced from the paths of rectitude by Whig
policy, and at all times honestly justified its name.

Of the Free Churches there was scarcely a representative in Parliament at that time ; and their
principles were still struggling for adequate expression
in the Press. In 1836 the *Patriot* was issued twice
a week, a time in its history recalled at a commemora-
tion banquet in 1853 in a speech made by one of the
staff, who said Mr. Josiah Condor, the editor, had

" the co-operation of the celebrated William Hone—a
name that we cannot mention without respect, when
we consider the struggles which he made, and the
honour they conferred on that noble institution trial
by jury. And when, under the ministry of Mr. Binney,
he had been led to renounce his early views and receive
the truths of Christianity, he applied himself with the
greatest diligence and with the most indefatigable
industry to his duties upon the paper. I recollect him
well, and always entertain for his memory the highest
respect. He seemed to my mind to be the very imper-
sonation of indefatigable industry and incorruptible
honesty and integrity. It was after the change from
a weekly to a bi-weekly issue that age and infirmities
compelled the resignation of Mr. Hone."

As a sub-editor Hone does not appear to have
possessed a free hand in the control of the paper's
policy. This is brought out in the matter of the controversy respecting the Scotch Bible monopoly. In

the *Times* of April 12, 1833, had appeared a long letter from J. R. and C. Childs, printers, of Bungay, protesting against a statement of Mr. Spottiswoode (one of the King's Printers) that as far as comparison could be made the price of Bibles and Testaments was less than half the price of other books, and making express reference to certain cheap editions of books published by Messrs. Childs, of Bungay. The letter is too long to quote here, but it cites the fact that Mr. Owen Rees (of the house of Longmans & Co.) had proved before a Parliamentary Committee that a King's Printer's Bible was sold at the same price as an unprivileged book equal in all particulars.

Another and a greater struggle, political as well as religious in its character, came to a head while William Hone was on the staff of the *Patriot*.

The struggle for the abolition of Church Rates extended over a period of nearly forty years, excited the keenest interest throughout the country both in and out of Parliament, and may be described as the greatest fight for religious and civil rights since the passing of the Toleration Act.

Organised opposition to Church Rates began in 1834, when a national convention of Nonconformists demanded their abolition. In that year the first Bill dealing with the matter was introduced into the House of Commons, but was withdrawn on the promise made by Lord John Russell that the Government would deal with the question. This promise was fulfilled by a proposal that the cost of repairing the fabric of Churches should be transferred to the Land Tax, but this was naturally so objectionable to the landowners and farmers—who argued that it would be prejudicial to agriculture—that it was withdrawn.

In 1837 the Government proposed that the Church Rates should cease, and the necessary funds should be obtained from Church lands and pew rents, but the majority in favour in the Commons was so small that nothing more was heard of it. In 1839 and 1840 the advocates of abolition were again defeated.

The part taken by Hone in this agitation was not altogether restricted to wielding the pen of a ready writer and an able advocate. His daughter Matilda was encouraged to employ herself in canvassing for the cause ; and on one occasion he left his desk to interview Sir Francis Burdett. It was the forenoon, and Hone was shown into the baronet's dressing-room whilst he was still at his toilet.

" Well, Hone, what can I do for you? " was the genial greeting he met with. But though he pleaded the Dissenters' cause with all his customary earnestness he could elicit no pledge from the wily old " reformer." It is difficult to estimate Hone's personal influence at this period of his life : Sir Francis probably regarded him as an extinct volcano.

The *Patriot* of February 6, 1837, reported that on Friday, the 3rd of that month, some four hundred delegates from local Church Rate Abolition Societies, from Independent and Baptist Churches in all parts of England, Scotland, and Wales had assembled in London, at the Crown and Anchor Tavern, preparatory to an interview by appointment with the Prime Minister. According to this report the delegates proceeded to Downing Street, and were introduced to Lord Melbourne by Mr. Joseph Hume, M.P. His lordship listened sympathetically to a statement of the grievances under which Dissenters laboured in respect of Church Rates ; and in his reply he concurred in the general principle stated by the speakers, tactfully promising on behalf of the Government that a Bill to deal with the subject would shortly be introduced by Lord John Russell. The promise, vague as it was, evidently satisfied the deputation, who withdrew quite pleased with the result of their efforts ; and at the subsequent meeting at the " Crown and Anchor," where resolutions, both congratulatory and declaratory, were unanimously passed by the delegates before their separation, Mr. John Childs was to the fore among the chief speakers.

At Bungay, in Suffolk, the war against Church Rates had been fought with great pertinacity by the Childs family, and a lengthy correspondence on the subject had passed between Hone and his friend John of that ilk.

Among the last of the letters to pass between the two on this topic was one of those amusing trifles which all famous men gifted with a sense of humour have thrown off in moments of leisure. The date appears to be November 5, 1839, and it runs :—

" DEAR JOHN,
   ' To-morrow never is, if not to-day—
   Time is, was and is as yesterday.'
                                Tuyfelsdrockh, Junr.

' There's Cruden for one ear, and Adams for t'other,
  And each is for both, as you'll have it so—Bother.'
                                   G. Wither, Junr.

" ' Celestial scenery '—' No Church Rates '—come !
  Dick of the Kirk, and John of Bungay, come !
  Secession he, and Nonconforming thee,
  At five o'clock this afternoon to tea.
  One lectured last night on Astronomy ;
  Each talks to-night on Nonconformity ;
  On Leighton, Bastwick, Prynne, who lost their ears
  In Palace Yard, and left their blood and tears
  A legacy to us—not braver they
  Than him, George Fox, the man of yea and nay,
  Of greater suffering, higher principle—he left
  The Hat to witness of him—Sturge anon.

Come at 5—I expect Dr. Dick of the same school.
                    " Thine, dear John,
                         " W. HONE."

Though the missive was nothing more than a whimsically worded invitation to tea, the literary allusiveness makes it really interesting. " Tuyfelsdrockh " was a fictitious German philosopher whom Carlyle has pretended to quote, and G. Wither, jun., was a playful pseudonym and allusion to the fiery Puritan poet, author of " Abuses Whipt and Stript," who sold his estate to raise a troop of horse for the Parliament. The first coined quotation appears to be a parody on Roger Bacon's " Time was, Time is, Time is past," adapted to fit the invitation to tea that day. What Hone meant to convey in the second " quotation " is not quite clear, unless it was to set in antithesis the crack-brained Cruden, author of the Concordance, and the Puritan theologian Thomas Adams. " Celestial scenery " unmistakably relates to the other invited guest, Dr. Dick, who seceded from the Church of Scotland and wrote among other works, scientific and religious, a book bearing the title of " Celestial Scenery." The somewhat obscure allusions in the last line apparently are, first, to the broad-brimmed " hat," of which Fox, the founder of Quakerism, set his sect the fashion ; and, secondly, to the writer's intention of saying, when time and opportunity served, something about the modern Quakerism of Joseph Sturge.

From the spirit of literary playfulness in which the note was penned it might be imagined that the storm of this great controversy had passed over their heads. This was not the case. John Childs writes to Hone, February 7, 1840 :—

" . . . All the people here are going to jollify on the 10th, except myself and Charles ; he is cited to appear in the Ecclesiastical Court of Norwich on that day, the only shop expected to be open, and the constable has a warrant to take my wife's boilers."

And again, more than two years later, he reports the ultimate success of their persistent contumacy :—

" . . . My Brother Charles, has, after a thousand miles travelled between Bungay and Norwich, in between thirty and forty journeys, to defend himself in the *Court Christian*, got a judgment in his favour, with costs, by which decision the Churchwardens of this parish are in a very *con*-siderable fix ! They thought their own Courts would justify them in doing as they listed ! "

Notwithstanding all these efforts the great grievance was not redressed in Hone's day. For more than twenty years after the struggle had to be carried on.

In 1861 the Abolition Bill was rejected by the casting vote of the Speaker, amidst a scene of wildest excitement ; and in 1868 the struggle was closed by the passing of a Bill brought in by Mr. Gladstone.

In theory there is still subsisting a common-law liability in parishioners for " necessary " repairs to the parish church and ornaments of the service, which ought to be discharged by Church Rates, but before the Act of 1868 it had become impracticable to enforce the making of a rate ; and since the Act it is impossible to enforce payment of a rate when made, except in special cases, as where such rates are payable under a statute or contract.

To consider our subject as a *littérateur* is to take the fullest and most comprehensive view of the man possible ; for he was author and publisher, or journalist and editor, the whole of his working life, and a bibliophile, if not a bibliolater, from his earliest to his latest years.

His earliest productions were in verse, and the only one to which his name was attached was a sonnet on November in the *Monthly Visitor* (1797) ; the earlier one he called " The Contrast," produced when a child of twelve, and presented to the Society at the Crown and Anchor Tavern, has already been mentioned (pp. 44-5).

Soon after his marriage he contributed papers on political economy to the *Monthly Magazine,* and became the conductor of an established review.

Had his energies as a writer, wielding so versatile a pen, been directed to personal objects, his efforts, only moderately rewarded, might have placed him and his family in prosperous circumstances. Neither by the writing of books nor the selling of them did he ever make a decent competency.

Prolific as William Hone's pen was, it is erroneous to suppose that it was the implement of a ready writer. His copy was not thrown off with that ease and rapidity his large output might lead us to credit. He wrote and he rewrote ; he struck out, and he interlined ; his proofs, too, were subjected to the same remorseless correction, with unstinted deletions and interpolations. A " revise " was strictly required, and even on that the insertion of many afterthoughts and emendations would severely try the temper of the compositors. He seemed never able to satisfy himself, his standard of excellence ever urging him to greater precision.

Honest William Hone confesses to a number of his works being compilations of the scissors and paste variety—to " work forfex-fashion " is a phrase of his coining. He acknowledges, too, that he often felt himself labouring under a heavy disadvantage in knowing no other language than his own.

Though his writing is without any particular distinction of style, Miss Rolleston's estimate of it, as given in her pamphlet, is fairly well justified :—

" A genuine Englishman he was, knowing no country but England, no language but his own, and over that (it is acknowledged) he had a complete mastery. Critics have referred with praise to ' the pure Saxon English ' of Hone and Cobbett."

It cannot be claimed for Hone that he was a man very variously endowed ; he was essentially a bookman and possessed of all that keenness of pursuit which is characteristic of the hunter transformed into the searcher for literary treasure. He was a regular reader at the British Museum, and evidently on familiar terms with the officials there.

A few years ago it was communicated to the Press by Mr. J. Spencer Curwen that an interesting letter was extant written in 1820 by Vincent Novello to William Hone, on behalf of " a friend of his," who had a few hundred pounds at command, and wished to embark on a business as a printer, but not being acquainted with the technical part wanted to meet with a partner who understood all that, so that he himself might be free to correct proofs and manage the literary part of the business. This " friend " is a good French, Italian, and Latin scholar, and has received a most excellent education. Now (says Mr. Curwen) William Hone was a noted publisher in his day—a Newnes or Harmsworth of the period—and it was natural Novello should appeal to him. But who was the " friend "? Scarcely Vincent Novello's son, Joseph Alfred, who was but nine years old at the time, and did not begin to publish his father's books till nine years later. Answering his own query, Mr. Curwen hazards the guess that Vincent Novello's letter was written on behalf of himself. " Here, then," he exclaims, " is the germ of the Novello business ! "

The suggestion, and from such an authority, is interesting, but not convincing, for the following reasons. At the date of his note Vincent Novello was an established musician, composer, and music publisher, who had devoted his whole life to music, and had little literary knowledge beyond that connected with his art. It was not at all likely, therefore, that he was ready to throw up his profession to undertake the superintendence of Hone's publications. Again, of what use would a musician have been to Hone, who knew nothing of music and had no dealings with musical composers? Nor was Hone at all a likely man for Novello to apply to for himself, for he took too keen an interest in the literary part of his business to entrust it to an inexperienced hand. From the " friend's " knowledge of French, Latin, and Italian, it is not unlikely that Novello was acting on behalf of some compatriot, though why Hone should be likely to regard a knowledge of such languages as conclusive of fitness for such a post is not very understandable. Or, possibly the " friend " might have been Charles Cowden Clarke, who commenced business as a book-seller about that date.

XXVII

RETIREMENT AND DEATH

IT became apparent to Hone's family and friends, if not to himself, that he was overtaxing his strength. If he were conscious that he was overworked, he never relaxed his efforts. That one incentive, responsibility to his wife and family, was all-sufficient to William Hone to keep him industriously at work.

The *Patriot* had now become a bi-weekly. On a Thursday at the beginning of May he writes :—

" Another *Patriot* on Monday, and the printer clamorous. I must stay in till I chop it presently at Anderton's Coffee House just at hand. This evening I appropriate to the Sunday School Meeting at Exeter Hall."

Though .William Hone was a capable and efficient journalist, he belonged to that type which always finds the disciplined methods of a newspaper office irksome.

In the June of 1837 he was lying ill in his room upstairs, unable to get down to the editor's room for the transaction of business.

These paralytic attacks, though crippling or enfeebling his body, did not permanently impair his intellect. They were invariably accompanied by a con-fusion of the mind, which passed away, though the consequent depression was more enduring. " I am without power to do anything," he writes on one occasion ; " a spell has bound my faculties, as it were, until now ; a sudden movement on the piano dispels the numbing influence on the sudden, and I hastily, snatch a pen to confess myself a fool." This was written at Bolt Court, where he could probably hear his own piano upstairs from his office.

Of his enforced holiday, first at Hampstead, afterwards at Ramsgate, Hone writes :—

" Thinking it possible that the voyage may rouse me, and sea air brace my lax nerves, I propose to go with my daughter to Ramsgate, and return on Monday.

" Mr. Conder thinks the notion good, and Mr. Boykett also cheerfully assents. My wife is busy unpacking our things from Hampstead, for my departure to Ramsgate. I am certainly better, but am unaccountably oppressed."

Every one on the staff at the *Patriot* office seems to have been particularly kind to the sub-editor, none more so than the Rev. George Ralph Miall, who in earlier years had been a regular subscriber to all Hone's works which came out in weekly numbers, and looked up to him with a respect bordering on reverence.

Twelve months later another attack of paralysis distorts his usually fine, clear handwriting ; so much that, in self-pity, he cannot help calling Miss Rolleston's attention to it in the opening sentence of the letter he addressed to her :—

" You see what is the matter. On Thursday I got Mr. Charles Lushington to give me a frank to you for to-day, for a long letter, and behold !

" Yesterday, 3rd. June, I entered on my fifty-ninth year. In the morning I found my faculties of expression by tongue and hand impaired—to-day they are feebler—my powers have been over-wrought. The mind, as mind, is clear and firm. I am only to others seeming idiotic—or idiot-like. With great difficulty I scrawl this. My surgeon says I must leave the scene awhile, and one of my daughters is gone to Hampstead for a quiet lodging for Mrs. Hone and me. I can neither speak nor write clearly. . . . Farewell.

"W. HONE."

It is evident that the salary of £2 a week, even when it is eked out with his earnings in other literary pursuits, is inadequate to meet his household expenses, to which sickness and invalidity always add so materially. So we find Hone selling his library, and the good man is not a little querulous at having to part with his treasures. In a letter dated December, 1838, after complaining of his loss of memory and failing strength, he grieves at the low prices his books sold at, and says he must have "another turn out" to make up another sale before the 1st of March. Unhappy book-lover !

How he was "retired" is gathered from "The Memoirs of Daniel Macmillan," on p. 95 of which it may be read :—

"Did I ever tell you that old Hone's only means of support is doing drudge work (chiefly reading morning papers, and making selections, and correcting the press) for the *Patriot?* He hates the paper and dislikes the kind of work ; but what was the poor man to do? Now, however, some good friends have resolved to get him rid of his burden, or, as he puts it, 'to send the old horse to grass.' Binney, who is a noble, generous-hearted fellow, is at the bottom of this."

Change of air was repeatedly tried, but without permanent benefit. In the September of 1839 he stayed a short time in Hackney, lodging at Shore Cottage, in Shore Road. He tried Richmond, and he visited Ripley.

In the summer of 1840 Hone found himself compelled to relinquish his editorial duties, welcome as the small but regular salary attached to that office had been to him and his family. It is generally believed that from the time of his retirement, in June, 1840, until his death, in November, 1842, the proprietors of the paper made him an allowance of £1 a week.

When presently the family settled at Tottenham it was devoutly hoped by his best friends that William Hone had cast anchor there to ride out the storm of life. But even there changes of residence had to be made—for a few months No. 9, James's Place was occupied, then No. 1, Church Road, and, finally, No. 8, Grove Place.

Here is an interesting extract from "Memoirs of the Life and Ministry of the Rev. Thomas Raffles, D.D., LL.D." (Jackson, Watford & Co., 1865):—

"Dr. Raffles has recorded in his autobiographical reminiscences, a circumstance which he always referred to with interest, and which occurred on his passing through London on his way home. It relates to William Hone, the celebrated political writer.

"Dr. Raffles says: 'I never saw Hone but once. That, however, was under circumstances which impressed him indelibly upon my memory. Mr. Upcott, of the London Institution, who knew him well, in 1822 gave him my Album, in which he wrote some beautiful verses. Between that date and 1837, a saving change was undoubtedly wrought by Divine grace in his heart, and from being a sceptic, he became a humble Christian, and a consistent member of the Church at the Weigh-House, under the pastoral care of the Rev. T. Binney.

"'In 1837, on my return from a tour on the Continent, I preached for Mr. Binney on a Sabbath evening. After the service Mr. Hone came into the Vestry, and introducing himself to me, referred to the fact of his having written in my Album some years ago; but now, said he, "I am another man; take this as an evidence and memorial of the change." Then

Lines written before Breakfast 3ᵈ June 1834

the Anniversary of my Birth Day in 1780

The proudest heart that ever beat
Hath been subdued in me;
The wildest will that ever rose
To scorn Thy cause, and aid Thy foes,
Is quelled, my God, by Thee.

Thy will, and not my will be done;
My heart be ever Thine—
Confessing Thee, the mighty Word,
I hail Thee, Christ, my God, my Lord,
And make Thy name my sign.

W Hone

Published by J. Unwin 31 Bucklersbury London.
The Profits will be devoted to the cause of Education.

FACSIMILE OF VERSES WRITTEN BY HONE, JUNE 3, 1834

To face p. 393

taking his Bible from his pocket, he tore out the fly-leaf, on which he had written the following lines, and which he begged me to accept as an addition to my collection of autographs :—

" ' " Lines written before Breakfast, 3rd. June 1834, the anniversary of my Birthday in 1780 :—

" ' " The proudest heart that ever beat
    Hath been subdued in me ;
The wildest will that ever rose
    To scorn Thy cause, and aid Thy foes
    Is quelled, my God, by Thee.

Thy will, and not my will be done ;
    My heart be ever Thine—
Confessing Thee, the mighty Word,
I hail Thee, Christ, my God, my Lord,
    And make Thy name my sign.
                W. HONE."

" ' On the leaf which contains the above I wrote at the time: " This leaf was torn out of his pocket Bible and given to me by Mr. Hone, in the vestry of the Weigh-House Chapel, London, July 16th. 1837. —T.R." ' "

Evidently Hone failed to keep a copy of these verses, for a holograph letter written by Dr. Raffles to him from Liverpool, December 12, 1838, encloses a " correct copy " of them, with the added note, " I am glad you are about to publish them."

On the removal of the family to Tottenham their transfer from the Weigh-House Chapel (Congregational) to the Tottenham Baptist Church was made in all due form, as appears on the records of the latter. On Sunday, November 1, 1840, Mr. and Mrs. Hone and Miss Ellen Hone were received into fellowship by their new pastor, the Rev. John Jordan Davies, and his congregation.

Though there is no record of his baptism there, Hone told the Rev. Mr. Davies that his antiquarian researches had convinced him that immersion was the original form of baptism. At his death were found in his pocket his Communion ticket ("Tottenham Baptist Chapel— Rev. J. J. Davies") and a ticket of membership of the Tottenham and Edmonton Mechanics' Literary Institution.

Absent-mindedness as well as loss of memory affected him at times. His house, No. 8, Grove Place, was one of a row, all alike and practically indistinguishable to the careless observer or the absent-minded. Hone returning home one evening, shortly before his final confinement to the house, found an open door, entered, and unconcernedly made himself one of a party assembled in a neighbour's house. It was some considerable time before he discovered he was not in his own home or among his own family. When it did dawn upon him that he was a self-invited guest in another man's house his apologies were profuse and sincere ; but when he essayed to take his departure the neighbours flatly refused to hear of it ; charmed with his conversation, they sent word to Mrs. Hone, and prevailed upon their newly made friend to remain with them the whole of the evening.

One day, towards the end, oblivious of the many recent visitors he had received, he observed to one of his daughters: " What a place Tottenham is to die in ! who would believe there could be a place so near London where a man could be buried alive by avoidance, as I have been ! "

" My dear father," was the reply, " it is not the place that conceals you. Once you were on the stilts of popularity—now you are hid in Christ, which is far better."

" Ah, yes, my child ! far, far better! "

At the commencement of the illness the patient's serenity of mind was disturbed by the strongly expressed desire of his daughter Emma to go out to South Africa as a missionary. In an affecting letter dictated by him and enclosed in a similar one from the loving mother she is told to take the course she herself believes to be right. " God's will be done," he says ; " my mind is not strong enough to ponder the subject."

From a family diary some particulars of his last illness are available :—

" 1 Oct., 1842.—Dressed for the last time—but retired to bed again, almost immediately—very disturbed night—breathing with great difficulty. Mr. Woollaston suggested an operation to relieve the breathing, a considerable amount of fluid having accumulated during the last 48 hours. He had no objection, and a pint of fluid was drawn off, affording immediate relief."

" 5 Oct., 1842.—Apparently our loved father is rather better. but we are assured by all recent changes that it is but the flickering of the lamp ; the end may be sudden when it does come. He is calm and truly happy. George Cruikshank and Charles Dickens saw him to-day."

" 6 Oct., 1842.—Although from the removal of a great weight from his mind, by the settlement of money matters on mother's behalf, and the reconciliation with George Cruikshank, his spirit is greatly relieved, and a calm cheerfulness prevails, at times almost deceiving us and leading us to hope, we dare not say he is better, because we know the disease is making rapid progress.

" George Cruikshank and Charles Dickens were here yesterday. Father was greatly delighted to see them ; they speak of calling again.

" This morning he asked me to read the death of Jacob ; you may well suppose it was a difficult task for me, and yet the clear and steady gaze with which he looked towards heaven as I read, strengthened and encouraged me to proceed, endeavouring to overcome my own feelings for the sake of his enjoyment of the passage. Speaking of his hope compared with that of the worldling, he said that he could not help thinking of George and his friend in this light, when they were here yesterday."

That evening a letter was written to her son Alfred :—

" Father desires me to write to you, telling you that he has had another visit from George Cruikshank, and with him Charles Dickens, with whom father was greatly pleased. Mr. Woollaston begged we would not hurry them ; they were with him about half an hour ; he held George's hand the whole time. They promised to come again soon."

On October 20th one of his daughters wrote to Miss Rolleston :—

" My father is gradually sinking—his sun is setting, and it reminds me of such a sunset as we often see at this season, when after a bright and calm day, the glorious luminary sinks serenely to his rest, without a cloud to obscure the last rays of his departing light."

A callers' book was kept during this last illness, and it bears among the names of members of his family, and of business friends and acquaintances, those of Charles Dickens and George Cruikshank. The signature of the former was written on a separate sheet and carefully dated.

The names of the Rev. T. Binney and the Rev. J. J. Davies appear several times, as well as those of several medical friends, in addition to that of his family doctor, Mr. Woollaston.

XXVIII

HONE'S FUNERAL—A DICKENSIAN EPISODE

THE fact that Charles Dickens attended the funeral of William Hone was, of course, alluded to in John Forster's Life of the great novelist. But, unfortunately, some of the circumstances associated with the incident were, to say the least of it, so grossly misdescribed that a controversy grew out of the disputed passage which has only recently been set at rest with the weight of real authority begotten of a full knowledge of the facts. For this consummation the literary world is indebted to "Claudius Clear" (Sir William Robertson Nicoll) in the columns of the *British Weekly*. As references to the irritating controversy have been creeping into the public Press from time to time for very many years, let us hope it may be accorded unto us for righteousness to quote this able authority at some length.

How unsatisfactory had been all previous attempts to settle the vexed points at issue may be gathered from the fact that John Forster, finding he had raised a hornets' nest by this particular passage in his "Life of Charles Dickens," inserted a lengthy note of explanation in an after edition of the work, and then subsequently saw fit to cut out the original passage, and with it, of course, the note, in his finally revised edition of the great biography. But a story of this kind cannot be easily forgotten ; nor, when characters have been cleared and reputations set right, is the tomb

of oblivion altogether desirable for a story which (as
" Claudius Clear " says) " is of value first from the
character and position of those concerned, and next
for the light it throws upon Charles Dickens's methods."

The controversy rages chiefly round the personali-
ties of three of those who attended Hone's funeral.
These were the Rev. Thomas Binney, who conducted
the service, the man to whom Hone owed his spiritual
regeneration, and whose intimacy ever since that epoch
had been almost equivalent to that of a " father con-
fessor " ; George Cruikshank, the famous etcher and
caricaturist, whose genius as an illustrator Hone had
been the first to recognise and encourage ; and last,
and least known (to the family), that great literary
luminary Charles Dickens, who was present merely as
one of the confraternity of the pen, paying the last
homage of respect to a departed brother.

Of Thomas Binney something has already been said
in these pages. He was unquestionably one of the
most eminent Nonconformist divines in London at that
time, a man of remarkably strong character, and a
force in the religious world. The man was in no sense
a " Stiggins "—he was a natural Boanerges.

George Cruikshank, the artist and caricaturist, was
about fifty. He had done many effective social and
political caricatures, of which the most effective was
the so-called " Bank Restriction Note," published by
Hone. It must be remembered that Cruikshank is not
entirely trustworthy. In his rather disreputable old
age he affirmed that he suggested the story and incidents of " Oliver Twist," but he completely failed to
make his claim even plausible.

The third and principal character in this interlude
was Charles Dickens, then a young man of thirty, but he
was at the very height of his glory, having just returned
from his overwhelming reception in America. His
spirits never were higher. He was about this time

attending the Unitarian Chapel of the Rev. Edward Tagart, but, as Sir Leslie Stephen says, "he seems to have held that every dissenting minister was a 'Stiggins.'" Binney was older, being then forty-four.

These three, Binney, Cruikshank, and Dickens, all men of note, met at the funeral of William Hone, and nothing more was heard about the business till, in 1872, the American publisher and editor J. T. Fields published his "Yesterdays with Authors." Therein he included a letter from Dickens to Mr. Felton, an American friend. H., of course, stands for Hone ; C. for Cruikshank ; and the unnamed clergyman is Binney. The letter is dated March 2, 1843 :—

"'You know H——'s Book, I daresay. Ah ! I saw a scene of mingled comicality and seriousness at his funeral some weeks ago, which has choked me at dinner-time ever since. C—— and I went as mourners ; and as he lived, poor fellow, five miles out of town, I drove C—— down. It was such a day as I hope, for the credit of nature, is seldom seen in any parts but these—muddy, foggy, wet, dark, cold, and unutterably wretched in every possible respect. Now, C—— has enormous whiskers, which straggle all down his throat in such weather, and stick out in front of him, like a partially unravelled bird's nest ; so that he looks queer enough at the best, but when he is very wet, and in a state between jollity (he is always very jolly with me) and the deepest gravity (going to a funeral, you know), it is utterly impossible to resist him, especially as he makes the strangest remarks the mind of man can conceive, without any intention of being funny, but rather meaning to be philosophical. I really cried with an irresistible sense of his comicality all the way ; but when he was dressed out in a black cloak and a very long black hatband, by an undertaker (who, as he whispered me with tears in his eyes—for he had known H—— many years—was " a character, and he would like to sketch him "), I thought I should have been obliged to go away. However, we went into a little parlour where the funeral party was, and God knows it was miserable enough, for the widow and children were crying bitterly in one corner, and the other mourners—mere people of ceremony, who cared no more for the dead man than the hearse did—were talking quite coolly and carelessly together in another ; and the contrast was as painful and distressing as anything I ever saw. There was an independent clergyman present, with his bands on, and a Bible under his arm, who, as soon as we were seated, addressed us thus, in a loud, emphatic voice : " Mr. C——, have you seen a paragraph respecting our departed friend, which has gone the round of the morning papers? " " Yes, sir," says C——, " I have," looking very hard at me the while, for he had told me with some pride coming down that it was his composition. " Oh ! " said the clergyman, " then you will agree with me, Mr. C——, that it is not only an insult to me, who am the servant of the Almighty, but an insult to the Almighty, whose servant I am." " How is that, sir? " said C——. " It is stated, Mr. C——, in that paragraph," says the minister, " that when Mr. H—— failed in business as a bookseller, he was persuaded by *me* to try the pulpit, which is false, incorrect, unchristian, in a manner blasphemous, and in all respects contemptible. Let us pray." With which, my dear Felton, and in the same breath, I give you my word, he knelt down, as we all did, and began a very miserable jumble of an extemporary prayer. I was really penetrated with sorrow for the family, but when C—— (upon his knees, and sobbing for the loss of an old friend) whispered me " that if that wasn't a clergyman, and it wasn't a funeral, he'd have punched his head," I felt as if nothing but convulsions could possibly relieve me. . . .' "

Apparently the publication of this letter by Fields attracted no immediate attention, but the situation was altered when, in the second volume of his biography, published a year later, Forster published the following. He begins with a quotation from Dickens :—

" ' I am going out to Tottenham this morning, on

a cheerless mission I would willingly have avoided. Hone, of the 'Every-Day Book,' is dying, and sent Cruikshank yesterday to beg me to go and see him, as, having read no books but mine of late, he wanted to see and shake hands with me before (as George said) " he went." There is no help for it, of course, so to Tottenham I repair, this morning. I worked all day, and till midnight, and finished the slavery chapter yesterday.'

" The cheerless visit had its mournful sequel before the next month closed, when he went with the same companion to poor Hone's funeral ; and one of his letters written at the time to Mr. Felton has so vividly recalled to me the tragi-comedy of an incident of that day, as for long after he used to describe it, and as I have heard the other principal actor in it good-naturedly admit to be perfectly true, that two or three sentences may be given here. The wonderful neighbourhood, in this life of ours, of serious and humorous things, constitutes in itself very much of the genius of Dickens' writing ; the laughter close to the pathos, but never touching it with ridicule ; and this small occurrence may be taken in further evidence of its reality.

" ' We went into a little parlour where the funeral party was, and God knows it was miserable enough, for the widow and children. . . .' " (Remainder as in preceding quotation.)

The passage is as in Fields, but the description of Cruikshank is omitted. It will be observed that Dr. Binney is not named ; but the identification was very easy, and the passage was at once challenged, as will be seen. Thirty years had passed, but several of those present at Hone's funeral were still alive, and came forward with their evidence.

Among the survivors were Dr. Binney, George Cruikshank, and the Rev. Joshua C. Harrison, the well-known Congregationalist minister, of Camden Town. The reply was penned by Dr. Binney, assisted in the preparation of it by the Rev. Joshua W. Harrison, and was published in the *Evangelical Magazine* for January, 1873 :—

" Everybody is acquainted with Dickens's wonderful power of description, both of incident and character. With all his exaggerations, and his tendency to make things and persons grotesque and ridiculous, he throws an air of reality over the scenes he depicts. His manner is very amusing while he deals with the fanciful and fictitious ; but it is altogether another thing when he professes to state *facts*, and to report exactly what he saw and heard. Mr. Dickens, having attended the funeral of the late William Hone, gave soon afterwards to a friend in America the following account of what he had witnessed."

The letter proceeds deliberately to challenge, and dispose of, the Dickens " facts " one after another. That no " other mourners " who really cared for the dead were present in the " little parlour " is untrue, for Dr. Binney and Mr. Harrison were there ; and the clergyman present, though certainly dressed in black, wore no bands and had no Bible under his arm. For the description of the minister's voice as " loud and emphatic " there was no warrant ; and to assert that he wound up his address by saying, " Let us pray," and " in the same breath began a miserable jumble of extemporary prayer " is a grotesque libel. The paragraph which had appeared in the *Herald* that Hone having failed at one " speculation " had " tried his powers of the pulpit " is proved to be a cruel fabrication and a grave reflection on the dead, though who was responsible for the statement is not so clear. As Dickens and Cruikshank did not sit together, and did not kneel side by side, they could not have whispered together, as alleged. In fact, the whole episode, after a severely critical examination, is dismissed as a " fancy piece " of writing. If further refutation were wanting, there is a letter, dated November 20, 1872, addressed to the *Daily Telegraph*, in which George Cruikshank distinctly states that the account of Hone's funeral given by Dickens " partakes more of the character of fiction than of reality." Forster, on this challenge, responded by taking the earliest opportunity for correcting the misstatements. The correction was first made by the insertion of a note in the 1874 edition ; two years later Forster decided to withdraw the whole passage, and in the 1876 edition the episode disappeared from his pages entirely.

Here at last the matter is brought to as satisfactory a conclusion as could possibly be expected of anything so highly controversial by the succinct and authoritative setting forth of all the facts, and the weighing of all the evidence, by " Claudius Clear," whose final comment is :—

" It is not necessary to comment at length on the incident. Dickens, it will be remembered, was not writing for publication. He seems, however, to have been fond of telling the story. His way was to work up from slight foundations an amusing narrative not to be taken seriously, but there cannot be any mistake as to his intense animus against Dissenting ministers, and the exact truth of Sir Leslie Stephen's comment. It is well that the story no longer disfigures the standard biography of Dickens, and it is also well that it should not sink wholly out of memory in estimating the strong and the weak features of a truly great character and genius."

There is one brief sentence in the statement of " Claudius Clear " which needs correction. He says near the beginning of his article that " Binney frequently allowed Hone to occupy his pulpit." This was not so. As already recorded in these pages, the only time William Hone was known to address a congregation was at a tent meeting organised by the Rev. George Verrall on Peckham Rye Common. One other point should be noted—that is the disclosure by Cruik-

23

shank of the name of the person who interpolated the offensive paragraph into the obituary notice.

The Hone family were deeply pained by the publication of this travesty of what took place at their father's funeral, and Mrs. Burn promptly denied the misstatements in Forster's Life as soon as they appeared in 1872. She said :—

" Of the twenty-four individuals present, fifteen were members of our family—our mother, myself, Fanny, Matilda, Alfred, Emma, Rose, Ellen, Alice, Samuel, Tom Hemsley, and the four grandsons, Tom, Willy, Henry, and Alan. There were the Rev. Thomas Binney, Rev. J. C. Harrison, Rev. J. J. Davies, Mr. Woollaston, Mr. Cruikshank, Mr. Hoskins, and Mr. Charles Dickens and two others. Mr. Dickens was the only one present with whom we had not been long associated in intimate friendship ; the friendship with George Cruikshank dating from an earlier period than that of any of the others."

Of the " two others " one was Mr. Jacob Unwin, father of Mr. T. Fisher Unwin, the publisher of this volume. Mr. Jacob Unwin was a friend of Hone and of Binney, and was connected with the *Patriot* newspaper.

William Hone was buried in Abney Park Cemetery, and his grave at one time was visible from the highroad. In a work entitled ".Walks in Abney Park," by James Branthwhite French (Clarke & Co., 1883), allusion is made to our subject :—

" Turning from this road into the path which leads towards the Elm Avenues, and going up it but a few paces, on the left may be observed a plain headstone with the inscription :—

The Family Grave of
WILLIAM HONE,
.Who was born at Bath the 3rd of June 1780, and died at Tottenham the 6th of November, 1842.

" So modest is this inscription that it would be passed by most people, oblivious of the fact that it records the name of one who made a great figure in his day. William Hone was the author of " The Every-Day Book," a work that has a charm for every book lover. But he gained a notoriety of quite another order than that which attaches to him from this and other of his literary works. He was the friend of Charles Lamb, and one of a coterie of literary celebrities of the last generation. In the latter years of the reign of George III., at the time of the Regency, Hone had excited the hot wrath of the Government by a succession of satires, for which that vicious Administration gave but too much cause. Hone was then a Deist, and the crimes of the Government, done in the name of a Christian State, seemed to him to be in some sort a reflection on Christianity."

After reference to the trials, and the public subscriptions afterwards raised for the victim of a spiteful prosecution, to Hone's conversion and the fruits of it, and other interesting biographical details, the writer says :—

" Such are the stirring events gathered up in the name so modestly inscribed on this tombstone."

Hone's gravestone also records the death of his wife, which took place in 1864, and of two infant grandchildren, also of his third daughter, Matilda, born in 1805 and died in 1884.

On the death of so well known a character a number of obituary notices, all of them more or less complimentary, were at once forthcoming in the public Press. The *Times* and the *Chronicle* dealt respectfully with " this literary character " ; the *Patriot*, of course, gave a long and intimate memoir ; the *Athenæum* notice, from the pen of Dr. Cooke Taylor, did full justice to Hone's character ; but the most elaborate character sketch was written by the Rev. Robert Fletcher for the *Nonconformist*. The necrologists did him full justice. In course of time came the personal recollections ; Samuel Carter Hall, who in early life had been a gallery reporter on the *New Times*, makes allusions to Hone in " A Book of Memoirs of Great Men and Women of the Age," and also in another work, " The Retrospect of a Long Life " ; but the most notable of these reminiscences are perhaps those of John Timbs the antiquary, which appeared in the *Leisure Hour* in 1871. Graceful allusions to Hone appear in the early reminiscences of Alexander Macmillan, and also in the " Memoirs of Daniel Macmillan " ; indeed, the house of Macmillan once proposed to publish a " Life of William Hone," to be written by an Anglo-Indian journalist, James Routledge ; though the project was never carried out, this writer devoted a large portion of his bulky volume, " The History of Popular Progress," to this subject. A portrait of Hone was painted in oils by George Patten ; it is now in the National Portrait Gallery.

APPENDIX

BIBLIOGRAPHY

IN dealing with the bibliography of an author who was also a publisher on a large scale, at a period when anonymity was often essential to the writer's safety, the chief difficulty lies in distinguishing between author and publisher. Hone lived at a period when the political pamphleteer had the fear of the law ever·before his eyes, and though there were plenty of such writers willing and ready boldly to assail the Government and the evils that prevailed, there were but few courageous enough to brave the risks of prosecution and imprisonment by attaching their names to their productions. Hone was one of the daring few. He was an ardent Radical, honest in his convictions, a detestor of the petty tyrannies of the law, ever ready to risk his liberty in the advocacy of the freedom of the Press. Nor, considering his temperament, was it to be wondered at that he threw down the gauntlet, when the terrible state of existing affairs was considered. The greater wonder is that such legal luminaries as Eldon, Stowell, Ellenborough, and Brougham should have been willing, without eloquent protests, to administer laws so Draconian in ferocity, and so utterly opposed to common sense, to good government, and the principles of justice and equity. When people were sent to the gallows for the most trivial offences ; when soldiers and sailors, the gallant defenders of their country, were flogged to death at the triangle

357

and the mast-head for mere incivilities ; when fathers of families were kidnapped in the streets by press gangs and shipped off to fight without taking leave of their wives and children ; when it was seditious to write or speak against a Government they had no voice in electing, we can understand why Hone threw himself heart and soul into the struggle for political liberty. The cause appealed to his emotions, and made him a writer of a kind of literature which was far beneath the level of his powers. That he might have done far more honourable service to literature is proved by the " Year Book," " Every-Day Book," and " Table Book," works which have elicited the warmest approval from many of the greatest writers of his day and since. He, however, was forced by stress of circumstances, unfavourable to the development of his finest qualities, to become a political pamphleteer, and to give up to it a large slice of his life which might have been more profitably employed in more intellectual pursuits. While Hone fearlessly attached his name to many pamphlets, there are many more about the authorship of which he was discreetly silent. In this attempt to give as complete a bibliography as possible, these pamphlets have been in many cases critically examined, errors of former bibliographers corrected, and a large collection of his letters and papers searched for anything that would throw light upon the authorship of the anonymous publications. The following list is as complete as it can be made from the materials at disposal.

1. Hone's first literary effort, as far as is known, was his editing of a new edition of Shaw's GARDENER, in 1806.

2. THE RULES AND REGULATIONS OF AN INSTITUTION CALLED TRANQUILLITY COMMENCED AS AN ECONOMICAL BANK. London, 1807. 8vo.

3. THE KING'S STATUE AT GUILDHALL. 1815. Broadside.

4. REPORT OF THE CORONER'S INQUEST ON JANE WATSON. 1815. 8vo.

5. REPORT OF THE EVIDENCE AND PROCEEDINGS BEFORE THE CORONER'S INQUEST ON EDWARD VYSE, shot dead during the Corn Bill Debates, from the House of the Hon. J. F. Robinson, M.P. With wood-cut illustrations.

6. THE CASE OF ELIZABETH FENNING. 1815. 8vo. Edited by Hone.

7. THE MAID AND THE MAGPIE. 1815. 8vo.

8. APPEARANCE OF AN APPARITION TO JAMES SYMPSON, OF HUDDERSFIELD, COMMANDING HIM TO DO STRANGE THINGS IN PALL MALL, AND WHAT HE DID, with coloured illustration by Cruikshank. 1816. Broadside.

9. VIEW OF THE REGENT'S BOMB, NOW UN-COVERED FOR THE GRATIFICATION OF THE PUBLIC IN ST. JAMES'S PARK. 1816. Broadside. With coloured view and illustrations in prose and verse.

10. AUTHENTIC ACCOUNT OF THE ROYAL MAR-RIAGE, containing memoirs of Prince Leopold and Princess Charlotte, with an engraving. 8vo. 1816.

11. INTERESTING HISTORY OF THE MEMORABLE BLOOD CONSPIRACY IN 1756, carried on by S. MacDaniel, J. Berry, J. Egan and J. Salmon, and their Trials and Sentences in 1756. With etched portrait of MacDaniel, by Cruikshank. 8vo. 1816. Edited only.

12. FOUR TRIALS AT KINGSTON, April 5, 1816, including Elizabeth Miller's for poisoning children, with 13 questions to Mr. Espinasse respecting Elizabeth Fenning. 8vo. 1816.

13. TRIAL OF LORD COCHRANE AT GUILDFORD, August 17, for escaping from the King's Bench Prison. 8vo. 1816.

14. AN ACCOUNT OF CHRISTIAN SLAVERY IN ALGIERS. 8vo. 1816.

15. THE LIFE OF WILLIAM COBBETT, written by Himself. 8vo. 1816.

16. AN ACCOUNT OF THE RIOTS IN LONDON,

Dec. 2, 1816. With Memoirs and Anecdotes of Preston, Dyall, the Watson family, and Thomas Spence. 3 parts. 8vo. 1816.

17. THE REFORMISTS' REGISTER AND WEEKLY COMMENTARY. Issued from the First of February, 1816, to October 25, 1817. 8vo.

18. THE WHOLE OF THE BURIAL PROCESSION AND OBSEQUIES OF THE PRINCESS CHARLOTTE. 8vo. 1817.

19. ANOTHER MINISTERIAL DEFEAT. THE TRIAL OF THE DOG FOR BITING THE NOBLE LORD [CASTLEREAGH] WITH THE WHOLE OF THE EVIDENCE TAKEN IN SHORTHAND. 16 pp. 8vo. 1817.

20. OFFICIAL ACCOUNT OF THE NOBLE LORD'S BITE, AND HIS DANGEROUS CONDITION. 8vo. 1817.

21. BARTHOLOMEW FAIR. 8vo. 1817.

22. BAG NODLE'S FEAST, OR THE PARTITION AND REUNION OF TURKEY, with two curious caricatures fol. 1817. [This is a ballad on the alleged meanness of Lord and Lady Eldon.]

23. THE BULLET TE DEUM, WITH THE CANTICLE ON STONE. 8vo. 1817.

24. MR. WHITBREAD'S LATTER DAYS AND DEATH WITH A MEMOIR AND REPORT OF THE INQUEST. Post 8vo.

25. THE LATE JOHN WILKES'S CATECHISM OF A MINISTERIAL MEMBER. 8vo. 1817.

26. THE SINECURIST'S CREED OR BELIEF, AS THE SAME CAN OR MAY BE SUNG OR SAID. 1817. 8vo.

27. THE POLITICAL LITANY DILIGENTLY REVISED, TO BE SAID OR SUNG UNTIL THE APPOINTED CHANGE COME. 1817. 8vo. (Nos. 26, 27, and 28 are the Parodies for which Hone was tried.)

28. A POLITICAL CATECHISM, DEDICATED WITHOUT PERMISSION TO HIS MOST SERENE HIGHNESS OMAR, BASHAN DEY, ETC., ETC., OF ALGIERS : THE EARL OF LIVERPOOL, LORD CASTLE-

THE QUEEN'S
MATRIMONIAL LADDER,

A National Toy,

WITH FOURTEEN STEP SCENES,

AND

ILLUSTRATIONS IN VERSE,

WITH EIGHTEEN OTHER CUTS

BY THE AUTHOR OF " THE POLITICAL HOUSE THAT JACK BUILT."

"The question is not merely whether the Queen shall have her rights, but whether the rights of any individual in the kingdom shall be free from violation."

Her Majesty's Answer to the Norwich Address.

" Here is a Gentleman, and a friend of mine."

Measure for Measure

Forty-fourth Edition.

LONDON:
PRINTED BY AND FOR WILLIAM HONE, LUDGATE-HILL.

1820.

The Pamphlet and the Toy together,
ONE SHILLING.

To face p. 301.

REAGH, & CO. BY AN ENGLISHMAN, ETC., ETC. 1817.

29. THREE TRIALS OF WILLIAM HONE, for publishing three PARODIES on three EX-OFFICIO INFORMATIONS, at Guildhall, during December, 1817, before three SPECIAL JURIES and MR. JUSTICE ABBOTT and LORD CHIEF JUSTICE ELLENBOROUGH.

30. FIRST TRIAL OF W. HONE. 1817. 8vo.

31. SECOND TRIAL. 1817.

32. THIRD TRIAL. 1817. 8vo. (Many editions of each trial were published.) THE THREE TRIALS, 1818; also WITH INTRODUCTION AND NOTES BY W. TEGG. 1876. 8vo.

33. DANCE IN CHAINS. BY THE AUTHOR OF THE POLITICAL HOUSE THAT JACK BUILT. 1819. 8vo.

34. THE POLITICAL HOUSE THAT JACK BUILT, with thirteen cuts, by G. C. 8vo. 1819.

34a. THE TRIUMPH OF THE PRESS. BY THE AUTHOR OF THE POLITICAL HOUSE THAT JACK BUILT. "*Knowledge is Power.*" Bacon. Illustrated with many woodcuts. 8vo.

34b. THE RADICAL HOUSE THAT JACK BUILT. 8vo. 1819.

35. TRIAL BY JURY. 8vo.

36. THE QUEEN'S MATRIMONIAL LADDER, a NATIONAL TOY. By the Author of the Political House that Jack Built. With 14 Step-scenes; and Illustrations in verse, with 18 other Cuts, by G. C.; viz. High and Low—He qualifies — declares — She accepts — He alters—imputes—She exculpates—emigrates—remigrates — consternates — He accuses — The Press watches—The British Lion awakes—He asks for his Crown and they give him the Bag—They degrade him—The End, Cats' Meat :—Teapot the great—Gone Sailing. 1819. London: Printed for William Hone, Ludgate Hill.

37. THE DROPT CLAUSES OUT OF THE BILL

AGAINST THE QUEEN : For Mr. Attorney General—to peruse and settle ; with a Refresher. Also, Price 6d.

38. Two shillings.—THE PREROGATIVES OF A QUEEN CONSORT OF ENGLAND ; particularly of her ability to make and receive gifts, to sue and be sued, and to hold Courts without the King ; of its being Treason to plot against her Life ; of the Modes of Trying her for Offences ; and of her ancient Revenue of Queen-Gold.

39. HONE'S POLITICAL SHOWMAN—AT HOME ! Exhibiting his surprising Artificial Cabinet, and the Wonderful Beasts and Reptiles, all alive ! alive O !—By the Author of The Political House that Jack Built. With twenty-four Cuts of the astonishing Curiosities and Creatures ! *viz.* The Monster. The Showman. The Show-cloth. Bags. A Crocodile. A Mask. The Locust. A Scorpion. The Lobster. A Prime Crutch. The Opossum. Black Rats. Rat-Bait. A Cadge-Anchor. A Water Scorpion. Dirkpatrick. Music. The Bloodhound. The Doctor. A Booby. A Twopenny Flat. The Slop-pail. My Eye. The Legitimate Vampire.

40. By the Author of the Political House that Jack Built.—In Parliament. THE DROPT CLAUSES OUT OF THE BILL AGAINST THE QUEEN. For Mr. Attorney-General. To peruse and settle. With a Refresher. Printed for William Hone, Ludgate-hill, Solicitor for said Clauses. Price sixpence.

41. THE QUEEN THAT JACK FOUND. 8vo. 1820.

42. THE QUEEN'S BUDGET OPENED. 8vo. 1820.

43. THE MAN IN THE MOON. A speech from the Throne to the Senate of Lunataria, with 15 illustrations by Cruikshank. 8vo. 1820.

44. THE MIDNIGHT INTRUDER, OR OLD NICK AT CARLTON HOUSE. 3 parts. 8vo. 1820. A poem in three parts.

45. THE POLITICAL APPLE PIE. Illustrated. 8vo. 1820.
46. A POLITICAL LECTURE ON HEADS. 8vo. 1820.
47. A POLITICAL CHRISTMAS CAROL. 2 illustrations. 8vo. 1820.
48. THE DOCTOR. A Broadside, with 2 illustrations. 1820.
49. The Englishman's Mentor, the PICTURE OF THE PALAIS ROYAL, describing its Spectacles, Gaming Rooms, Coffee Houses, Restaurateurs, Tabagies, Reading Rooms, Milliners' Shops, Gamesters, Sharpers, Mouchards, Artistes, Epicures, Courtesans, Filles, and other Remarkable Objects in that High Change of the Fashionable Dissipation and Vice of Paris, with Characteristic Sketches and Anecdotes of its Frequenters and Inhabitants, *long folding* COLOURED *front. by* G. Cruikshank, 12mo, boards.
50. NON MI RECORDO : BEING A FREE PARODY ON A LATE EXTRAORDINARY CROSS-EXAMINATION. Illustrated with three cuts. 1820.
51. THE FORM OF PRAYER, WITH THANKSGIVING TO ALMIGHTY GOD, to be used Daily by all devout People throughout the Realm for the Happy Deliverance of Queen Caroline from the late most traitorous Conspiracy. 1820. 8vo. (Five editions.)
52. BUONAPARTEPHOBIA : the Origin of Dr. Slop's Name. 1820 (ten editions).
53. PLENIPO AND THE DEVIL. 1820. 8vo.
54. THE APOCRYPHAL NEW TESTAMENT : being all the Gospels, Epistles, and other Pieces now extant attributed in the first four centuries to Jesus Christ, His Apostles, and their Companions, and not included in the New Testament by its Compilers, translated from the Original Tongues and now first collected into One Volume. 1820. 8vo. Several editions.
55. THE BANK-RESTRICTION BAROMETER. 1820.

The original edition was printed as a large
open half-sheet to serve as an envelope for
Cruikshank's " Bank Note not to be imitated,"
printed on thin bank paper.

56. THE TRIAL OF THE KING V. JOHN HUNT.
Feby. 21, 1821.

57. AN IMAGINARY INTERVIEW BETWEEN W. HONE
AND A LADY. 8vo. 1822.

58. THE RIGHT DIVINE OF KINGS TO GOVERN
WRONG. 2 woodcuts by G. C. 1821. A
Rifacimento of one of De Foe's works, with
a Preface by Hone.

59. THE MIRACULOUS HOST TORTURED BY THE
JEW, under the reign of Philip le Bel, in
1290 : being the Legend which converted the
three Daughters of Douglas Loveday, Esq.,
under the reign of Louis the XVIII. in 1821 ;
from the original French .Work authorised by
the College of Theology, at Paris, in the
Publisher's possession. With Ten Cuts copied
from the same work, viz.—The Arms—Bargaining — Receiving — Delivering — Stab-
bing — Flagellating — Lancing — Boiling —
Recovering—Burning. 8vo. 1822.

60. A SLAP AT SLOP AND THE BRIDGE ST. GANG.
8vo. 1822.

61. BUONAPARTEPHOBIA, with a Portrait of Napoleon, price 1s. THE ORIGIN OF DR. SLOP'S
NAME ! Showing how he cursed himself,
through Napoleon, into the name of Dr. Slop,
and exemplifying the truth of the old saying,
that " a Living Ass is better than a Dead
Lion." 8vo. 1822.

62. HONE (William, 1780-1842, *Author and Bookseller*) ANCIENT MYSTERIES DESCRIBED,
especially the English Miracle Plays, including Notices of Ecclesiastical Shows, Festivals
of Fools and Asses, etc. ; illustrated with
plates after George Cruikshank, etc., that of
the " Giants in Guildhall " being finely
coloured. First Edition. 8vo. Orig. boards,
uncut, with label. Lond. 1823.

63. ASPERSIONS ANSWERED : an Explanatory Statement to the Public at large and every Reader
of the "Quarterly Review." 1824. 8vo. Five
editions.

64. THE QUARTERLY REVIEW OF THE APOCRYPHAL
NEW TESTAMENT REFUTED. By William
Hone.—At the same time, THE SUPERFLUX.
By the same. Price 1s.

65. ANOTHER ARTICLE FOR THE "QUARTERLY
REVIEW." 1824. 8vo. Five editions. No. 55
was noticed in the *Quarterly Review*, Aug.,
1824 ; this is a reply.

66-8. Hone's Works.—THE EVERY-DAY BOOK, or
Guide to the Year, relating to Popular
Amusements, Sports, Ceremonies, Manners,
Customs, and Events in Past and Present
Times, a series of 5,000 anecdotes and
facts ; THE TABLE BOOK and THE YEAR
BOOK, containing Remarkable Men and
Manners, Times and Seasons, Solemnities and
Merry Makings, Antiquities and Novelties,
with a Key to the Almanack, by William
Hone, Complete Set, with Indexes, illustrated
with 550 engravings by Geo. Cruikshank and
others of curious customs, pastimes, antiqui-
ties, etc. 4 thick vols. 8vo. 1826-7. Con-
tains contributions by Charles Lamb in
Every-Day Book, entitled The Months, Sir
Jeffery Dunstan, Captain Starkey, The Ass,
In re Squirrels, Remarkable Correspondent,
The Humble Petition of an Unfortunate Day,
Quatrains to the Editor ; in the Table Book,
Mrs. Gilpin's Riding to Edmonton, The Defeat
of Time, Gone or Going, and the 46 Extracts
from Garrick's Plays ; and in the Year Book,
two poems.

69. POOR HUMPHREY'S CALENDAR. An Almanack.

70. FACETIÆ AND MISCELLANIES, with 120 illustrations by G. C. First collected edition of these
Tracts. 1827.

71. FULL ANNALS OF THE REVOLUTION IN
FRANCE. 8vo. 1830.

The following were edited only by Wm. Hone:—

72. THE SPORTS AND PASTIMES OF THE PEOPLE OF ENGLAND, with 140 engravings selected from ancient and curious paintings and illuminations. By Joseph Strutt, with many additions, and an Index by Wm. Hone. Large 8vo. 1830.

73. Dr. Knox's Spirit of Despotism. In the Press, handsomely printed in a large Octavo Volume, price 10s. 6d. in boards. THE SPIRIT OF DESPOTISM. By the late Vicesimus Knox, D.D. With a Preface by the Author ; and interesting Particulars, by the Editor, of his Interview with Dr. Knox, in February last, authenticating the Work. With Preface by Hone.

74. In a handsome volume, in foolscap 8vo. with a Historical Plate, price 6s. in boards, SIXTY CURIOUS AND AUTHENTIC NARRATIVES AND ANECDOTES RESPECTING EXTRAORDINARY CHARACTERS ; illustrative of the tendency of Credulity and Fanaticism ; exemplifying the imperfections of circumstantial Evidence ; and recording singular instances of voluntary human suffering, and interesting occurrences. By John Cecil, Esq.

75. In a pocket volume, with a large folding coloured Engraving, price 5s. in extra boards. THE PICTURE OF THE PALAIS-ROYAL ; describing its Spectacles, Gaming-houses, Coffee-houses, Restaurateurs, Tabagies, Reading-rooms, Milliners' Shops, Gamesters, Sharpers, Mouchards, Artists, Epicures, Courtesans, Filles, and other remarkable objects in that High Change of the fashionable dissipation and vice of Paris. With characteristic Sketches and Anecdotes of its Frequenters and Inhabitants.—Printed for William Hone, Ludgate Hill.

76. Important Legal Argument. Price eighteen pence, THE RIGHT ASSUMED BY THE JUDGES

TO FINE A DEFENDANT, WHILE MAKING HIS DEFENCE IN PERSON, DENIED: being a Shorthand Report of the important Legal Argument of Henry Cooper, Esq., Barrister at Law, in the King v. Davison, on moving for a New Trial. With a Preface. Printed for .William Hone, 45, Ludgate-hill.

There were no doubt a number of other squibs and pamphlets that Hone was the author of, but being pseudonymous or anonymous it is difficult now to distinguish them. Nor does it materially affect the completeness of this bibliography, as they did probably little credit to his ability and certainly added no leaf to his literary laurels.

77. THE EARLY LIFE AND CONVERSION OF WILLIAM HONE, by Himself, edited by his son, .Wm. Hone. 1841. 8vo.

78. SOME ACCOUNT OF THE CONVERSION OF THE LATE .W.. HONE, with further particulars of his Life, and Extracts from his Correspondence. 1853. Sm. 8vo. Frequently confounded with No. 77.

Biographical notices in *Gent. Mag.*, May, 1843, pt. I., p. 96; "Some Account of the Conversion of .W. Hone," 1853; *Notes and Queries*, 1st ser., iv. 25, 105, 241; vii. 154; 3rd ser., iv. 429; 4th ser., x. 351, 399, 528; 5th ser., i. 477; viii. 446; 6th ser., i. 92, 171, 354, 522; ii. 31, 283; iii. 426. "The Three Trials of .W. Hone," with Introduction by .W. Tegg. 1876. 8vo. For Hone's connection with Cruikshank see G. W. Reid's Catalogue, 1871, 3 vols, 4to; .W. Bates's "G. Cruikshank," 1879, 4to; B. Jerrold's "Life of G. Cruikshank," 1891; and F. G. Stephens's "Memoir of G. Cruikshank," 1891. For Bibliography see Lownde's Bibl. Man. (Bohn) ii. 1103-5; *Notes and Queries*, 6th ser., xii. 271-2; see also lists at the end of Hone's "Political Showman," 1820, and advertisements of Hone's editions, 1820.

The chronological list of works illustrated by George

Cruikshank, given in Stephens's Memoir of the artist, include these among Hone's publications: —

"The Englishman's Mentor": a picture of the Palais Royal, 1819. "Facetiæ and Miscellanies," by Wm. Hone (120 engravings), published for William Hone by Hunt & Clarke (1819-22), containing: "Political House that Jack Built" (13 cuts), 1819. "Man in the Moon," etc. (15 cuts), 1820. "Political Christmas Carol" (2 woodcuts), 1820. "The Doctor" —one leaf with 2 woodcuts, 1820. "Queen's Matrimonial Ladder"—14 step scenes, and 18 other cuts, 1820. "Non Mi Ricordo," etc. (3 woodcuts), 1820. "Form of Prayer with Thanksgiving" (woodcut on title-page), 1820. "Political Showman—at Home" (24 cuts), 1821. "Bank Restriction Note, with Bank Restriction Barometer," 1821 ; "Slap at Slop and the Bridge Street Gang" (3 large folding woodcuts and 23 smaller cuts), 1822. "The Spirit of Despotism" (woodcut on title), 1821. "Ancient Mysteries Described" (2 coloured etchings of the "Giants in Guildhall," and "The Fools' Morris Dance," 1823. "Every-Day Book." By William Hone. 2 vols. (11 woodcuts by G. C.), 1826-7. "Table Book." By William Hone. 2 vols. (1 woodcut—of "Botocudo Indians"), 1827-8.

Blanchard Jerrold's "Life of George Cruikshank" adds to the list :—

Hone's "Interesting History of a Memorable Blood Conspiracy" (portrait of Stephen Macdaniel, etched by G. C.), 1816. "Official Account of the Noble Lord's Bite" (woodcut vignette on title-page by G. C.), 1817. "Another Ministerial Defeat" (woodcut vignette on title-page by G. C.), 1817. "The Right Divine of Kings to govern wrong" (2 woodcuts by G. C.), 1821. "The Miraculous Host by the Jew under the reign of Philip the Fair in 1290" (illustrated by 10 cuts), 1822.

See also Sotheby's Catalogue of the Truman Collections of the Works of George Cruikshank, sold May 7–12, 1906, particularly Lot 365 with G. C.'s interesting note on a portrait head of Hone.

INDEX

ABNEY Park, 354
" Ancient Mysteries," 218, 243-4, 275, 364, 368
Antiquaries, &c., 70-73, 243
Apocryphal New Testament, 218, 243, 363
Arminianism, 24, 28
" Aspersions Answered," 196, 209, 243, 268, 364
Aspland, Rev. R., 239, 240
Athenæum, 281, 355

" BANK Restriction Note," 191, 198-205, 210-11, 218, 348, 368
" Bank Restriction Barometer," 200, 368
Bankruptcy of Hone, 73, 164, 291, 320
Bath, 22, 59, 187, 317
Belsize, 30-32, 39
Bettridge, Dame, 25-8
Binney, Rev. Dr., 306-11, 317, 322, 328, 342, 346, 348-9, 351-2
Birmingham, 139, 251, 334
" Black Dwarf, The," 117, 138, 146
Bolton, 291
Bone, Mr., 73-4, 76, 78
Book auctions, 46, 78, 187, 208-9

Booksellers, bookselling, 38-9, 40, 54, 69-71, 78, 80-90, 100, 103, 106, 116, 134, 141, 148, 212, 214, 247, 357
Borrow, George, 89
Bowyer, 70
Brand (Antiquary), 258
" Bridge Street Gang," 224, 368
Burdett, Sir Francis, 79, 86-8, 91, 123, 146, 179, 332
Burn, Mrs., 18, 81, 84, 97, 130, 180, 189, 195, 203, 206-8, 216, 354
Butler, Samuel, 244

CANONBURY, 251
Carlile, Richard, 116
Cartoons, 172-3, 193
Cartwright, Major, 147
Carvelho, 223
Catchpenny publications, 104
Catnach Press, 103
Caxton, 43
Chatham, 56, 66-7, 69, 75-6
Childs, John, 182-3, 187, 210-11, 220, 289, 322, 331-3
"Christmas Carol, Political," 223-6, 368
Church rate abolition, 330-35

" City of London Tavern," 93, 121, 177

Clowes, William, 294

Cobbett, William, 74, 119, 120, 126–9, 130, 133, 170, 177–8, 194, 299, 336, 359

Cochrane, Lord, 96–8, 160, 171, 179, 359

Condor, Josiah, 330, 340

Cowden Clarke, Charles, 263–4, 288, 338

Creery, 212

Creevy, Thomas, 179

" Crown and Anchor," 45, 53, 146, 187, 332, 335

Cruden, 333–4

Cruikshank, George, 92, 101, 104, 106, 110, 138, 172, 189–97, 201–4, 210, 220, 225–8, 230, 236, 248, 289, 320, 348, 351, 354, 368

Cruikshank, Isaac, 102

Curwen, J. Spencer, 337

DAVIES, Rev. J. J., 343–4, 346

De Foe, 212, 276, 292–3, 320

" Derry-down-Triangle," 115, 185, 221–2

Dick, Dr., 333–4

Dickens, Charles, 107, 345–9, 350, 352, 353–4

" Doctor, the," 115, 194, 218, 222 236

Dolby, 219

ELLENBOROUGH, LORD, 96, 122, 136–8, 154, 159, 160, 165–7, 172, 174, 215, 234, 357

" Every-Day Book," 15, 62, 79, 181, 193, 195, 217, 246–59, 262, 265, 268–9, 273–4, 277, 286, 294–6, 320, 351

" FACETIÆ," 189, 192–3, 219, 229, 365, 368

Fenning, Eliza, 98–101, 103, 359

Filby, 261

Fores, 173, 190

" Form of Prayer," 192, 363

Forster, John, 347, 350, 353–4,

Forster, Dr. T. I., 301

Foxe's " Book of Martyrs," 35–7

Francis, Philip (" Junius "), 170, 177

French Revolution, 11, 34–5, 44–5, 55, 77, 149, 299, 311, 365

" Friends of Liberty," 178, 180

GASPEY, Thomas, 323–5

Gatton, 125

Gentleman's Magazine, 70–73

Globe, the, 104

Godwin, 54, 148

Goodyear, Joseph, 251

Gordon Riots, 13, 252

HALL, S. CARTER, 320, 356

Hampstead, 23, 24, 30

Hardy, 188

Harrison, Joshua C., 351–2, 354

Hazlitt, 209, 212, 228, 236, 267, 279, 293

Hemsley, Thomas, 308, 318, 322, 354

Hill, Rowland, 57, 59

" History of Three Days' Revolution," 62

Hobhouse, J. Camden, 130

Holcroft, 54–5, 148–9

Homewood Farm, 63

Hone, Alfred, 32, 190, 214, 253, 354

Hone, Alice, 318, 354

Hone, Ellen, 318, 325, 343, 354

Hone, Emma, 308, 318, 325, 344
Hone, Fanny, 318, 354
Hone, John, 259, 260, 261, 282
Hone, Joseph, 63, 174, 256, 304
Hone, Matilda, 284, 290, 310, 354-5
Hone, Rose, 318, 354
Hone, Samuel P., 216, 322, 354
Hone, Sarah, 318
Hone, William (son) 259, 260, 261
Hone, William (senr.) 22, 23, 34, 35, 56-9, 63, 176
Hone, William—his character and temperament, 14, 20-22, 32, 47, 65, 67, 68, 73, 77, 293; his opinions, 91, 95, 102; his politics, 14, 51, 53, 91, 104, 112-16, 242, 299-318, 357; his religion, 14-17, 34, 36, 51-3, 56-7, 61, 68, 156, 273, 299-318, 329; his philanthropy, 92-5, 103, 320; his literary style, 336; as a citizen of London, 103, 177, 294-5, 327; his hallucinations, 207-8, 286; his ill-health, 18, 19, 77, 186-8, 285, 319, 339; his death, 18, 345-6, 354
Hone, William—his various residences, lodgings, and offices: Lambeth Walk, 64; St. Martin's Lane, 68; Albion Place, Blackfriars, 76; Strand, 78, 164-7; Old Bailey, 79, 134, 154, 177; 55, Fleet Street, 101; 45, Ludgate Hill, 177, 181, 207-8, 211, 234, 252, 257, 267; Belvedere Place, 180, 252, 257, 260, 288; 2, Great Suffolk Street, 252, 255; Peckham Rye, 273, 304, 317, 319-27, 353; Grasshopper Coffee-house, Gracechurch Street, 276, 278, 295-6, 300, 304, 321; Penton-

ville, 141, 286; Newington Green, 291: Camberwell, 305, 319; Kingsland, 315, 321; 5, Bolt Court, 327, 340; Tottenham, 63, 342-4, 350-51
" House that Jack Built, Political," 104, 185, 191-4, 198, 218, 220-22, 225, 227-8, 237
Howard, J. E., 176, 326
Hunt, Leigh and John, 170, 212, 228, 288
Hunt and Clarke, 229, 253-4, 256, 259, 265, 283, 286-7, 294
Huntingdon, Rev. W., 24, 28
Hurst, Thomas, 292

INFORMATIONS, ex-officio, 53, 89, 96, 110, 133, 146, 154, 161, 171-2, 220
Inns—"Adam and Eve," 23; "Albion Tavern," 78; "Horn Tavern," 75; "Hole-in-the-Wall," 130; "Old King's Head," 23; "Pied Bull," 249

JOHNSON, MRS., 34, 59, 64, 65, 84
" Joss and his Folly," the, 236
Jury system, 151-4, 168, 173, 188

KING'S BENCH, 61, 87, 96-7, 136, 150, 187, 195, 252, 264, 282-93

LAMB, CHARLES AND MARY, 19, 257-8, 263, 266-81, 324, 355
Lambeth, 34-57, 59, 64, 66, 84
Lawrence, Dr. W., 176, 285, 287
Literary Fund, 279, 323-4
London Corresponding Society, 53, 66
L'Overture Toussaint, 83-4
Lowton, 73

Lucas, E. V., 266
Lunatic asylums, 92–5
Lushington, Charles, 340

MACMILLAN, DANIEL, 341, 356
" Maid and Magpie," the, 100–101, 359
" Mat de Cocagne," 106, 189
Methodism, 49, 77
Miall, G. R., 340
Morgan, Lady, 105
Moxhay, 283, 286–7, 297
Murray, Lady Augusta, 80–82, 88

NAPOLEON, 80, 96, 106–9, 189, 225
New Philosophy, the, 51, 55, 311
New Road, 41
Nicholl, Sir W. R., 347–8, 353
Nichols (of *Gentleman's Magazine*), 70–72
" Non mi ricordo," 152, 192, 228, 368
Norris, William, 93–5, 103
North, Christopher, 265
Novello, Mary, 263–4
Novello, Vincent, 337

OGLE, ROBERT, 145–6
" Old Bags," 115, 185, 218
Olive, Princess, 84–6
Owen, Robert, 51

PADDINGTON, 23
Paine, Tom, 45, 148
Pancras Church, 24
Parkes, Mr., 286
Parliament Houses, 63
Parodies, 15, 16, 18, 60, 61, 104, 111, 179, 196, 210, 213, 225, 236, 291, 339, 341
Parr, Samuel, 179, 185, 215–16

Patriot, the, 19, 319, 327–38, 355
Patten, George, 356
Pearson, Charles, 151
Percy, 210
Phillips, Charles, 99, 106–7, 184, 240
Phillips, Richard, 88–9
" Pilgrim's Progress," 28, 30, 33, 40
Place, Francis, 88, 90, 120, 125
" Political Showman," 191–2, 218, 225, 362
" Poor Humphrey's Calendar," 289, 365
Price, Dr., 291
Printers' Address to Queen Caroline, 238
Pynson, 43

QUAKERISM, 279, 305, 333–4
" Queen's Matrimonial Ladder," 192, 218, 223, 227, 229, 236–7, 361

RAFFLES, DR., 292, 342–3
Red Lion Square (and Court), 33, 41, 42, 72
Rees, Owen, 30, 331
Reformists' Register, 104, 110, 119–27, 134, 138, 144, 146, 153–4, 360
Register Extraordinary, 121
Richmond, 63, 341
" Right Divine," 192
Riots, 88, 96, 102, 123–4, 145, 299, 359
Rochester, 68
Rolleston, Miss, 236, 273, 319, 320, 325, 336, 346
Romanism, 36, 233
Royal Exchange, 29, 59, 96

Routledge, James, 201, 356
Russell, Fuller, 320

SADLER'S WELLS, 49
Savings Bank, 73
Scott, John, 175, 280, 323
Serres, Olivia, 84–6
Skeffington, Sir Lumley, 82–3
"Slap at Slop," 223–5, 229, 235, 365, 368
Socialism, 51
Society for Abolition of Poor Rate, 75–6
Spa Fields riots, 102, 299
Spy system, 96, 116, 130, 138–43
Stationers' Company, 290
Stawell, 22
Stoddart, Dr., 224–5
Strutt's "Sports and Pastimes," 265, 366
Sturge, Joseph, 334
Southey, 227, 276–7, 280, 297–8
Southwark, 46, 73
Surrey Chapel, 57, 59, 306, 318

"TABLE BOOK," 62, 181, 217, 246, 259–65, 274–7, 294–8, 351
Tallies, 63
Tegg, 172, 277, 294–6, 361
Thelwall, 149, 188
Thompson, 47
Timbs, John, 356
Times, the, 62, 119, 355
Tooke, John Horne, 54, 149, 150, 188
Townley, 65

Townson, 67
"Tranquillity," 74–6, 358
Traveller, the, 102, 104

UNITARIANISM, 16, 50
Unwin, Jacob, 354
Upcott, Mr., 342

VAUXHALL, 64
Venning, 66, 68–9, 76
Verrall, George, 321, 353

WAITHMAN, ALDERMAN, 92, 122, 177–80, 184
Wakefield, Edward, 92–3
Wakefield, Gilbert, 180
Ward, Lock & Co., 296
Warren Street, 23–4
Watts's Songs, 33, 56, 312
"Weekly Commentary," Hone's, 119
Weigh-house Chapel, 336, 315–17, 321–2, 342–3
Wesley, John, 24, 28, 37
White (artist), 217, 248
White, Joseph Blanco, 301
Wilkes, John, 71, 111, 146, 150, 170–71
Williams (artist), 217, 248
Williams (banker), 167
Williams's, Dr., library, 239
Wilson, C. C., 262
Wilson, Effingham, 278
Wilson, Walter, 276, 292–3

"YEAR BOOK," 62, 79, 246, 294–8, 351

The Gresham Press,
UNWIN BROTHERS, LIMITED,
WOKING AND LONDON.

Lightning Source UK Ltd.
Milton Keynes UK
UKOW05f0703030214

225750UK00006B/41/P